PASS

Cambridge BEC 1

Teacher's Guide

Pass Cambridge BEC 1 Teacher's Guide

ISBN 1-902741-02-1

 Published by Summertown Publishing Ltd
26 Grove Street
Summertown
Oxford
OX2 7JF
United Kingdom

Produced by the Linguarama Group Pedagogical Unit, 89 High Street, Alton, Hants, GU34 1LG, United Kingdom.
© Linguarama International 1999 Edition 1.

Acknowledgements

Linguarama would like to thank the following companies for their kind permission to reproduce photographs and other copyright material. Linguarama is particularly grateful to the individuals named below for their help in contributing to the content of the units.

First Great Eastern	Juliet Sharman, Communications Manager
Holiday Inn	Kevin Smith, Deputy Manager Holiday Inn, London - Nelson Dock
Raupack Ltd	Wolfgang Rauch, Managing Director
UPS	Connie Lydon, Marketing Department
Direct Line Insurance plc	George Watt, National Sales Manager

Direct Line, Direct Line Insurance and the red telephone on wheels are registered trade marks of Direct Line Insurance plc and are used with its permission.

Rank Xerox for the advertisement which appeared in **Arena**, Feb-March 1998.

Agfa Gevaert for the advertisement which appeared in **Arena**, Feb-March 1998.

Every effort has been made to trace copyright holders.
The publishers would be interested to hear from any not acknowledged.

Printed in the United Kingdom

Introduction

Pass Cambridge BEC 1 provides support material for courses leading to the Cambridge Business English Certificate 1 examination.

The following introductory pages to the *Pass Cambridge BEC 1 Teacher's Guide* are an expanded version of the Introduction in the Student Book and contain the following:

- The Cambridge BEC examination

- *Pass Cambridge BEC 1*

- Language development in *Pass Cambridge BEC 1*

- Preparing students for Cambridge BEC 1

- Questions and answers

The Cambridge BEC examination

The Cambridge Business English Certificate (BEC) is a new international Business English examination. It was introduced by the University of Cambridge Local Examinations Syndicate (UCLES) in Europe in 1998 and takes place six times a year. It offers a language qualification for learners who use, or will need to use, English for their work.

Cambridge BEC is available at three levels, linked to the levels of traditional Cambridge examinations.

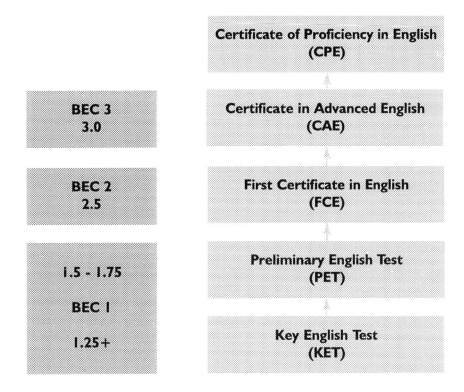

Cambridge BEC 1 covers both KET and PET levels. This book assumes that students are aiming for a good pass; students should therefore have a Linguarama level of approximately 1.5 before starting the examination preparation course.

Cambridge BEC 1 is a practical examination that focuses on English in business-related situations. There is little focus on grammar in the examination. The major emphasis is on the use of language skills: reading, writing, listening and speaking. The examination can be broken down as follows:

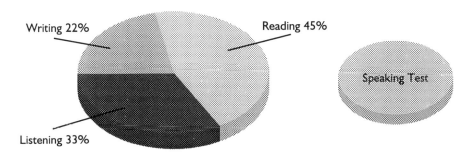

Candidates receive two separate grades: a combined grade for the Reading, Writing and Listening Tests and one for the Speaking Test. There are four possible grades for the former (A, B, C or D) and two for the Speaking Test (1 or 2).

Pass Cambridge BEC I

Student Book

The Student Book contains:

- **Introduction**: An introductory unit which provides information about the examination
- **Core units**: Twelve double units which cover a wide range of business-related topics
- **Exam focus units**: Six units which prepare students directly for the examination
- **Activity sheets**: Pairwork activities and games at the back of the book
- **Self-study**: A section in every core unit for consolidation of coursework and examination practice
- **Answer key**: Answers to Self-study
- **Essential vocabulary**: A list of the key vocabulary of each unit
- **Tapescripts**: The content of the cassette
- **Irregular Verbs**: A list of common irregular verbs.

Cassettes

There are two cassettes:

- *Pass Cambridge BEC I*: The listening material for the core units (approximately 60 minutes)
- *Pass Cambridge BEC I Exam Focus*: The listening material for the three Exam focus units which are accompanied by a cassette (approximately 60 minutes).

Cards

- There are sets of cards to accompany ten of the units. Extra sets are available from Alton.

Teacher's Guide

The Teacher's Guide contains an A5 version of the Student Book with the following additions:

- Full teacher's notes with answers to all exercises
- Expanded Introduction
- Black and white copies of the cards for reference.

The Teacher's Guide does not contain the list of irregular verbs which is in the Student Book. Moreover, Essential vocabulary, Tapescripts and the Answer keys to Self-study can be found in the units themselves rather than at the back, as in the Student Book.

Language development in *Pass Cambridge BEC 1*

• Grammar

 The book assumes a certain level of grammatical knowledge. Therefore, grammar is systematically reviewed in the **Don't forget!** sections in each unit but not presented in great detail.

 If students need to look at a grammar point in more depth, they should refer to **Linguarama English Reference Guide 2**. The Reference Guide symbol will tell them which unit to refer to.

If students are not sure of basic verb forms, they should look at the **Irregular verbs** list at the back of the book.

• Functions

The book also reviews basic functional language such as phrases for making requests, asking for permission, making suggestions and arranging an appointment. These are presented in authentic situations and recycled throughout the book. For Cambridge BEC 1, candidates also have to be able to express such functions in writing.

• Vocabulary

Important vocabulary is systematically recycled in the **Self-study** section of each unit and then throughout the core units of the book. This progression means later units are lexically denser and require a certain amount of familiarity with earlier units. At the back of the Student Book there is **Essential vocabulary**, which lists the key vocabulary for each unit. This section is designed as a revision aid for both teachers and students, with each unit providing a manageable, thematically-based vocabulary list, which can be used for classroom-based activities or copied onto flash cards for self-testing. Please note that in the Essential vocabulary lists in the Teacher's Guide (which can be found in the units themselves rather than at the back of the book) certain words are written in italics. This means that they are not items on the official Cambridge BEC 1 Vocabulary List provided by UCLES. However, they have been included because they are essential for discussion of the topic or because they represent useful vocabulary for people who use English for work.

Students will probably meet words that they do not know in the Reading and Listening Tests so it is important to have strategies for dealing with difficult words. Unit 3, the **Exam focus: Vocabulary** unit, provides ideas for helping students to guess the meaning of words. It also provides ideas for storing and building vocabulary.

• Reading

Reading is the most tested skill in the examination. The book therefore contains extensive reading practice, using authentic, semi-authentic and examination-style texts representing a wide variety of genres. UCLES policy requires items targeted in the examination to be drawn only from the official Cambridge BEC 1 Vocabulary List. As some words on this list might still be unfamiliar to students, they should be trained not to panic if they do not understand every word of a text.

However, students should also be trained to read very carefully when answering examination questions; sometimes the most obvious answer on the first reading is not correct.

• Listening

The examination also has a heavy bias towards listening skills. Therefore, the book includes a wide variety of listening material in the majority of units. The **Tapescripts** to the cassette can be found at the back of the Student Book and in the relevant units of the Teacher's Guide.

> For both reading and listening, the emphasis in the examination is on looking for specific information rather than understanding gist. Although teachers' priority is to train their students in examination skills, it is also useful if teachers include additional activities to develop general reading and listening skills when time permits.

• Writing

In the Cambridge BEC 1 examination students have to write short memos and notes as well as longer memos and formal letters. The Writing Test is potentially the most difficult for students due to the requirement of word limits, the specific nature of the instructions and the fact that students are probably unfamiliar with the genres and conventions involved. Success in the Writing Test is not simply a matter of committing spoken language to paper but of recognising the genre required by the question. Moreover, candidates always need to pay very careful attention to task fulfilment. Students will need to learn and practise the necessary writing skills in order to perform well in the Writing Test. The book focuses on these skills in Unit 4b (notes and memos), Unit 8b (formal letters) and Unit 9 (**Exam focus: Writing**). Further practice is provided throughout both the core and Exam focus units.

• Speaking

The Speaking Test for Cambridge BEC 1 is short and not particularly demanding; given Linguarama's traditional emphasis on oral skills, few students should find it difficult. It is possible for a candidate who fails the Speaking Test still to receive a certificate giving credit for a pass in the other elements of the examination; however, the reverse is not possible. Although preparation time is thus likely to be more profitably spent preparing for the Reading, Listening and Writing Tests, students may be nervous about the Speaking Test and will need to be fully prepared for it. Unit 15 **Exam focus: Speaking** outlines the format of the Speaking Test and strategies to help students perform well in it. The unit also includes materials for the teacher to stage Part Two of a mock Speaking Test. Furthermore, all core units provide fluency practice and opportunities for students to work together in pairs and groups.

Preparing students for Cambridge BEC 1

What is available?

The following are available in your centre:

- *Pass Cambridge BEC 1* (Linguarama)

- *BEC 1: Teachers' Information Pack* (Linguarama)

- *Cambridge BEC Handbook* (UCLES)

- *BEC 1 Sample Papers* (UCLES)

- *Linguarama Cambridge BEC 1 Practice Tests 1 and 2*

Each Linguarama centre has someone responsible for administering the examination who should be able to answer any questions you may have.

Examination preparation in *Pass Cambridge BEC 1*

- **Introduction**

  The **Introduction** presents the content of the examination and focuses on important examination dates. Students will also do a quiz about the book and start to think about how to study for the examination.

- **Core units**

  The core units contain general exercises and activities as well as examination-style exercises such as *multiple-choice* and *matching*.

- **Examination focus**

  Four **Exam focus** units in the book provide information about the examination and train students directly in techniques for successful performance. They are yellow to help identify them.

Unit 6	Exam focus: **Reading**
Unit 9	Exam focus: **Writing**
Unit 12	Exam focus: **Listening**
Unit 15	Exam focus: **Speaking**

- **Exam practice**

  The final exercise in the **Self-study** section of each unit is **Exam practice**. The yellow background tint explicitly signals that the exercise provides examination practice and is identical in format to a question on the Cambridge BEC 1 examination paper.

  The final unit of the book, Unit 18, provides four pages of examination practice. Once again, it is yellow so that students know they are preparing for the examination.

Specific examination exercises in *Pass Cambridge BEC 1*

Activities which are specifically related to the Speaking Test are outlined below. Exercises which are related to the Reading, Writing and Listening Tests are signalled in the grid opposite.

Most examination-specific exercises are to be found in Self-study or Exam focus units. However, certain examination-specific exercises can be found in the body of the units themselves.

In general, Self-study exercises carefully recycle vocabulary; however, the vocabulary in examination practice exercises is not restricted to that of the unit. Therefore, should teachers wish to practise a specific examination question, they can jump to examination practice exercises in later units.

Activities related to the Speaking Test

Unit 15 Exam focus: **Speaking** prepares students specifically for both parts of the Speaking Test. In addition, the following units contain relevant material.

Part 1 (Personal information)

Unit 1a involves students talking about their jobs.

Part 2 (Information exchange)

Units 4a, 5a and 11a contain information exchange activities. Teachers can usefully supplement these, if desired, with information exchanges from a wide range of published material.

The numbers refer to each part of the specific tests. A description of parts of each test can be found in the relevant Exam focus units (6, 9 and 12).

Unit		READING 1	2	3	4	5*	6	WRITING 1	2	3	LISTENING 1	2	3	4
1a	Job descriptions						X							
1b	Working conditions					X								
2a	Company history		X											
2b	Company activities				X									
3	Exam focus: Vocabulary													
4a	Telephoning	X												
4b	Internal communication								X					
5a	Facts and figures			X										
5b	Performance			X										X
6	Exam focus: Reading	X	X	X		X	X							
7a	Product description						X							
7b	Product development	X												
8a	Business equipment				X									
8b	Correspondence									X				
9	Exam focus: Writing							X	X	X				
10a	Business hotels												X	X
10b	Commuting	X			X									
11a	Arranging a conference								X	X				
11b	At a conference	X										X		
12	Exam focus: Listening										X	X	X	X
13a	Production								X					
13b	Quality control		X										X	X
14a	Direct service providers						X							
14b	The banking sector					X								
15	Exam focus: Speaking							X	X	X				
16a	Delivery services	X				X								
16b	Trading		X			X							X	X
17a	Recruiting staff			X										
17b	Applying for a job				X					X				
18	Exam practice	X		X			X	X	X	X	X			X

* Part Five consists of two types of exercises.

Questions and answers

I have never taught an examination class before. Can you give me any advice?

The main difference with examination classes is that your objectives are especially clear. You have a syllabus and a certain amount of time to teach it in. Plan the course as a whole but set short-term objectives to check that you are on schedule. Do not fall behind your schedule; overloading students close to the exam will not compensate for bad planning at the start.

You need to be realistic about timing. You have a lot to do to get through the examination syllabus; if you do other things just for interest, you may run out of time. You will need to manage carefully any time spent going over homework in class. You should also be prepared for a lot of marking of written work.

Give your students a mock test before the examination. If course length permits, a preliminary mock examination just before the final entry date also gives students feedback on likely performance before they commit their time and money by entering for the examination. In addition, it will encourage them to revise seriously if necessary.

If you do not know much about Cambridge BEC examinations, there is plenty of information in your Linguarama centre. Look at the Introduction unit (Teacher's Guide) for a list of things to help you. The best way to familiarise yourself with the examination is to do a past paper.

Can I depart from the book or do I need to follow it exactly?

It is sensible to follow the order of the book if there is no particular reason not to; the sequence has been planned carefully to lead students towards success in the examination. However, the syllabus leading to the examination may not correspond exactly to your students' needs: they may have particular strengths and weaknesses or need specific language for their jobs in addition to general business-related language for the examination. If time permits, tailor the course to the interests and needs of your students.

I'm American. Do I have to teach British English?

Any material needs to be internally consistent and, as Cambridge BEC is a British examination, British English has been chosen as the norm for this book. However, there is a range of nationalities on the cassette and candidates can use British English, American English, Australian English - or any other native speaker variety - as long as they are consistent. Therefore, teachers should simply teach the language they usually speak.

There's a lot of self-study in the book but my students don't have time for homework.

You need to point out to students that taking an examination course is a commitment; examination courses tend to be intensive and demanding. Make it clear to students that the self-study and examination practice sections are essential for recycling and internalising the language presented in the book.

My Cambridge BEC students all work for the same company. Some of the pairwork activities won't work with them.

If a speaking activity is irrelevant for your students, adapt it to create a reason for speaking. For example, change the task so that there is an information gap. Or adapt the task to provide an outcome, e.g. ask students to agree on a ranking or to present the results of their discussion formally to the rest of the class.

My students are pre-experience. They can't talk about their job or company because they haven't got one.

Once again the speaking activities in the book need to be adapted. Many of the activities involve giving personal opinions and, with a little adaptation, can be done by anybody. For the activities involving companies, the teacher could ask students to talk about companies they know. (This may involve using information about famous companies in the book or asking students to speak about famous local or national companies. It may even involve asking students to do research and find out information before the class.)

I have only one student taking Cambridge BEC 1. Is the book suitable for 1:1 lessons?

Yes - obviously with a little adaptation of some of the oral activities.

Do I have to use the whole book or can I concentrate on the exam practice?

Unlike more general Business English material, this book has been designed to provide extensive preparation for the Cambridge BEC 1 examination. The core units are essential for developing skills, learning vocabulary used by UCLES in the examination and training students in effective examination techniques.

My students like to talk a lot. Will they find the exam course boring?

Discuss expectations at the start of the course. Make sure students realise that as the examination is so heavily biased towards receptive skills, the majority of time will be spent developing reading and listening. Fluency practice will still be an important and integral part of every lesson but topics will be dictated by the syllabus, rather than the students' interests. The book includes games, pairwork activities, puzzles and cards to maintain variety throughout the course.

Contents

			Language	Skills

			Language	Skills

Introduction

Objectives: To give Ss general information about Cambridge BEC 1
To provide useful study strategies for the Cambridge BEC 1 course
To familiarise Ss with the content of *Pass Cambridge BEC 1*

Materials needed: None

Unit overview

- **Cambridge Business English Certificate 1**

  T does essential briefing for the start-up of a new course.

  T elicits Ss' knowledge, experience and opinion of examinations.

  T goes through the weighting of the different parts of the examination.

- **An overview**

  T describes the examination content and relates it to real-world skills. T talks Ss briefly through the content of the examination.

- **Important Cambridge BEC dates**

  Ss complete a table with their essential Cambridge BEC 1 dates.

- **Introductions**

  Ss obtain personal information from one another and complete cards.

  Ss do a *Find someone who ...* activity.

- **Learning for Cambridge BEC 1**

  Ss work in pairs and brainstorm ideas to add to a diagram about studying for the examination.

  Ss discuss and complete a questionnaire on the usefulness of various language learning practices.

- **Quiz: *Pass Cambridge BEC 1***

  Ss do a quiz to familiarise themselves with *Pass Cambridge BEC 1*.

Cambridge Business English Certificate 1

If T is unfamiliar with Cambridge BEC 1, he/she should look at the following:

- *BEC 1: Teachers' Information Pack*
- *UCLES BEC1 Sample Papers*
- *Linguarama Cambridge BEC 1 Practice Tests 1 and 2.*

T needs to emphasise that a Cambridge BEC 1 exam course will require Ss to learn and practise techniques which will help them to be successful in the exam itself. In addition, they will learn and practise language which is relevant to their professional lives.

1   If this is the first lesson of a new group of Ss, T spends some time on introductions and sorting out practical details such as lesson times.

2   **Warmer (books closed):** T writes *examination* on the board and asks Ss all the words they can think of which are associated with examinations (e.g. *candidate, examiner, test, paper, exercise, mark, certificate, stress, nerves, results, take/pass/fail an examination*). T then elicits Ss' past experience of examinations.

3   Ss open their books and read the information about the examination. T takes Ss through the information about the grades and the weighting of the different tests.

An overview

4   T talks Ss through the overview of the examination using the table. T then elicits from Ss what type of reading, writing, listening and speaking they have to do in English related to their jobs. For example, Ss may have to look at graphs and charts and read notices and product descriptions. T relates any of these types to the content of the exam. The different tests tend to cover the following:

Reading: notices, advertisements, graphs, charts, product descriptions and short texts
Writing: notes, memos and formal letters (all with strict word limits)
Listening: short conversations, telephone conversations, announcements, longer conversations and monologues

Speaking: giving personal information and exchanging factual information.

5   T reassures Ss that the course will provide practice in all four skills. T shows them the **Contents** pages of the book to indicate the coverage of reading, listening and writing in the skills column. T points out that in addition to the specific focus on reading, listening and writing, the book contains a lot of general speaking practice, often in pairwork. T also draws attention to the **Exam focus** units, which concentrate on each skill in the exam and provide extensive exam practice. Further exam practice is supplied in the **Self-study** section of each core unit.

6   T uses the **Contents** pages to show Ss the range of business topics in the language column. T points out that BEC 1 tests a wide range of general business vocabulary. T tells Ss that **Unit 3 Exam focus: Vocabulary** concentrates on helping Ss learn vocabulary effectively and also directs them to the **Essential vocabulary** section at the back of the book.

Important Cambridge BEC 1 dates

7   Before the lesson, T should have found out about Cambridge BEC 1 dates from the Linguarama Centre Manager. T tells Ss the various dates, which Ss should write in the boxes. It is impossible to be specific about the Speaking Test at this stage; however, Ss should be warned to keep weekends free within the period specified. It is essential that all students make a record of this information at the start of their course. All latecomers or students who join the group later in the course must also receive this information.

Introductions

8   **Ex ❶:** T now changes the focus of the lesson from information about the exam itself to a focus on the Ss. T sets up the information exchange activity. Ss go round the group asking and answering questions to complete their cards. T may wish to set a time limit in order to have time to focus on the rest of the activities in this lesson. However, T should allow time for Ss to report back if they are strangers to one another. If Ss are from the same company, T adapts the exercise to make it relevant to the group.

Introduction

Cambridge Business English Certificate 1

Successful Cambridge BEC 1 candidates receive two grades: one for Reading, Writing, Listening and one for the Speaking Test.

Writing 22%
Reading 45%
Listening 33%

Speaking Test

Single grade (A, B, C, D or Fail)

Separate grade for the Speaking Test (1, 2 or No grade)

An overview

The following table gives an overview of the different parts of the examination, how long they take and what they involve.

	Test	Length	Contents
1	Reading & Writing	70 minutes	Reading: 6 parts (40 questions) Writing: 3 parts (form filling, memo or note, formal letter)
2	Listening	40 minutes	4 parts (30 questions) Approx.12 mins of listening material played twice
3	Speaking	10 minutes	Interview: 2 examiners and 2 or 3 candidates

Important Cambridge BEC 1 dates

Your teacher will give you some important dates at the start of your course. Write these dates in the boxes below.

Cambridge BEC 1 examination

Your teacher will give you the dates of the written papers but can only give you the date of the Speaking Test after your entry has been confirmed by Cambridge.

- PAPER 1 Reading & Writing Test
- PAPER 2 Listening Test
- Speaking Test (to be confirmed)

Between   and

Entry date

This is the date by which Linguarama must receive your exam entry.

- Entries must be confirmed by

Grades and certificates

Cambridge sends out results 6-8 weeks after the examination. Successful candidates receive their certificates about four weeks after that.

- Results should be available by

Introductions

Introduce yourself to the people in your class. Find out the following information from them.

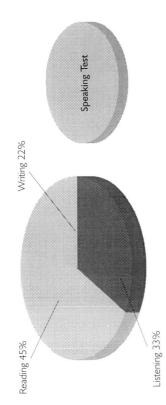

Name ....
Company ....
Position ....
Why is he/she doing Cambridge BEC 1? ....

Name ....
Company ....
Position ....
Why is he/she doing Cambridge BEC 1? ....

Name ....
Company ....
Position ....
Why is he/she doing Cambridge BEC 1? ....

Name ....
Company ....
Position ....
Why is he/she doing Cambridge BEC 1? ....

9 **Ex ❷**: Ss go round the group finding people who match one or more of the seven descriptions. T encourages Ss to ask and answer one or two further questions in order to promote fluency practice. T organises a relatively brief feedback as the exercise is primarily to enable Ss to get to know one another better.

Studying for Cambridge BEC 1

10 **Ex ❶**: T ensures that Ss are clear about their task before they work in pairs adding ideas to the diagram. In this exercise Ss are simply asked to brainstorm ideas for studying for the exam. Later, in **Ex ❷** Ss will be asked to evaluate options and discuss ideas in more detail. T can stop the group after a set time, elicit some ideas and then ask students to complete the diagram for homework. During feedback, T may wish to remind Ss of Linguarama study aids: *Linguarama English Reference Guide 2* for general language reference (which students are referred to throughout the book) and *Postscript*, the self-study magazine now on the Internet (http://www.linguarama.com). T may also like to refer to the brochure *Effective Self-Study with Linguarama*, which gives a range of ideas for self-study.

11 **Ex ❷**: T asks Ss to consider in more detail how to learn a language effectively. Ss change partners and discuss the various possibilities. This activity should provoke a lot of discussion. In feedback T should not only deal with any points arising but also use this as an opportunity to inform Ss about their forthcoming course, e.g. Ss will be doing a substantial proportion of pairwork, relatively little grammar practice but will have a lot of examination practice.

Quiz: *Pass Cambridge BEC 1*

12 **Ex ❶**: T explains that the final activity of the lesson is to introduce Ss to the book. T may wish to introduce a fun element by either imposing a time limit or getting Ss to work in teams with the winning team being the first to finish.

1 *Unit 1b, page 11*
2 *Unit 2a, page 14 (Volkswagen Beetle)*
3 *First Great Eastern: Unit 5b, pages 37 to 40*
   Holiday Inn: Unit 10a, pages 65-68
   UPS: Unit 16a, pages 105-108
4 *Unit 10b: The Commuter Game, Activity Sheet, page 129*
5 *Unit 4b, page 30*
6 *Unit 5b, page 38*
7 *Irregular verbs, page 157*
8 *Unit 11a, page 74*
9 *Unit 10b, page 72 and Unit 14b, page 100*
10 *Unit 17a, page 115 and Unit 17b, page 117*
11 *Unit 7b, pages 49 and 50*
12 *Exam focus units: 6 - Reading, 9 - Writing, 12 - Listening and 15 - Speaking*

In feedback T ensures Ss are aware of the other sections in the book. T mentions that all the units have a **Self-study** section for consolidation/review purposes, which will be set as homework. T impresses upon students the importance of completing Self-study exercises as they are an essential form of revision and internalisation of vocabulary and grammar. T also points out that at the back of the book Ss can find: **Essential vocabulary**, **Tapescripts** and the **Answer key** to **Self-study**. T asks Ss to read the *Pass Cambridge BEC 1* Introduction for homework.

2 Now find someone in your class who ...

- has already taken an English examination.
- knows someone who has a Cambridge BEC 1 certificate.
- uses English regularly at work.
- has been to the UK or USA on business.
- has an English-speaking colleague.
- reads the same newspaper/magazine as you.
- has the same interests as you.

Studying for Cambridge BEC 1

1 Work in pairs. Look at the diagram below and complete it with ideas for studying for Cambridge BEC 1.

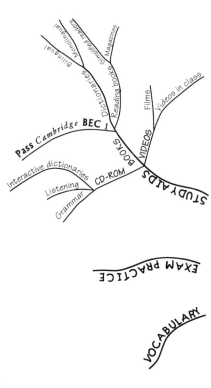

2 Work in pairs. How useful are the following?

useless   useful   very useful

1 Using a bilingual dictionary
2 Using an English-English dictionary
3 Having the teacher correct all my mistakes
4 Doing pairwork with other students
5 Keeping vocabulary in a list
6 Writing new words on cards
7 Listening to a lot of cassettes
8 Reading tapescripts
9 Recording myself to check pronunciation
10 Doing a lot of grammar practice
11 Doing a lot of examination practice
12 Reading through class notes regularly
13 Reading for pleasure
14 Keeping a learner diary

Quiz: Pass Cambridge BEC 1

1 Where would you find the following in this book? Write the unit or page numbers.

1 Terms and conditions of employment
2 A picture of a very famous car
3 Information about the companies on this page
4 A game where you have to get to work before 9am
5 Advice on how to write memos
6 Information about the use of the present perfect
7 A list of irregular verbs
8 Information about hotels in Prague
9 A crossword
10 A job advertisement
11 An article about drug development
12 Useful tips for each of the Cambridge BEC 1 tests

First
Great Eastern

Holiday Inn®

Job descriptions

Objectives:	To enable Ss to talk about jobs
	To practise listening for specific information
	To review the present simple
Materials needed:	Cassette – *Pass Cambridge BEC 1*

Unit overview

- **Duties**

Warmer	T elicits to what extent Ss use business cards.
Listening 1	Ss listen to identify speakers at a Chamber of Commerce meeting.
Listening 2	Ss predict two people's duties and listen to confirm their predictions before listening again to complete notes about the people.
Language focus	Ss review the form of the present simple.
Reading	Ss scan questions for key vocabulary and decide which person from the business cards each question is for.
Speaking	Ss do a *Find someone who ...* activity.

- **Talking about your job**

Vocabulary	Ss match sentence halves about one of the people from the business cards and focus on language for talking about jobs.
Speaking	Ss work in pairs and interview their partner about his/her job in preparation for writing a newsletter article.

- **Self-study**

Vocabulary	Matching exercise (verbs and nouns). Ss then think of another noun to go with each verb.
	Word-building exercise (nouns and verbs). Gap-fill exercise using the nouns and verbs.
Writing	Ss write a newsletter article about the person they interviewed.
Exam practice	*Multiple-choice gap-fill text (Reading Test Part 6).*

Duties

1 Warmer (books closed): T asks Ss how important business cards are to them (their own/other people's).

2 Ex ❶: T introduces the Chamber of Commerce and gives more information if requested (it is an organisation which operates on a local basis; it helps businesses by promoting the area; it offers business opportunities for its members through a variety of services and events).

T focuses Ss' attention on the business cards and clarifies job vocabulary where necessary. Ss listen to six new Chamber of Commerce members speaking and number the business cards in the order in which the people speak.

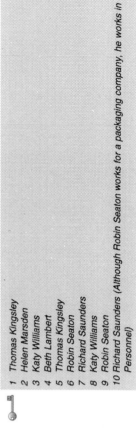

```
2  Helen Marsden
3  Thomas Kingsley
4  Beth Lambert
5  Richard Saunders
6  Robin Seaton
```

3 Ex ❷: T focuses Ss' attention on two of the cards: Helen Marsden's and Robin Seaton's. T elicits from the group what they think their duties are.

Ss listen to Helen Marsden and Robin Seaton in order to find out whether their predictions were correct. T should not give too much information at this stage as Ss will listen again and take notes in Ex ❸.

4 Ex ❸: Ss read the notes about Helen Marsden and Robin Seaton before listening to the cassette again. T explains any difficult vocabulary where necessary. T uses the feedback to check whether Ss have problems with the third person -s when talking about the people's jobs.

Helen Marsden:
1 *Works for a company that produces vaccines and sells them to doctors*
2 *Discusses new products with doctors*
3 *Deals with designers and printers*
4 *Deals with the health authorities in central Europe*
5 *Travels a lot*
6 *Organises conferences for the medical press*

Robin Seaton:
1 *Recruits people*
2 *Writes job advertisements*
3 *Chooses the applicants to interview*
4 *Interviews the applicants with the department manager*
5 *Contacts successful and unsuccessful candidates*
6 *Deals with employees' problems*
7 *Informs employees if the management isn't satisfied with their work*

5 Before Ss look at the **Don't forget!** section, T elicits the form of the present simple from Ss. T then draws Ss' attention to the **Don't forget!** section, which focuses on the main problem areas encountered when using the present simple: third person -s and negative and question forms using the auxiliary *do*. T points out that *-es* is added to words ending in *-s, -ch, -sh,* or *-o* (e.g. *discusses, watches, wishes, does*). T may wish to point out that there are three possible pronunciations for third person *-s* endings: /s/, /z/ and /ɪz/. However, only /ɪz/ is likely to be problematic.

6 Ex ❹: Ss decide individually (or in pairs) which person each question is for. The exercise recycles some of the vocabulary from the tapescript but also includes some as yet unseen vocabulary, which T may need to explain.

```
1   Thomas Kingsley
2   Helen Marsden
3   Katy Williams
4   Beth Lambert
5   Thomas Kingsley
6   Robin Seaton
7   Richard Saunders
8   Katy Williams
9   Robin Seaton
10  Richard Saunders (Although Robin Seaton works for a packaging company, he works in Personnel)
```

This activity can be used to make the point that it is often not necessary to understand every word in order to extract sufficient meaning for the reader's purpose. This point is emphasised in the accompanying **Reading tip**. T may wish to ask Ss to underline the vocabulary which suggested the answer (e.g. in Question 8 the mention of *software* immediately suggests that the question is for Katy Williams, the IT consultant).

Job descriptions

Duties

Listening 1 **1** The Chamber of Commerce is an organisation for business people. Listen to six new members. Number the business cards in the order the people speak.

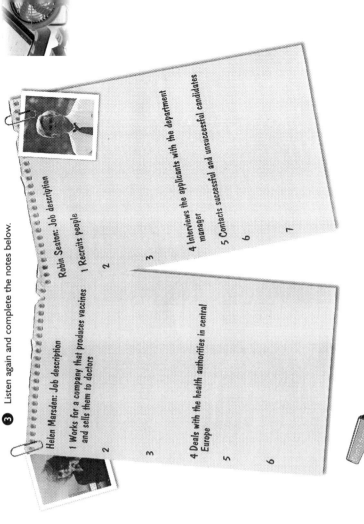

REGAL FROZEN PRODUCTS
105-109 Valley Road, Staines,
Middlesex, ST12 4JW
Tel: 01784 933 6525
Fax: 01784 933 6522

RICHARD SAUNDERS
Production Manager

94 THE SQUARE
BRIGHTON
SUSSEX
BN1 6DJ

TEL: 01273 656 872
FAX: 01273 656 818

KATY WILLIAMS
CONSULTANT

INFORMATION TECHNOLOGY
SERVICES PLC

Meridian Financial Products

Thomas Kingsley
Sales Executive

Meridian House
Cole Street
London EC4 2AF

Tel: 0171 236 4925
Fax: 0171 236 119
e-mail: TKingsley@MFP.co

Robin Seaton
Human Resources
Manager

V a c u p a c k
Units 5-10
Hayes Business Park
Watford
WA6 3AG
Tel: 01923 465 222
Fax: 01923 465 710
e-mail: rs@vacupack.co.uk

L S P Lister Steetley
Pharmaceuticals

Becton House
Becton Court
Tunbridge Wells
TW16 2QD

Tel: 01892 340 170
Fax: 01892 326 462

Helen Marsden
Marketing Manager

RTLP
CONSULTANTS

BETH LAMBERT
ACCOUNTANT

METRO HOUSE
95 THE COMMON
READING RG2 9LH

TEL: 01734 318 222
Fax: 01734 318 419

Listening 2 **2** Helen Marsden and Robin Seaton talk about their jobs. Before you listen, decide what their duties are. Then listen and check your answers.

3 Listen again and complete the notes below.

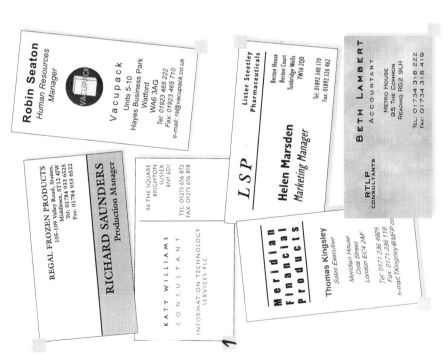

Helen Marsden: Job description

1 Works for a company that produces vaccines and sells them to doctors

2

3

4 Deals with the health authorities in central Europe

5

6

Robin Seaton: Job description

1 Recruits people

2

3

4 Interviews the applicants with the department manager

5 Contacts successful and unsuccessful candidates

6

7

Present simple

- The third person singular form takes **-s**.
  She work**s** in marketing.

- Negatives are formed with **don't** or **doesn't**.
  I **don't** work with other people.
  He **doesn't** travel on business very often.

- Questions are formed with **do** or **does**.
  Do you work in an office?
  Does she work at head office?

Unit 1

Reading **4** Look at the business cards again. Who is each question for?

1 How many sales meetings do you attend each month?

2 What advertising do you want to organise for this product?

3 Why do we need to update our current network?

4 When do you want to discuss the balance sheet?

5 Could you give me some advice on investing money?

6 Do you want me to interview the short-listed candidates?

7 How do you plan to increase output at the factory?

8 What kind of after-sales service do you provide for this software?

9 When do you want the successful applicant to start?

10 Do I need to keep a record of the number of packs we produce a day?

Reading tip:
You do not need to know every word to understand the meaning of what you read. Concentrate on the words that you do know!

6

7 **Ex ➎**: Ss mingle in order to find out the information. This activity allows Ss to use the present simple and some of the vocabulary that has already been presented. It also allows T to monitor the use of the present simple and give further practice where necessary.

Talking about your job

8 **Ex ➊**: Ss match sentence halves about Beth. This enables Ss to review some general work-related vocabulary which they will need in order to speak about their jobs. Before Ss begin, T elicits what an accountant's job might involve. T then ensures that Ss are aware that prepositions are followed by a noun or -ing, e.g. *I deal **with questions**: I'm responsible **for checking**.* T also draws Ss' attention to the fact that *involve* is followed by a noun or -ing, e.g. *My job also **involves** giving financial advice.* T points out that Reading /redɪŋ/ is a town in the south of England and that its pronunciation is different from the general *reading*.

🗝 2 *I'm responsible for checking companies' accounts/giving financial advice.*
3 *My job also involves giving financial advice/checking companies' accounts.*
4 *I deal with questions people have about their accounts.*
5 *As part of my job I have to produce financial reports.*
6 *I'm based in Reading, not far from London.*

9 **Ex ➋**: Ss work in pairs to find out about their partner's job. This allows Ss to practise the present simple and some of the vocabulary from the unit. Ss need to take notes as they will write an article about their partner's job in the **Self-study** section. T reminds Ss that they can use the phrases used by Beth Lambert in **Ex ➊**.

Self-study 📖

Ex ➊: 2 provide a service
3 interview an applicant
4 deal with a problem
5 attend a meeting
6 keep a record
7 organise a conference

Ex ➋: *Suggested answers:*
1 give a presentation
2 provide support
3 interview a candidate
4 deal with people
5 attend a training session
6 keep a diary
7 organise a holiday

Ex ➌: product   produce
sale   sell
organisation   organise
interview   *interview*
applicant   apply
advertising   advertise

1 interview
2 organise
3 advertise
4 applicants
5 products
6 discussion
7 sales

Ex ➏: 1 A   2 C   3 B   4 A   5 A   6 B   7 A   8 C   9 C   10 B

Essential vocabulary

Jobs
accountant
consultant
human resources (HR) manager
marketing manager
production manager
sales executive

Work
to work as (+ job)
to work for (+ company)
to work in (the food industry)

Duties
to attend (a meeting)
to deal with (a problem)
to discuss (problems)
to give (advice)
to interview (applicants)
to involve (+ -ing)
to keep (a record)
to organise (a conference)
to provide (a service)
to be responsible for (+ -ing)

General
to advertise
applicant
to be based on
department
financial products
head
personnel

The words in italics are not on the Cambridge BEC 1 wordlist.

Speaking 5 Write about the person you interviewed for the Chamber of Commerce newsletter. Write about 50-60 words.

6 Exam practice
- Read the text below from the 'New Members' section in the Chamber of Commerce newsletter.
- Choose the correct word from A, B or C to fill each gap.
- For each question, mark the correct letter A, B or C.

Meet Thomas Kingsley

Thomas Kingsley works for Meridian Financial Products in East London. He works (1) ..... a sales executive. He (2) ..... with a large number of small and medium-sized businesses in the London area. He (3) ..... them on the best financial products for their needs.

He is only in his office in the morning when he discusses clients (4) ..... the Sales Manager. Then he travels around London to see his clients. He informs them (5) ..... new products on the market. He keeps a (6) ..... of any changes in the clients' information so that he can offer advice if necessary. He (7) ..... his paperwork and arranges (8) ..... from home or from his car between appointments.

If any members would like (9) ..... advice on insurance or any financial product, please phone Thomas (10) ..... 0171 236 4925. He will be happy to help you if he can!

	A	B	C
1	as	like	in
2	discusses	provides	deals
3	advise	advises	advised
4	with	to	from
5	about	on	to
6	notice	record	reference
7	does	record	deals
8	meets	meet	meetings
9	an	a	some
10	to	on	under

---

1 Match the verbs with the nouns. Then look back through the unit and check your answers.

1	give	a problem
2	provide	a record
3	interview	a conference
4	deal with	advice
5	attend	a service
6	keep	a meeting
7	organise	an applicant

2 Think of another noun to go with each verb.
1 give
2 provide
3 interview
4 deal with
5 attend
6 keep
7 organise

3 Complete the table below.

Noun	Verb
discussion	discuss
product	
sale	
	organise
interview	
applicant	
advertising	

4 Now complete the following sentences with the correct form of the words from the table above.
1 We're going to _____ ten applicants for the position of accountant.
2 Could you _____ the room for the meeting tomorrow?
3 Are we going to _____ our new sports shoes on the radio or only on television?
4 There were forty _____ for the job but we short-listed only five of them.
5 My company sells financial _____.
6 We had a very interesting _____ about increasing output at the factory.
7 Peter works in the _____ department. His job involves a lot of travelling to visit clients.

Job descriptions

Speaking 5 Find out about people in your group. Find someone who ...
- organises things. What does he/she organise?
- attends meetings. What sort of meetings does he/she attend?
- deals with different nationalities. Which ones and why?
- provides a service. What service?
- travels a lot. Where to and why?

Talking about your job

Vocabulary 1 Match the sentence halves about Beth Lambert.

1	I work as	questions people have about their accounts.
2	I'm responsible for	an accountant with RTLP.
3	My job also involves	produce financial reports.
4	I deal with	checking companies' accounts.
5	As part of my job I have to	Reading, not far from London.
6	I am based in	giving financial advice.

RTLP CONSULTANTS

Speaking 2 Work in pairs. You are going to write an article about your partner's job for the Chamber of Commerce newsletter. Interview your partner about his/her job and take notes. Start your questions with the words below.

| Do you ...? | Are you ...? | Where ...? | Who ...? |
| When ...? | What ...? | Why ...? | How often ...? |

Job descriptions

Tapescript: Listening 1

Conversation 1

Richard: So, are you from London then - or just here for the meeting?
Katy: No, I'm not from London, but my company has offices here.
Richard: What kind of company is it?
Katy: I work for an IT company. I'm a consultant.

Conversation 2

Robin: Where do you work?
Helen: I work for a large pharmaceutical company.
Robin: And what do you do?
Helen: I'm the head of the marketing department.

Conversation 3

Katy: So what kind of products do you sell?
Thomas: Anything that helps people make money.
Katy: How do you mean?
Thomas: Financial services. I sell investment products.

Conversation 4

Thomas: Tell me, does your consultancy work with big companies?
Beth: No, we do the accounts for small and medium-sized companies.
Thomas: Ah, I see. Do you have clients in London?
Beth: Some but not many. Most of our clients are in Reading.

Conversation 5

Helen: So, you work in the food industry?
Richard: Yes, I'm a factory manager.
Helen: Oh, really? What do you make?
Richard: We produce frozen food.

Conversation 6

Beth: And what do you do?
Robin: I'm a manager in Personnel.
Beth: What kind of company do you work for?
Robin: We make packaging for fresh food.

Tapescript: Listening 2

Helen Marsden

Hello, I'm Helen Marsden. I work as a marketing manager for a large pharmaceuticals company. My department produces vaccines against hepatitis and so on. We normally sell our vaccines directly to doctors so one of my jobs is to discuss our new products with doctors. Marketing managers don't always do this, but I do as I'm a qualified doctor. I'm also responsible for our publicity material so I have to deal with designers and printers. My area is central Europe, so I have to deal with the health authorities in those countries. That means my job involves a lot of travelling. And finally, when we produce a new vaccine, it's my job to organise a conference for the medical press so that they can ask us questions about it.

Robin Seaton

Hello, I'm Robin Seaton. I work for a company called Vacupack. I'm responsible for employing most of the people in the company. I write the job advertisements and then I have to choose which applicants I want to interview. Usually, I interview the applicants with the head of the department where the vacancy is. I then have to contact the applicants after the interview, both the successful and unsuccessful ones. Another duty is dealing with employees' problems. Of course many of them are work-related, but people do sometimes come to discuss personal problems with me. My job also involves informing employees if the management isn't satisfied with their work, which isn't a pleasant part of the job.

Working conditions

Objectives:	To enable Ss to talk about working conditions
	To practise reading for gist and for specific information
	To review adverbs of frequency

Materials needed: None

Unit overview

• Comments about work

Warmer	T asks Ss whether they have a suggestions/comments box at work.
Reading	Ss look at comments made by employees and answer comprehension questions.
Language focus	Ss place adverbs of frequency on a cline according to meaning and review word order of adverbs of frequency.
Speaking	Ss use the adverbs of frequency to talk about what they do at/outside work. Ss then decide how they would deal with the problems/comments in the comments box.

• Terms and conditions of employment

Vocabulary	Ss match vocabulary in preparation for the reading task.
Reading	Ss gist-read a Terms and Conditions of Employment document. They then read the text again and answer multiple-choice comprehension questions.
Speaking	Ss discuss their own conditions of employment.

• Self-study

Vocabulary	Recycling of vocabulary from the unit.
	Word search.
	Gap-fill exercise (prepositions).
Writing	Ss write about their own conditions of employment.
Exam practice	*Vocabulary matching exercise (Reading Test Part 5 - second part).*

Comments about work

1 **Warmer:** T asks Ss whether they have a suggestions box or a comments box at work. If so, what kind of things do people write about? If not, T asks what other system they have for dealing with problems/complaints at work. T asks what typical problems they have at work.

2 **Ex ❶:** Ss read the comments in order to answer the questions.

1 They are rarely for him/her.
2 They frequently run out of stationery.
   There isn't a sensible system for ordering supplies.
3 They don't receive overtime pay when they work late.
   They get their bonus annually but one person would prefer it monthly.
4 Equipment breaks down during presentations.
   There isn't a sensible system for ordering supplies.
   One person thinks they have too many meetings.
   One person answers the phone a lot but it is never for him/her.
5 The only person who makes a suggestion as well as a comment is the person who writes about the bonus system.

3 **Ex ❷:** T asks Ss to underline any adverbs of frequency in the exercise and write them in the appropriate place on the cline. They then compare their order with a partner.

never rarely occasionally sometimes frequently/often usually **always**

4 **Ex ❸:** Ss look at the comments again in order to work out the position of adverbs of frequency. They then complete the **Don't forget!** section.

> ### Adverbs of frequency: word order
>
> * Words such as always, *usually*, **often**, frequently, **sometimes**, occasionally, rarely and **never** usually come before the verb.
> * However, these words come **after the verb** to be.
> * Words such as hourly, daily, **weekly**, **annually** and **monthly** come after the verb, often at the end of the sentence.

5 **Ex ❹:** Ss work in pairs to discuss routines: both work-related and personal.

6 **Ex ❺:** T might wish to get Ss to change partners. Ss look at the comments again and make suggestions as to how to deal with them.

Terms and conditions of employment

7 **Ex ❶:** Ss match items of vocabulary with the appropriate meaning in order to prepare for **Ex ❷**. T could ask Ss to scan the Terms and Conditions of Employment text in **Ex ❷** to see if they can work out the meaning of unknown words.

2 salary   money a person receives for work
3 to review   to look at something again in order to change it
4 overalls   work clothes that people wear to keep their own clothes clean
5 regulations   rules people have to follow
6 overtime   extra hours a person works
7 leave   holiday from work
8 line manager   the person you are directly responsible to
9 break   time to have a rest and possibly something to eat or drink
10 to provide   to give somebody something he/she needs

Working conditions

Comments about work

Reading **1** The staff at Amberley Advertising have a comments box. Read the comments and answer the questions.

1 Why is one employee unhappy about taking calls?
2 What kind of supply problems does the office have?
3 What are the problems with pay?
4 What stops people from doing their job efficiently?
5 One person makes a suggestion as well as a comment. What is it?

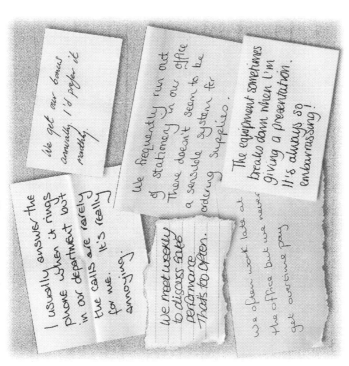

We get our bonuses annually. I'd prefer it monthly.

I usually answer the phone when it rings in our department but the calls are rarely for me. It's really annoying.

We frequently run out of stationery in our office. There doesn't seem to be a sensible system for ordering supplies.

We meet weekly to discuss sales performance. That's too often.

The equipment sometimes breaks down when I'm giving a presentation. It's always so embarrassing!

We often work late at the office but we never get overtime pay.

Vocabulary **2** Put the words into the correct order on the line below.

never   sometimes   always

usually ——→ How often? ←—— often

rarely   occasionally   frequently

never
⋮
always

Work in pairs. Compare your order with your partner.

Grammar **3** Look at the comments on the previous page. What do you notice about the position of the adverb in each one? Complete the information below.

Adverbs of frequency: word order

- Words such as always, _____, _____, frequently, _____, occasionally, rarely and _____ usually come before the verb.
- However, these words come _____ the verb to be.
- Words such as hourly, daily, _____, _____ and _____ come after the verb, often at the end of the sentence.

Unit 29

Speaking **4** Work in pairs. Find something that you both do:

frequently   occasionally   annually   weekly

5 Work in pairs. Look at the comments again. How would you deal with them?

Terms and conditions of employment

Vocabulary **1** Match the following words with the correct meaning.

1 shift — work clothes that people wear to keep their own clothes clean
2 salary — rules people have to follow
3 to review — a period of work which starts when another one finishes
4 overalls — money a person receives for work
5 regulations — the person you are directly responsible to
6 overtime — holiday from work
7 leave — to look at something again in order to change it
8 line manager — to give somebody something he/she needs
9 break — extra hours a person works
10 to provide — time to have a rest and possibly something to eat or drink

Working conditions

8 **Ex 2:** Ss read the Terms and Conditions of Employment text for gist and decide what type of work the document refers to.

*Factory work (**shifts, safety regulations, overalls**).*

Ss then read the multiple-choice questions before looking for the answers in the text.

1 B   2 B   3 C   4 A

9 **Ex 3:** Ss work in pairs to discuss their conditions of employment. Some ideas have been given but Ss do not have to discuss all of them. They may also have ideas of their own. The pairs then give feedback to the whole class on what was the same for both partners.

Self-study

Ex 1: *Suggested answers:*
- *paper, stationery, supplies, time, money*
- *holidays, overtime, salary, problems*
- *holidays, overtime, orders, stock*
- *computers, telephone calls, customers*

Ex 2:

```
r o e e m i t r e v o
p e m p l o y m e n t
s r g t n q f b e r f
u s d u q h j m w r i
p o s a l a r y v e h
p f w z w a a n t v s
l e k v d m t u s i e
i t x b b g a i f e w
e   s l a r e v o w s
c o n t r a c t n x
s x e o v y t e f a s
```

Ex 3: *1 with   2 about   3 at   4 of*
       5 of   6 in   7 at/in   8 with

Ex 5: *1 B   2 E   3 G   4 F*

Essential vocabulary

Frequency words
annually
daily
monthly
rarely
weekly

Working conditions
at (the current) rate
bonus
break
day off
employment
equipment
health and safety
leave (holiday)
line manager
overalls
overtime
regulations
salary
shift
supplies

General
annoying
to arrange
to break down
to consult
efficient
in operation
instead of
a review
to run out of
stationery

The words in italics are not on the Cambridge BEC 1 wordlist.

2 Read this page of Fibretech's conditions of employment. What type of work is it?

FIBRETECH PLASTICS

TERMS AND CONDITIONS OF EMPLOYMENT
These terms and conditions should be read before you sign your contract.

SALARY
Your starting salary is £14,000. This is reviewed annually.

HOURS
The normal hours of work are eight hours a day, Monday to Friday. A shift system is in operation. The shifts are:
A 06:00 - 14:00   B 14:00 - 22:00   C 22:00 - 6:00.

There are three shift groups and the following system is in operation.

Week one:	Group one	Shift A	Group two	Shift B	Group three	Shift C
Week two:	Group one	Shift B	Group two	Shift C	Group three	Shift A
Week three:	Group one	Shift C	Group two	Shift A	Group three	Shift B

For your first shift, week commencing ___8/6___ you will be in Group ___3___ and Week ___3___ will be in operation. On the first morning report to your line manager ___John Knight___.

HEALTH AND SAFETY
Please read the safety regulations attached. If you have any questions, contact the Health and Safety Officer, whose name is at the top of the regulations sheet. If you have any health problems, please inform the Senior Nurse, ___Jane Thomas___. If you cannot work because of illness, please telephone the factory before your shift is due to start.

ANNUAL LEAVE
During your first year of employment you are allowed twenty days' leave. This should be arranged with your line manager.

OVERTIME
If you work more than forty hours a week, you will be paid at the current overtime rate. Your line manager will keep a record of the overtime you work. If you work on public holidays, you will be paid at the current rates. If you prefer, time can be taken instead of extra pay for public holidays and overtime.

CLOTHING
The Supplies Department provides overalls. Inform Supplies of your size two days before you need them. You can also order any other special equipment you need for your job from Supplies.

Choose the correct option to complete the sentences.

1 This employee will start work at
   A 06.00.
   B 14.00.
   C 22.00.

2 Employees consult their line manager about
   A health problems.
   B their annual holidays.
   C a salary review.

3 If employees work on public holidays, the company will give them
   A only extra money.
   B only days off.
   C extra money or days off.

4 The company provides
   A special clothing.
   B no special clothing.
   C a uniform.

Speaking **3** Work in pairs. Discuss your conditions of employment. Use the ideas below.

hours   overtime   leave   clothing   health and safety

Which things are the same for you and your partner?

---

1 Write two things at work which:
• you can run out of.
• you discuss with your line manager.
• you keep a record of.
• you find really annoying.

2 Look at the word search below. Find ten words from the Terms and Conditions of Employment sheet on the opposite page. You can move backwards, down and as well as forwards. You can move across, down and diagonally.

```
r o e e m i t r e v o
p e m p l o y m e n t
s r g t n q f b e r f
u s d u q h j m w r i
p o s a l a r y v v e h
p f w z w a a n t v s
l e k v d m t u s i e
i t x b b g a i f e w
e s l a r e v o w s
s c o n t r a c t n x
s x e o v t e f a s
```

3 Complete the sentences with the prepositions below. You can use the prepositions more than once.

about   at   in   with   of

1 You should arrange your holiday ___ the line manager.
2 I need to consult my boss ___ that.
3 If you work more than 40 hours, you will be paid ___ the current overtime rate.
4 If you want, you can have time off instead ___ overtime pay.

5 We need to keep a record ___ the hours you work every month.
6 A shift system is ___ operation.
7 I don't work late ___ the office very often.
8 We have a lot of problems ___ pay.

4 Choose three of these areas. Write about your own conditions of employment.

hours   overtime   leave
clothing   health and safety

Exam practice
• Look at the Terms and Conditions of Employment again.
• For questions 1-4, use the information in the text to match each sentence with one of the company departments A-G.
• For each question, mark the correct letter A-G.
• Do not use any letter more than once.

1 Someone in this department helps people who feel ill at work. ___

2 Employees who need special boots for their job go to ___

3 If employees have problems with their pay, they should speak to someone in ___

4 If employees think something in the workplace is dangerous, they should contact ___

A Production
B Medical
C Catering
D Human Resources
E Supplies
F Health and Safety
G Accounts

Company history

Objectives: To enable Ss to describe companies and their histories
                    To practise reading for specific information
                    To review the past simple and prepositions of time

Materials needed: No cassette needed
                       Cards – 8 Cards: *Pass Cambridge BEC 1 Unit 2a* One set per pair/group

Unit overview

- ### The history of Volkswagen

Warmer	T elicits any knowledge/experience of VW/Beetles.
Reading	Ss do a quiz about Volkswagen in pairs then scan a text to find answers to the quiz. Ss then answer multiple-choice questions.
Vocabulary	Ss scan the text again to pick out target vocabulary.
Language focus	Ss review the form of the past simple.
Speaking	Ss exchange information about their own company's history.

- ### Company profile

Vocabulary	Ss match company descriptions with definitions.
Speaking	Ss order cards to make a company organigram then describe the company structure.
	Ss exchange information about the present situation of their own companies.

- ### Self-study

Language focus	Gap-fill exercise (past simple).
Vocabulary	Sorting exercise (prepositions of time: *in, at, on*).
	Odd-one-out collocation exercise (verbs and nouns).
Exam practice	*Vocabulary matching exercise (Reading Test Part 2).*
	Note-writing exercise (Writing Test Part 2).

The history of Volkswagen

1 **Warmer (books closed):** T asks Ss if they know what the most successful car ever is: the Volkswagen Beetle. T then asks Ss what they know about Volkswagen (VW) and VW Beetles. T can ask if any Ss own/have owned a Beetle and what they thought about the car.

2 **Ex ❶:** The quiz focuses Ss' attention on the subject matter of the unit and introduces Ss to the history of Volkswagen. Ss do the quiz in pairs. T does not give the correct answers as Ss will have to scan the text to find them in **Ex ❷**.

3 **Ex ❷:** Ss check their answers to the quiz by scanning through the text on page 14. T reminds Ss that they are scanning the text for relevant information only and do not need to read for detailed comprehension. Ss will look for vocabulary in Ex ❹ so it is probably best if T does not answer questions concerning the vocabulary in the text at this stage.

1 B	2 B	3 A	4 C	5 B

4 **Ex ❸:** Ss read the text again and answer the multiple-choice questions. T makes sure Ss identify the relevant passage of text in support of their answers. Ss should always read the questions carefully, paying attention to features such as absolutes (e.g. *completely* in Question 2). These are traps for Ss reading the questions too quickly.

1 C	2 B	3 A	4 B	5 C

Company history

The history of Volkswagen

Speaking **1** How much do you know about Volkswagen? Work in pairs and do the quiz below.

1 The company was first registered in

   A 1912.   B 1938.   C 1947.

2 The company produced its first car in

   A 1920.   B 1938.   C 1947.

3 The company exported the first Beetle to the USA in

   A 1949.   B 1957.   C 1976.

4 How many Beetles have been produced?

   A 3 million.   B about 12 million.   C over 20 million.

5 The company opened a Chinese joint venture in

   A 1977.   B 1982.   C 1994.

Volkswagen
a history

Ferdinand Porsche started work on the 'people's car' with money he received from the German government in 1934. First of all he travelled to America to learn about car production. Then in 1938 he returned to Germany, founded Volkswagen GmbH and started production with his new American machinery in Wolfsburg, Lower Saxony.

Commercial production stopped during the war and the factory and its 9,000 workers fell into British hands in 1945. After the war the British helped the local economy by ordering 20,000 cars but decided not to take over the company as they did not think it had a future. Instead, Heinrich Nordhoff took over as Managing Director and the Volkswagen success story began.

Within five years annual production went from 20,000 to 230,000 cars and the company founded its first South American subsidiary, Volkswagen do Brasil S.A. In 1949 the first exports to the USA arrived in New York, where they were described as 'beetle-like' and the VW Beetle legend was born. Thirty-two years later the 20 millionth Beetle rolled off a Volkswagen de Mexico production line. In 1960 Volkswagen became a public limited company valued at DM600m.

The company continued its globalisation by setting up its own production facilities in Australia (1957), Nigeria (1973) and Japan (1990) while expanding into the USA (1976) and Spain (1986) by buying car manufacturers. The company also set up a joint venture in China (1982). Political events at the end of 1989 gave VW the opportunity to move into central Europe, where it soon began production in the former East Germany and expanded into the Czech Republic.

Today Volkswagen AG is Europe's largest car-maker with 242,770 employees and a turnover of $65bn. With new versions of two of the world's most successful cars, the Beetle and the Golf, the future for VW looks every bit as bright as its past.

3 Choose the correct option to complete the sentences.

1 Porsche produced the first Volkswagen car

   A ten months after he received government money.

   B three years after he received government money.

   C four years after he received government money.

2 During the war the company

   A stopped producing cars completely.

   B stopped producing cars for sale to the public.

   C continued producing cars as before.

Company history

1957

1990

1982

1973

1938

1986

1950

1976

Self-study 🔑

Ex ❶:

1 tried	2 visited	3 found	4 were
5 decided	6 sold	7 expanded	8 began
9 had	10 bought	11 had	12 set up
13 went	14 announced		

Ex ❷:

IN:	December	1992	summer	the 1980s
AT:	10.30	Christmas	the weekend (UK)	the weekend (US)
ON:	Friday	23 July	Tuesday morning	

Ex ❸: 1 stop 2 produce 3 make

Ex ❹: 1 E 2 C 3 A 4 F 5 D

Ex ❺: *Suggested answer: (19 words)*
New sales brochures have arrived. Could you please collect your copies from the Marketing Dept as soon as possible?

Essential vocabulary

Companies	**Activities**	**General**
holding company	to buy	facilities
joint venture	to expand	*partnership*
parent company	to export	plant
public limited company (plc)	*to found*	stake
subsidiary	to manufacture	to survive
	to own	turnover
	to produce	
	to register	
	to set up	
	to take over	

The words in italics are not on the Cambridge BEC 1 wordlist.

---

5 **Ex ❹:** Ss now read the text once more for detailed comprehension, searching for specific vocabulary to match a list of definitions. T ensures that Ss know that the words are in the same order in the text. When Ss report back, T asks for the whole sentence and not just individual words, thus encouraging Ss to use the new vocabulary in context. Only when the feedback has been completed does T invite questions concerning any remaining vocabulary problems from the text.

🔑 1 take over   2 subsidiary   3 public limited company
   4 globalisation   5 setting up production facilities   6 turnover

6 Ss will undoubtedly be familiar with the past simple; therefore, the **Don't forget!** section simply reminds them about the use of auxiliaries in question-forming and negatives.

T should ensure that Ss are confident about the pronunciation of past tense endings. It is probably sufficient for T to point out that most past tense endings do not require the addition of another syllable: /ɪd/ is required only if the verb ends in *t* or *d*. T may wish to look at the **Language note** at the end of the T's notes for this unit for further information.

T could ask Ss to scan quickly through the text about Volkswagen again and put all of the regular past simple verbs into the three categories:

/t/   *stopped, helped*
/d/   *received, travelled, returned, arrived, described, rolled, continued*
/ɪd/   *started, founded, decided, expanded*

7 **Ex ❺:** If the class is an in-company group, Ss could pool their knowledge of their company's history to present to the class. Alternatively, groups could compete to provide the most information within a time limit, with other groups challenging the accuracy of the information. On the other hand, open groups would suit a genuine information exchange. T should encourage Ss to ask for information and not just transcribe their partner's monologue. If necessary, T quickly brainstorms useful questions that will help Ss complete the task.

Company profile

T may wish to omit this section of the unit with very weak groups. The vocabulary enables Ss to talk about their companies. However, little of the vocabulary is in the BEC 1 wordlist.

8 **Ex ❶:** Ss can do the task individually or in pairs. *Subsidiary* and *public limited company* both appeared in **Ex ❹** in the previous section. The exercise is therefore a combination of vocabulary consolidation and input, preparing Ss for **Ex ❷**.

🔑 1 A public limited company is owned by shareholders.
   2 A parent company has a controlling stake in another company.
   3 A wholly-owned subsidiary is completely owned by another company.
   4 A holding company only administers other companies in a group.

9 **Ex ❷:** T explains the task to Ss before handing out the cards. Ss lay out the cards on the table and form an organigram. They then present their organigram on the board. The class challenges anything they are not happy with and reaches consensus before T provides any necessary correction. The answer appears at the end of the T's notes for this unit.

10 **Ex ❸:** T encourages Ss to ask their partner a lot of questions. T also encourages Ss to make notes and present a quick profile of their partner's company to the class if time permits. Alternatively, the quick profile could be set as a homework writing task.

3 The British did not take over the company because

A they did not think it would survive.
B they did not have enough money.
C Heinrich Nordhoff had already bought it.

4 Between 1945 and 1950 production increased

A every year by 20,000.
B from 20,000 to 230,000.
C by 20,000 to 230,000.

5 Volkswagen expanded globally by buying other car companies

A and forming partnerships.
B and building its own car plants.
C and also building new car plants and forming partnerships.

Vocabulary **4** Find words in the text which mean the same as the following.

1 buy more than 51% of a company ....
2 a company partly, or wholly, owned by another company ....
3 a company partly, or wholly, owned by shareholders ....
4 worldwide expansion ....
5 organising and building a factory ....
6 income of a company ....

Past simple

- All regular past simple verbs end in **-ed**. For a list of useful irregular verbs, see the back of this book (page 157).
- Negatives are formed with **didn't**.
  The British **didn't** think Volkswagen would survive.
- Questions are formed with **did**.
  When **did** the company produce *its first car?*

Unit 3
Unit 96

Speaking **5** Work in pairs. Find out five things about the history of your partner's company.

Company profile

Vocabulary **1** Match the company descriptions with the definitions.

1 A subsidiary .... is owned by shareholders.
2 A public limited company .... is at least 51% owned by another company.
3 A parent company .... only administers other companies in a group.
4 A wholly-owned subsidiary .... has a controlling stake in another company.
5 A holding company .... is completely owned by another company.

Speaking **2** Work in pairs. Your teacher will give you some cards. Read about the eight companies in the MNE group and form an organigram of the group structure.

Speaking **3** Work in pairs. Find out about your partner's company today. Use the ideas below.

size   turnover   locations   products   markets   subsidiaries

---

3 Delete the verbs which do not go with the nouns.

a company: found / set up / stop / take over

a subsidiary: produce / open / own / found

production: stop / make / continue / begin

1 Complete the history of the clothing company Gap, Inc. Put the verbs in brackets into the correct past simple form.

It started in San Francisco in 1969 when Donald G. Fisher (1 *try*) _____ to buy a pair of jeans. He (2 *visit*) _____ store after store but only (3 *find*) _____ jeans departments that (4 *be*) _____ disorganised and difficult to shop in. So in August that year Fisher and his wife Doris (5 *decide*) _____ to open a well-organised store that (6 *sell*) _____ only jeans.

The company soon (7 *expand*) _____ rapidly throughout the USA and in 1974 it (8 *begin*) _____ selling its own-label products. Ten years later it (9 *have*) _____ 550 stores and in 1983 it (10 *buy*) _____ Banana Republic, a mail-order business. In 1985 Gap President Mickey Drexler (11 *have*) _____ a bad experience buying clothes for his children so he (12 *set up*) _____ GapKids in 1986. The following year the company (13 *go*) _____ international with a store in London.

In 1991 the company (14 *announce*) _____ that it would sell only its own-label merchandise. Gap, Inc. now has stores in Canada, France, Germany, Japan and the UK and turnover of over $5bn a year.

2 Write the following time expressions in the correct group below.

December	23 July
Friday	1992
10.30	summer
Christmas	Tuesday morning
the weekend	the 1980s

in	at	on
December		

Exam practice

4
- Look at the list of industries **A-H** below.
- For questions **1-5**, decide which industry **A-H** each person works in.
- For each question, mark the correct letter **A-H**.
- Do not use any letter more than once.

> **A** Financial services
> **B** Manufacturing
> **C** Telecommunications
> **D** Leisure
> **E** Retail
> **F** Construction
> **G** Pharmaceutical
> **H** Publishing

1 We have a chain of supermarkets all over Britain.
2 The company specialises in video-conferencing facilities.
3 We invest our clients' money on the stock market.
4 Our company is involved in major engineering projects.
5 I manage the local sports centre.

Exam practice

5
- Your company has just received new company brochures from the printers.
- Write a note to the Sales Manager:
  * saying the brochures have arrived
  * saying which department they are in
  * asking her to collect her copies immediately.
- Write **about 20 words**.

Language note: Pronunciation of -ed in regular verbs

- If the infinitive ends in *t* or *d*, the *-ed* ending is pronounced /ɪd/.

  e.g. **t** *started* /stɑːtɪd/

  d *expanded* /ɪkspændɪd/

- If the infinitive ends in a voiceless sound, the past simple ending is pronounced /t/, which is also voiceless.

  e.g. **p** *stopped* /stɒpt/

- If the infinitive ends in a voiced sound, the past simple ending is pronounced /d/, which is also voiced.

  e.g. **b** *described* /dɪscraɪbd/

Ex ❷: Company profile

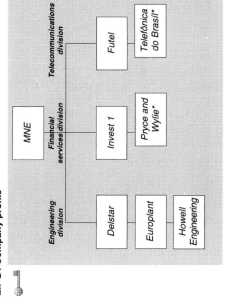

Company activities

Objectives:	To enable Ss to describe company activities
	To practise reading for specific information
	To raise awareness of cohesion and connectors of addition and contrast
	To review the present continuous
Materials needed:	None

Unit overview

• Investing in central Europe

Warmer	T introduces the topic and elicits Ss' experience/knowledge.
Reading	Ss answer questions based on a diagram showing investment in central Europe.
Language focus	Ss review the present simple/continuous contrast and stative verbs.
Speaking	Ss discuss reasons for inward investment.

• Driving eastwards

Reading	Ss do a jigsaw reading exercise, before scanning the text to answer 'Right, Wrong, Doesn't say' questions.
Vocabulary	Ss scan the text for connectors of addition/contrast then use the connectors to link information from the text.
Speaking	Ss draw and explain maps of their companies' activities.

• Self-study

Vocabulary	Gap-fill exercise (present continuous).
Language focus	Gap-fill exercise (present simple vs continuous).
Vocabulary	Matching exercise (companies, nationalities and activities).
Exam practice	Multiple-choice gap-fill text (Reading Test Part 6).

Investing in central Europe

1 Warmer (books closed): T asks Ss for examples of companies investing overseas and reasons why. For Ts working in central and eastern Europe, T asks Ss for examples of inward investment and the changes it brings. T brainstorms car companies and locations they might choose for foreign investment.

2 Ex ❶: Ss look at the visual on page 17. T checks vocabulary such as *plant, model, van, assembly* and abbreviations such as *m* and *bn*. Ss then look at the questions and scan the visual for the answers. T asks Ss to support their answers with relevant information.

1 Fiat ($1.8bn)
2 Volkswagen (in Mosel)
3 Volkswagen (in the former East Germany, Hungary, Czech Republic, Slovakia, Poland)
4 Poland ($3.52bn)
5 Slovakia ($120m)

3 Ex ❷: This exercise is a reminder of the different uses of the present tenses. Ss sort the uses into two groups. T asks Ss to give an example of each use.

Present simple	Present continuous
General facts (*Volkswagen manufactures cars.*) **Routines** (*I work for Audi.*) **States** (*VW now owns 70% of Skoda.*)	**Something happening now** (*Daewoo is now building a new plant.*) **Temporary situations** (*Many firms are investing a lot of money in central Europe.*) **Changing situations** (*Costs are rising slowly.*)

4 T reminds Ss about stative verbs and refers them to the **Don't forget!** section. The exception of *I think/I am thinking* hints at further complexity regarding the use of these tenses. However, T need not focus on more complex issues beyond the scope of Cambridge BEC 1.

5 Ex ❸: The pairwork activity allows Ss to discuss the unit topic and also acts as a prediction exercise for the text and a chance to introduce some relevant vocabulary. Ss work in pairs/groups and list possible reasons for investment, which can be written on the board. Before Ss do **Ex ❶** in the next section, they can quickly check their predictions by scanning through the text.

Reasons given in the text:
Cheap workforce
Generous government inward investment grants
Slow economic growth at home
Strong growth in central/eastern European car markets
Possible to take over existing facilities/companies cheaply
Good locations for exporting to the former Soviet Union

Other possible reasons not mentioned in the text:
By manufacturing in Europe, Asian and US companies avoid restrictions on imports into Europe
Investing in the area boosts local economies and adds to market growth
Higher returns on investments due to low costs
Shareholder pressure to increase performance

Driving eastwards

6 Ex ❶: The jigsaw reading task is not an exam-style exercise but introduces the subject of cohesion. Texts can be made cohesive through the use of various devices. In this case the text is made cohesive through lexical cohesion (e.g. the mention of *VW* and *Fiat* in paragraph 3 refers back to *the world's largest car-makers* in paragraph 2. The writer also uses (italicised) connectors of addition and contrast. Ss quickly read through the five extracts (skimming) to establish context and content. Then Ss read the text again and order the extracts. Ss may find the exercise easier if T photocopies the page and cuts up the paragraphs for them to re-assemble. When reporting back, Ss explain their decisions and quote relevant passages. T corrects as necessary and invites questions concerning difficult vocabulary in the text.

Suggested answers:
2 In addition to the cheap labour, ...
3 Volkswagen, for example, ...
4 Companies such as VW and Fiat ...
5 However, in spite of all these advantages ...

Company activities

Investing in central Europe

Reading ❶ Look at the diagram showing car company investment in central Europe. Answer the questions.

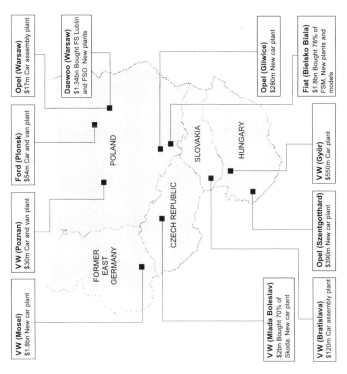

VW (Mosel)
$1.8bn New car plant

VW (Poznan)
$30m Car and van plant

Ford (Plonsk)
$54m Car and van plant

Opel (Warsaw)
$17m Car assembly plant

Daewoo (Warsaw)
$1.34bn Bought FS Lublin and FSO. New plants

Opel (Gliwice)
$280m New car plant

Fiat (Bielsko Biala)
$1.8bn Bought 78% of FSM. New plants and models

FORMER EAST GERMANY

POLAND

CZECH REPUBLIC

SLOVAKIA

HUNGARY

VW (Mlada Boleslav)
$2bn Bought 70% of Skoda. New car plant

VW (Bratislava)
$120m Car assembly plant

Opel (Szentgotthárd)
$390m New car plant

VW (Györ)
$550m Car plant

1 Who is investing the most in Poland?

2 Who is building a new car plant in the former East Germany?

3 Who is investing in five central European countries?

4 Which country is receiving the highest total investment?

5 Which country is receiving the least investment?

Grammar ❷ When do we use the present simple (I work) and present continuous (I am working)? Write each description in the correct group at the top of the opposite page.

general facts   something happening now   routines

states   temporary situations   changing situations

Present simple	Present continuous
general facts	

Stative verbs

We do not use the continuous form to express the following:

opinions (*think, believe*)
senses (*see, hear*)
emotions (*like, love*)
ownership (*own, have*)

❗ *I think it's a good idea.* (opinion)
I'm thinking of changing my job. (process of thinking)

Speaking ❸ Work in pairs. Why are companies investing so much in central Europe?

Driving eastwards

Reading ❶ Put the five extracts below into the correct order to complete the newspaper article.

Driving eastwards

By Paul Taylor

Istvann Mateew, a 32-year-old production engineer, works at Audi's engine plant in Györ, western Hungary. He earns about $400 a week *but* he would earn around eight times as much for doing the same job in Germany. Low wages are just one of the attractions for the world's leading car companies that are investing in eastern and central Europe.

Companies such as VW and Fiat have other reasons for investing so heavily in the east. With low-cost Asian imports in western Europe, they believe that cheaper production in the east is *not only* a way of developing new markets *but also* necessary for protecting those at home. *Moreover*, the big investors are already looking beyond to the former Soviet Union and the huge profits they hope to make there.

However, in spite of all these advantages, not all car-makers are ready to buy or build production facilities in the east. Some manufacturers expect wages and costs to rise quickly. *Although* there are signs that wages are climbing, it will be years before salaries reach western levels.

In addition to the cheap labour, generous state investment grants have *also* brought car-makers to central Europe. What really attracts them, however, is the fact that sales are growing by up to 41 per cent in countries like Poland and the Czech Republic. With low growth at home, the world's largest car-makers think their money is better spent abroad.

Volkswagen, for example, is spending $1.8bn on new car and engine plants in the former East Germany. *Furthermore*, VW has spent over $2bn buying and modernising Skoda, the leading Czech car-maker. Similarly, Fiat has acquired 80 per cent of FSM, the largest car-maker in Poland, *and* is spending $830m on developing two new models by 2002.

7 **Ex 2**: T advises Ss to read through all the questions before scanning through the text. Ss should check carefully whether there is enough evidence in the text to declare the statements either 'Right' or 'Wrong'. If there is not, Ss should choose 'Doesn't say'.

| 1 B | 2 A | 3 A | 4 C | 5 B | 6 B |

8 **Ex 3**: T checks Ss understand what connectors of *Addition* and *Contrast* are and elicits examples. T asks Ss to find the italicised connectors in the text and put them into the correct group. When reporting back, Ss identify the passage and read the connector in context.

If *not only ...* is used before the verb, the verb needs to be inverted. However, if it is used after the verb, there is no problem. At this level T is safest avoiding the subject of inversion with Ss. T must therefore be careful when constructing sentences with this phrase.

Although Ss are unlikely to need to use *in spite of* or *despite* at Cambridge BEC 1 level, they need to understand them. T may wish to point out that both *in spite of* and *despite* are followed by: 1) a noun, 2) -*ing* or 3) *the fact that*; they are not followed by the infinitive.

Addition	Contrast
and	*but*
in addition	*however*
furthermore	*although*
moreover	*in spite of*
also	
not only ... but also	

9 **Ex 4**: As the example shows, there are several ways of connecting the ideas. Weaker Ss can complete the exercise successfully by using just *and* or *but*. T elicits different options to illustrate these alternatives. For further practice Ss could use the connectors to make sentences about their own companies/jobs.

Suggested answers:
2 Opel is opening a new car plant in Poland. *Moreover/Furthermore/In addition, it is opening a plant in Hungary.*
   Opel is not only opening a new car plant in Poland but also a plant in Hungary.
3 Wages are lower in central Europe. *Moreover/Furthermore/In addition, workers are more flexible.*
   Wages are not only lower in central Europe but workers are also more flexible.
4 Wages are increasing in eastern Germany but they are 15-25% lower than in the west.
   Although wages are increasing in eastern Germany, they are 15-25% lower than in the west.
   In spite of an increase, wages in eastern Germany are 15-25% lower than in the west.
5 VW has bought companies in central Europe but also built new factories there.
   VW has not only bought companies in central Europe but this is not the only reason companies are investing there.
6 Wages are lower in central Europe but this is not the only reason companies are investing there.
   Although wages are lower in central Europe, this is not the only reason companies are investing there.

10 **Ex 5**: T asks Ss to draw a map showing their company's markets and activities. T reminds Ss that the maps are only diagrams and need not be works of art. Ss then mark on important locations and exchange maps with a partner. Ss take it in turns to ask each other what the locations are and what activities take place there. Ss should be encouraged to ask follow-up questions.

Self-study

Essential vocabulary

Addition	Contrast	Activities	General
also	although	assembly	to attract
furthermore	however	to build	attraction
moreover	in spite of	to develop	to climb
not only ... but also		to grow	costs
		to invest	to earn
		investment	*flexible*
		to modernise	low
			model
			to receive
			van
			wages

The words in italics are not on the Cambridge BEC 1 wordlist.

② Say whether the following sentences are 'Right' or 'Wrong'. If there is not enough information to answer, choose 'Doesn't say'.

1 Low pay is the biggest attraction for investors.

   A Right   B Wrong   C Doesn't say

2 Central European governments are trying to attract inward investment.

   A Right   B Wrong   C Doesn't say

3 Central European markets are growing faster than western markets.

   A Right   B Wrong   C Doesn't say

4 Fiat intends to buy the remaining 20% of FSM.

   A Right   B Wrong   C Doesn't say

5 Wages in the east will soon be equivalent to those in western Europe.

   A Right   B Wrong   C Doesn't say

6 The big car-makers are interested in selling cars only in central Europe.

   A Right   B Wrong   C Doesn't say

Vocabulary ③ Look at the words in *italics* in the text. Write the words in the correct group below.

Addition	Contrast
and	but

④ Now use the words to connect the following ideas.

1 production is cheaper in central Europe / car plants are expensive to build

   Production is cheaper in central Europe but car plants are expensive to build.

   Although production is cheaper in central Europe, car plants are expensive to build.

2 Opel is opening a new car plant in Poland / it is opening a plant in Hungary

3 wages are lower in central Europe / workers are more flexible

4 wages are increasing in eastern Germany / wages are 15-25% lower than in the west

5 VW has bought companies in central Europe / VW has built new factories there

6 wages are lower in central Europe / not the only reason companies are investing there

Speaking ⑤ Work in pairs. Draw a map showing your company's markets. Explain to your partner what is happening in these places at the moment.

Company activities

Exam practice

- Read the newspaper article below about Japanese car companies.
- Choose the correct word from **A**, **B** or **C** to fill each gap.
- For each question, mark the correct letter **A**, **B** or **C**.

Japanese car-makers increase European production

Japan's third largest car manufacturer, Honda Motors, has announced plans to build a third model in England. The model, a small car to compete **(1)** ..... the Ford Fiesta in the UK, will be produced at its Swindon plant in south-west England and not at a new location in central Europe. The move will **(2)** ..... Swindon's output to 250,000 cars a year.

The expansion follows the decision in January by Nissan, Japan's second biggest car-maker, to build a third model at **(3)** ..... Sunderland plant in north-east England.

The car-makers' plans come **(4)** ..... a time when Japan's biggest car company, Toyota, is considering **(5)** ..... its third European model at a new plant in northern France **(6)** ..... than expanding its present production facilities in England. Toyota is already looking at a possible location in a **(7)** ..... near the Belgian border. The area has a very high rate of unemployment, so generous government **(8)** ..... would be available to the company to create new jobs.

Toyota's strategy is to **(9)** ..... the French market, where sales for all Japanese car-makers have been weak due **(10)** .....strong competition from Renault and Peugeot-Citroën. Toyota said the plans were still being studied and that a decision would be made early next year.

	A	B	C
1	for	to	with
2	rise	raise	build
3	its	it's	his
4	on	at	in
5	building	build	built
6	other	instead	rather
7	country	land	region
8	grants	fund	money
9	start	leave	enter
10	to	of	at

---

① Complete the sentences with the present continuous form of the verbs below.

grow   invest   build   develop   earn   modernise

1 Siemens _____ some new offices in London.

2 We _____ a new product at the moment.

3 Markets in central Europe _____ rapidly and are now more attractive to large companies.

4 They _____ the offices this month so it's very hard to concentrate with all the noise.

5 The department _____ a lot of money in new computers at the moment.

6 Most workers _____ more money than before.

② Put each verb in brackets into the present simple or continuous.

1 They (work) _____ a lot of overtime at the moment.

2 The company usually (spend) _____ a lot on foreign investment.

3 We (think) _____ about moving into central Europe.

4 Normally a car maintenance engineer in central Europe (not / earn) _____ as much as an engineer in Germany.

5 They (build) _____ a new car plant in Poland this year.

6 Ford (not / invest) _____ a lot in central Europe right now.

7 Central European markets (grow) _____ fast.

8 Some car-makers (think) _____ that the other companies (take) _____ a big risk investing so much in central Europe.

9 Central European governments (want) _____ to attract investment so they (offer) _____ generous investment grants at the moment.

10 Although wages (climb) _____ , it will be a long time before they reach western levels.

③ Match the names, nationalities and activities. Then write complete sentences.

Aeroflot is a Russian airline.

1 Aeroflot	USA	chocolate manufacturer
2 Nokia	Switzerland	airline
3 Reuters	Russia	food group
4 Timberland	France	software distributor
5 ABN Amro	Finland	bank
6 Daewoo	Britain	electronics company
7 Godiva	Korea	clothes manufacturer
8 Swatch	Netherlands	press agency
9 Softbank	Belgium	car manufacturer
10 Danone	Japan	watch manufacturer

Company activities

Exam focus: Vocabulary

Objectives:	To provide Ss with useful strategies for coping with unknown vocabulary
	To present useful ways of organising and storing new vocabulary
Materials needed:	Optional – **Blank cards for vocabulary cards activity**
	A set of cards (taken from any teaching material) showing collocations or opposites

Unit overview

● **Vocabulary in the examination**

Warmer: T writes up the words *vocabulary* and *grammar* to introduce the topic. T ensures Ss understand why vocabulary is an **Exam focus** unit.

● **Understanding words**

Ss identify types of words then label the types of words gapped in sentences and complete the gaps.

Ss guess the meaning of potentially unfamiliar words through the use of context.

● **Storing new vocabulary**

Ss discuss the advantages and disadvantages of five ways of physically recording vocabulary.

Ss then look at examples of five ways of organising vocabulary and discuss which they use and how they are useful. Ss then assign groups of words to the most appropriate means of storage.

● **Vocabulary cards**

Ss look at an example of a vocabulary storage card and complete cards in a similar way. Ss work in pairs and discuss which types of information they would choose to store on cards.

T highlights the use of cards for vocabulary building (collocations, opposites etc.).

● **Building your vocabulary**

Ss focus on word families and note ways of changing form through suffixes, prefixes etc. They then build up words and write example sentences.

For homework/self-study Ss are asked to identify and store useful vocabulary from the previous units.

Vocabulary

1 **Warmer (books closed):** T writes the words *grammar* and *vocabulary* on the board and asks students to say which is more important when learning a language. T explains that as the exam is heavily biased towards reading and listening, vocabulary is far more important than structure. T also explains that Ss are likely to encounter words in the texts which they do not know. T states the aims of the unit: to establish useful ways of guessing the meaning of words and storing and building new vocabulary.

2 **Ex ❶:** Ss work in pairs to identify the types of words.

2 *nouns*	*industry, company*
3 *prepositions*	*on, with*
4 *articles*	*a, the*
5 *connectors*	*but, although*
6 *adjectives*	*sharp, interesting*
7 *adverbs*	*slowly, soon*
8 *relative pronouns*	*which, that*

Ss then identify which type of word can fill the gaps and complete the sentences.

Suggested answers:
1 **adjective** - *sharp*
2 **preposition** - *in*
3 **adverb** - *soon*
4 **relative pronoun** - *which / that*
5 **article** - *the*
6 **connector** - *but*
7 **noun** - *technology*

3 **Ex ❷:** Before Ss do this exercise, T may wish to make up some sentences using nonsense words to make the point about information around the unknown word indicating its meaning (*e.g. I **boggle** my teeth every morning, I **gripple** for Linguarama etc.*). After Ss have done the exercise, T can elicit the language which helped them to guess the meaning of the words.

Storing new vocabulary

4 **Ex ❶:** Ss might wish to work in pairs as they discuss the advantages and disadvantages of the five ways of physically storing vocabulary. In feedback T also asks Ss which of the ways they themselves use. T encourages Ss to report any other ways they know and which they can recommend to other Ss.

5 **Ex ❷:** The increased emphasis on vocabulary in English language teaching over the last few years has resulted in many useful strategies for more effective organisation and learning of new vocabulary. Ss may not be aware of these, however, and the exercise is to introduce five basic strategies for organising and recording vocabulary.

T and Ss discuss the five ways and T elicits further uses of each type of visual.

Diagrams T elicits other useful areas which lend themselves to hierarchical diagrams (e.g. company organigram).

Tables T asks for other examples of collocation which can be stored in tables (e.g. *make/take/answer a call/enquiry*).

Keywords T asks Ss to think of a keyword relevant to them individually and suggests they build up partnerships (at least five) for homework.

Scales T asks for an example of another range of words which can be stored on a scale (e.g. *boiling, hot, warm, cool, cold, freezing*).

Word fields T suggests that, as with keywords, Ss may like to identify an important topic word and build other words around it. T makes the point that the words do not need to form partnerships with the keyword but simply be related in topic.

T refers Ss to the **Essential vocabulary** section at the back of the book and shows how the vocabulary is broken down by topic (word fields). T elicits other ways in which the **Essential vocabulary** of a particular unit could be stored.

Exam focus: Vocabulary

Vocabulary in the examination

You are not tested directly on vocabulary in the examination. However, you need to be able to deal with words you do not know in the Reading and Listening Tests. You also need to build your vocabulary so that you can read and listen successfully in the examination.

Understanding words

1 During the Cambridge BEC 1 examination you will have to guess the meaning of words from their type and the context. Match the following types of words with the examples.

1 verbs — sharp, interesting
2 nouns — buy, produce
3 prepositions — a, the
4 articles — which, that
5 connectors — industry, company
6 adjectives — on, with
7 adverbs — but, although
8 relative pronouns — slowly, soon

What type of word can fill each of the following gaps? Now complete the sentences.

1 There was a _____ rise in the number of unemployed.
2 I spoke to someone _____ the Marketing Department.
3 I expect the orders to arrive _____.
4 Here are the brochures _____ you asked for.
5 Barbara works for _____ same company as me.
6 I like the job _____ the money isn't very good.
7 The company invests a lot of money in _____.

2 Try to guess the meaning of the words in italics from the information in the rest of the sentence.

1 I would like to live in the city centre. Every day I have to *commute* to work and the train can be very slow!
2 The bank offers very cheap *mortgages* for people buying their first house.
3 We're going to *launch* the new product next week with TV advertisements.
4 Would you like me to *staple* all the pages together? Then if you drop them, it won't matter.
5 The company has cut jobs *despite* making large profits last year.
6 We've had a lot of telephone *enquiries* about the new product.
7 You don't need to worry about the expense of a taxi. The hotel has a *courtesy* bus which will take you to the airport whenever you want to go.

Storing new vocabulary

Speaking **1** As you learn new words on your course, it is important to store them effectively. You will need to find these words quickly, add to them and practise them. What are the advantages and disadvantages of storing new words in the following places?

- In your course book in the unit where you learn them
- On a separate sheet of paper
- In a separate vocabulary book in alphabetical order
- On cards
- On a computer

2 Look at the following ways of storing vocabulary. Which do you use?

Diagrams
Diagrams clearly show relationships that have some kind of hierarchy.

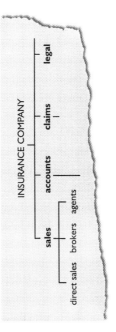

INSURANCE COMPANY
— sales — accounts — claims — legal
— direct sales — brokers — agents

Tables
These are particularly good for showing how words are used together. By using tables, you learn vocabulary in groups rather than single words. Write example sentences to make the table even more effective.

	a meeting	a conference	a training session	an appointment
have	✓	✓		✓
hold	✓	✓	✓	
attend	✓	✓	✓	
arrange	✓			✓

Keywords
You can show which words combine with a keyword. You also need to write example sentences.

travel		company
home	insurance	policy
car		claim
life		premium

6   Ex **3**: Ss work in pairs and decide how best to store the groups of words. Ss refer to the five ways illustrated earlier.

> *Suggested answers:*
> 1 scale
> 2 word field (*with the topic word being* **sales**)
> 3 table
> 4 diagram (*to show the hierarchy of the organisation*)
> 5 word field (*with topic word being* **terms and conditions**)
> 6 scale
> 7 diagram (*company organigram*)
> 8 keyword (*with words arranged to the right and left of the keyword* **bank**)

Vocabulary cards

7   Ex **1**: T may wish to hand blank cards to Ss to complete this exercise. T introduces the concept of vocabulary cards and elicits what kind of information would be useful on the cards. Ss then look at the example card in the book. Ss then produce their own cards for the words in the box. Ss compare versions in pairs before a group discussion on the advantages of including the various different types of information on a card. T also asks how Ss think they can best display their information on a card (both sides, colour coding etc.) and also how they can use the completed cards during their course.

8   The card illustrated is an example of the use of cards for the storage of vocabulary. T extends the discussion to illustrate cards for vocabulary building by showing cards for matching collocations and opposites etc. T can take in and demonstrate any relevant cards that he/she has made for other lessons or that he/she has taken from published materials. T suggests Ss might like to make their own cards and test themselves/each other by playing Pelmanism and Snap etc.

Building your vocabulary

9   Ex **1**: T directs Ss to look at some common ways of changing the form of words. T also makes the general point that although these ways are extremely useful, Ss will, of course, still need to double-check in their dictionaries as there are exceptions.

10 Ex **2**: Ss work in pairs and brainstorm as many different forms of the words as possible. T accepts any suitable answers but may challenge Ss to provide example sentences to ensure they can use the words correctly.

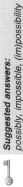

> *Suggested answers:*
> possibly, impossible, (im)possibility
> developer, development, developing, under/overdeveloped
> operator, operation, (in)operative, operational, operating
> safety, safely, unsafe
> generalise, generalisation, generally
> organisation, organiser, organised, disorganised
> privately, privatise, privatisation
> employer, employee, (un)employment, (un)employed

Ss write example sentences which are useful for them personally. T accepts -ise / -ize (*generalise / generalize*) spellings and explains that both are possible but all written work has to be consistent. The same applies to *our / or* (*colour / color*) spellings. T selects random samples from across the group.

11 T concludes by setting Ss a homework task: to look through the previous units in the book and select particularly useful vocabulary for themselves. T points out that vocabulary also includes phrases, idioms and collocations and not just single words. T encourages students to record items that they find useful or simply like. T also reminds students of the **Essential vocabulary** section which can be used for revision purposes.

Vocabulary cards

1 Cards can be an effective and flexible way of learning vocabulary. You can read them on the way to work if you travel by bus or train. Look at the example below and make cards for the following words. Use a dictionary to help you.

equipment   steady   available   receipt

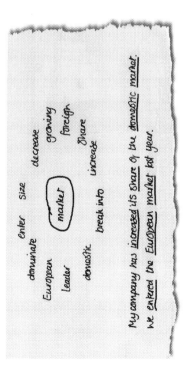

a translation
a definition
examples
other useful words
pronunciation
word grammar

subsidiary (Tochtergesellschaft)
- a company that is owned by another company
- countable noun - subsidiaries
- My company is a subsidiary of Siemens.
- We have several foreign subsidiaries.
- a subsidiary is owned by a parent company.

Building your vocabulary

1 Many words have several forms (produce, production, producer, productive and productively). Look at the following ways of changing the forms of words.

Change	Add	Example
Noun to verb	-ise	globalise, standardise
Verb to noun	-tion/sion/ment	confirmation, employment
Verb to person/company/machine	-er/or	manufacturer, investor
Adjective to noun	-ity/ty	probability, loyalty
Adjective to adverb	-ly/ily	normally, steadily
Adjective to its opposite	un-/im-/in-	uninteresting, improbable
To add the meaning "do again"	re-	relaunch, rewrite

2 Work in pairs. How many different forms of the words below can you think of? Use a dictionary to check your answers.

possible	develop	operate	safe
general	organise	private	employ

Now write example sentences for two forms of five of the words.

Scales

Groups of words that all measure the same thing can be stored together in order. The scale does not provide context so you need to write example sentences.

Frequency words

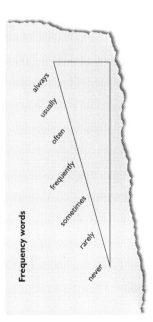

always
usually
often
frequently
sometimes
rarely
never

Word fields

If a group of words is connected with the same topic, store them in a word field. Decide what the topic word is and place the other words around it. It does not matter what type of word they are. Then write example sentences.

dominate   enter   size   decrease   growing   European   (market)   foreign   leader   share   domestic   increase   break into

My company has increased its share of the domestic market. We entered the European market last year.

3 Work in pairs. Now look at the groups of words below. What is the best way of storing them?

1 slightly, steadily, sharply, dramatically
2 commission, contract, target, results, figures, executive
3 send a package, send documents, send a shipment, send a letter, post documents, post a letter
4 group, holding company, division, subsidiaries, offices
5 pension, salary, leave, hours, duties
6 a long time ago, recently, currently, in the near future, long term
7 chairman, sales director, regional sales managers, sales executives, agents, head of production, production manager, shift managers
8 merchant bank, bank loan, bank transfer, bank manager, investment bank

Telephoning

Objectives: To practise telephoning language (including leaving and taking messages)
To practise listening for gist and specific information

Materials needed: Cassette - *Pass Cambridge BEC 1*
Activity sheets A and B

Unit overview

● Getting through

Listening 1	Ss listen to six telephone calls and match the calls with the correct descriptions.
Speaking	Ss produce appropriate responses to telephone phrases. Ss then listen again to identify the actual responses used in the calls.
Language focus	Ss review *will* for immediate decisions, offers and promises. Ss then do a matching exercise with phrases with *will*.
Reading	Ss find a telephone conversation in a maze.
Speaking	Ss select two items from the maze to make their own telephone conversation.

● Reasons for calling

Listening 2	Ss listen to a telephone receptionist take a message and note down the information before listening again for specific phrases.
Speaking	Ss do an information-gap activity, giving and taking telephone messages. (**Activity sheets** on pages 125 and 131)

● Self-study

Reading	Ordering exercise (telephone conversation).
	Gap-fill exercise (telephone conversation).
Exam practice	*Multiple-choice reading comprehension exercise (Reading Test Part 1).*

Getting through

1 **Warmer (books closed):** T asks Ss about their current use of English for telephoning. This is a chance to check basic vocabulary (*call, caller, make a call, leave/take a message*). T may wish to lead a brief discussion of the problems Ss experience in this area.

2 **Ex 1:** Ss listen to six phone calls and identify their content.

Call 2 *The receptionist connects the caller.*
Call 3 *The other person is not available so the caller will phone again later.*
Call 4 *The caller leaves a message.*
Call 5 *The caller waits for a short time then the receptionist connects her.*
Call 6 *The caller was cut off and phones again.*

Ss compare answers in pairs before feedback. T clears up any vocabulary points (*connect, cut off*).

3 **Ex 2:** T either does this as a T-led exercise or Ss work in pairs to produce suitable responses. Ss are not expected to replicate the responses on the cassette at this stage - but to suggest any possible answers. Ss then listen to the cassette again and compare with what the speakers actually said.

Answers (i.e. what is actually on the cassette):
1 a person's name (e.g. Lewis Taylor)
2 *No, it's all right thank you. I'll call back in about ten minutes.*
3 *Who's calling, please?*
4 *I'm afraid he's in a meeting. Can I take a message?*
5 *He should be available after lunch.*
6 *Right. I'll tell her you called back.*
7 *I'm afraid the line's busy.*
8 *Oh, sorry about that. I'll try to reconnect you.*

4 T draws Ss' attention to phrases with I'll (i.e. *I'll call back later, I'll put you through, I'll tell her you called back, I'll hold, I'll try to reconnect you*). T elicits from Ss that *will* in this context expresses an immediate decision, an offer or a promise. T then draws Ss' attention to the **Don't forget!** section.

5 **Ex 3:** Ss match the statements and responses. T may prefer to copy the language on to cards for Ss to match. When Ss have completed the exercise, T asks Ss to cover up the second column. Ss work in pairs with one S reading a statement for the other S to respond.

2 *Could I have extension 236, please?*	*Thank you. I'll put you through.*
3 *The phone's ringing.*	*I'll get it.*
4 *I'm afraid he isn't in the office at the moment.*	*It's OK. I'll phone back later.*
5 *It's Dave Rogers again for Joe West.*	*Sorry. I'll try to reconnect you.*
We were cut off.	
6 *Could you tell Mrs Rycroft that I called?*	*Yes, of course. I'll give her your message.*

6 **Ex 4:** Ss do the telephone language maze in pairs. T first ensures the task is clear to Ss by starting the maze as a full group activity: T asks Ss which squares on the first line would be possible to start a conversation ending with *Fine, Mr Murphy. I'll give him your message.* (Only three are possible.) T then asks Ss to scan the rest of the maze to look for names which recur to help them to eliminate some of the options. Ss then find the only route which leads to the end of the maze. T may wish to round off the maze activity by eliciting the correct conversation across the group or getting one pair of Ss to role-play the dialogue.

Good morning. Anna Jones speaking.	Good morning. Davis and Sons. Can I help you?	Hello. My name's Pete Brown. Can you put me through to Craig Wilson, please?	**Good morning. Walton's. Can I help you?**	**Yes. Can you put me through to Ellen Symes, please?**
Extension 471, please.	Hello Anna. It's Marion again. We were cut off.	I'm afraid he's in a meeting. Can I take a message?	Do you know when he'll be free?	**Who's calling, please?**
I'm sorry. Could you repeat that?	I'm calling about a problem with the delivery dates.	**Could you repeat the name of the company, please?**	**Alan Murphy from RSL Finance.**	He should be available in about an hour.
Hold the line, please. I'll put you through to Sales.	RSL	**The line's busy at the moment. Would you like to hold?**	Right. I'll call back later. Thank you.	Did you say 'F' for Freddie or 'S' for Sugar?
Yes, I'll tell him that. Shall I ask him to call you back?	I'm sorry. He won't be free until this afternoon.	OK	I'm afraid I can't hold. Could you take a message?	It's 'S' for Sugar.
Yes, please. I'll be in the office all afternoon.	**I'm sorry, the line's still busy. Can I take a message?**	**Yes, please. Could you tell Ms Symes I'll have to cancel our meeting on Thursday?**	**Could you repeat your name, please?**	**Alan Murphy.**
Fine. I'll tell her that. Thank you. Bye.	Thank you for your help.	I'll ask her to call you as soon as possible.	**Fine, Mr Murphy. I'll give her your message.**	Yes, I'll tell Ms Lewis it's urgent. Thank you. Bye.

Telephoning

Getting through

Listening 1

1 Clare MacPherson is a receptionist for Baker and Kerr, a manufacturer of cosmetic products. Clare takes six calls. Listen and number the descriptions of the calls.

A The receptionist connects the caller.

B The caller leaves a message.

C The caller will phone again soon. 1

D The caller will phone again later.

E The caller was cut off and phones again.

F The caller waits for a short time then the receptionist connects her.

2 Look at the telephone phrases below. What are the possible responses?

1 Who's calling?

2 Can I take a message?

3 Can I have extension 184, please?

4 Can I speak to William Grogan, please?

5 Do you know when he'll be free?

6 I'm returning her call.

7 Is Keith available?

8 We were cut off.

Now listen to the conversations again. How do the speakers respond?

Immediate decisions with will

We use **will** to express an immediate decision, offer or promise.
(In spoken English **will** becomes 'll.)
I'll call back in about ten minutes.
I'll put you through.

3 Match the telephone phrases below with the responses.

1 I'm afraid the line's busy.	It's OK. I'll phone back later.
2 Can I have extension 236, please?	It's OK. I'll hold.
3 I'm afraid he isn't in the office.	Sorry, I'll try to reconnect you.
4 Could you tell Sarah that I called?	I'll put you through.
5 It's Dave Rogers again for Joe West. We were cut off.	OK. I'll give her your message.

Reading **4** Work in pairs. Look at the maze below. Use the language in the squares to make a telephone conversation. To start, find the correct square. Then follow the conversation to the end. Move in any direction except up.

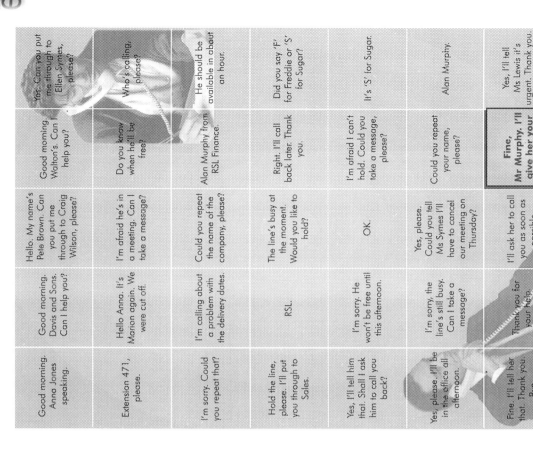

Good morning. Anna Jones speaking.	Good morning. Davis and Sons. Can I help you?	Hello. My name's Pete Brown. Can you put me through to Craig Wilson, please?	Good morning. Walton's. Can I help you?	Yes. Can you put me through to Ellen Symes, please?
Extension 471, please.	Hello Anna. It's Marion again. We were cut off.	I'm afraid he's in a meeting. Can I take a message?	Do you know when he'll be free?	Who's calling, please?
I'm sorry. Could you repeat that?	I'm calling about a problem with the delivery dates.	Could you repeat the name of the company, please?	Alan Murphy from RSL Finance.	He should be available in about an hour
Hold the line, please. I'll put you through to Sales.	RSL.	The line's busy at the moment. Would you like to hold?	Right. I'll call back later. Thank you.	Did you say 'F' for Freddie or 'S' for Sugar?
Yes, I'll tell him that. Shall I ask him to call you back?	I'm sorry. He won't be free until this afternoon.	OK.	I'm afraid I can't hold. Could you take a message, please?	It's 'S' for Sugar.
Yes, please. I'll be in the office all afternoon.	I'm sorry, the line's still busy. Can I take a message?	Yes, please. Could you tell Ms Symes I'll have to cancel our meeting on Thursday?	Could you repeat your name, please?	Alan Murphy.
Fine. I'll tell her that. Thank you. Bye.	Thank you for your help.	I'll ask her to call you as soon as possible.	**Fine, Mr Murphy. I'll give her your message.**	Yes, I'll tell Ms Lewis it's urgent. Thank you. Bye.

7 **Ex ⑤**: Ss work in pairs and take turns to choose two squares from the maze to build up a complete telephone dialogue. T may wish to remind Ss to attempt dialogues which involve taking or leaving messages. T could conclude the exercise by having some Ss role-play their conversations to the rest of the class.

Reasons for calling

8 **Ex ❶**: Ss listen to a telephone conversation and complete the phone message form.

Name of caller	David Whelan
Company	Health and Safety Council
Message	Has confirmed *First Aid course week beginning 13 May but can only take 25 participants not 29.*

In feedback T can ask Ss to compare the telephone message with their own practice. Do Ss for instance note down other information such as the caller's telephone number and time of call? T may need to explain the meaning of *First Aid*.

9 **Ex ❷**: Before Ss listen again for the relevant telephone phrases, T asks Ss to predict the language.

1 Could you spell ...?
2 I'm calling about ...
3 Sorry, did you say ...? So, that's ...

10 **Ex ❸**: Ss work in pairs and use the activity sheets on pages 125 and 131 to give and take telephone messages. They should check each other's messages at the end of the activity. T may wish to have Ss role-play their conversations to the rest of the group.

Self-study

Ex ❶:

[11] Right Mr Abraham. I'll give Mr Green the message.
[3] I'm afraid the line's busy. Can I take a message?
[13] You're welcome. Bye.
[1] Good morning, Priory Hotel.
[7] And what's the message, please?
[5] Could you spell your surname, please?
[9] Did you say 7:15 or 7:50?
[4] Yes, please. Could you tell him Alan Abraham called.
[12] Thank you very much.
[8] Could you tell him I've booked a table at Marcel's restaurant for 7:15 this evening and I'll meet him there.
[6] A-B-R-A-H-A-M.
[2] Hello, could you put me through to Mr Green in room 105, please?
[10] 7:15. Quarter past seven.

Ex ❷: Suggested answers:

1 Can I take a message?
2 Could you spell your surname, please?
3 Sorry, did you say?
4 I'm calling about ...
5 Could you tell her ...?
6 I'll give her the message.

Ex ❸: 1 C   2 B   3 A   4 A   5 C

Essential vocabulary

Telephone phrases
Can I speak to ...?
Can I have extension 204, please?
Is Keith available?
Who's calling?
Hold the line, please.
I'll put you through.
I'm afraid the line's busy.
I'm afraid he's not available.
Do you know when he'll be free?
Can I take a message?
I'm calling about ...
I'm returning his call.
I'll call back later.
I'll give him the message.
Could you repeat that?
Could you spell that?
Did you say ...?
We were cut off.
Thank you for calling.

Speaking **5** Work in pairs. Choose two squares from the maze. Make them into a conversation.

Reasons for calling

Listening 2 **1** Clare takes another call. Listen and complete the message.

PHONE MESSAGE

Message for   Sharon Thomson

Name of caller ....

Company ....

Message ....

....

....

....

2 Listen again. Write the phrases that the speakers use ...

- to ask for spelling ....
- to give the reason for calling ....
- to check what the other speaker said ....

Speaking **3** Work in pairs. Student A: Look at the Activity sheet on page 125. Student B: Look at the Activity sheet on page 131.

Exam practice

3
- Look at questions 1-5.
- In each question, which phrase or sentence is correct?
- For each question, mark the correct answer **A, B or C.**

1
Sally phoned. She said your e-mail was deleted by accident. Could you send it again?

The e-mail message
A did not arrive.
B was sent to the wrong address.
C was destroyed.

2
Ms Haan called. Our order's been delayed due to problems with a supplier.

The order has
A arrived late.
B not arrived yet.
C been cancelled.

3
Tuesday, 6pm
Alex
Sebastian Page returned your call from yesterday. He'll try again in the morning.

Sebastian Page is going to
A call Alex tomorrow.
B wait for Alex to call back later.
C call Alex again later today.

4
UPS called to say they'll collect the parcel at 3 o'clock this afternoon.

The delivery service
A will pick the parcel up today.
B intends to deliver the parcel at 3pm.
C came for the parcel at 3pm.

5
Chris
Call Annette Pohl. She's on her way to a meeting so try her mobile on 0486 366 57.

Annette Pohl is in
A her office.
B a meeting.
C her car.

1 Look at the telephone conversation below. Put the conversation into the correct order.

Receptionist
- [ ] Thank you, Mr Abraham. I'll give Mr Green the message.
- [ ] I'm afraid the line's busy. Can I take a message?
- [ ] You're welcome. Bye.
- [ ] Good morning, Priory Hotel.
- [ ] And what's the message, please?
- [ ] Could you spell your surname, please?
- [ ] Did you say 7.15 or 7.50?

Caller
- [ ] Yes, please. Could you tell him Alan Abraham called?
- [ ] Thank you very much.
- [ ] Could you tell him I've booked a table at Marcel's restaurant for 7.15 this evening and I'll meet him there?
- [ ] A-B-R-A-H-A-M.
- [ ] Hello, could you put me through to Mr Green in room 105, please?
- [ ] 7.15. Quarter past seven.

2 Robin Hobson applies for a job at Baker and Kerr. He telephones to arrange an interview. Read the conversation and fill the gaps.

Clare   Baker and Kerr. Can I help you?
Caller   Hello. I'd like to speak to Louise Sanderson, please.
Clare   I'm afraid she's out of the office this morning.
     (1) ....?
Caller   Yes, please. My name's Vic Hobson.
Clare   (2) ....?
Caller   H-O-B-S-O-N.
Clare   (3) ....
     B-S or P-S?
Caller   B for book - S. (4) ....
     the position as sales executive.
Clare   Yes?
Caller   Ms Sanderson left a message on my voice-mail asking if I could come for an interview at 2pm on 16 May. (5) ....
     that I'll be able to come then?
Clare   So, that's 2 o'clock on 16 May.
Caller   That's right.
Clare   Fine. (6) ....
Caller   Thank you. Bye.

Tapescript: Listening 1

Call 1

Clare: Good morning, Baker and Kerr. Can I help you?

Caller: Could you put me through to Elaine Pearson, please?

Clare: Who's calling, please?

Caller: Lewis Taylor of SRT.

Clare: One moment please, Mr Taylor ... Hello, Mr Taylor. I'm afraid the line's busy. Can I take a message?

Caller: No, it's all right, thank you. I'll call back in about ten minutes.

Clare: OK. Thank you for calling.

Call 2

Clare: Good morning, Baker and Kerr. Can I help you?

Caller: Yes, please. Could I have extension 184, please?

Clare: Who's calling, please?

Caller: Jack Symes.

Clare: Thank you. I'll put you through.

Caller: Thank you.

Call 3

Clare: Good morning, Baker and Kerr. Can I help you?

Caller: Can I speak to William Grogan, please?

Clare: I'm afraid he's in a meeting. Can I take a message?

Caller: Do you know when he'll be free?

Clare: He should be available after lunch.

Caller: Right. I'll call back then. Thanks.

Call 4

Clare: Good morning, Baker and Kerr. Can I help you?

Caller: Jasmine Singh, please.

Clare: I'm afraid she's interviewing all day. Can I take a message?

Caller: Yes, my name's Mary Banks, from Walkers. She called me earlier. I'm returning her call.

Clare: Mary Banks, from Walkers. Right. I'll tell her you called back.

Caller: OK. Thanks.

Call 5

Clare: Good morning, Baker and Kerr. Can I help you?

Caller: Hi Clare. It's Fiona. Is Keith available?

Clare: I'm afraid the line's busy, Fiona.

Caller: It's OK. I'll hold.

Clare: Fiona?

Caller: Yes.

Clare: The line's free now. I'll put you through.

Caller: Thanks.

Call 6

Clare: Good morning, Baker and Kerr. Can I help you?

Caller: Hi. It's Fiona again. We were cut off.

Clare: Oh, sorry about that. I'll try to reconnect you. Hold the line.

Caller: Thanks.

Tapescript: Listening 2

Clare: Good afternoon. Baker and Kerr. Can I help you?

Caller: Good afternoon. Can you put me through to Sharon Thomson, please?

Clare: I'm afraid she's out of the office at the moment. Can I take a message?

Caller: Yes, my name's David Whelan from the Health and Safety Council.

Clare: I'm sorry. Could you spell your surname, please?

Caller: W-H-E-L-A-N.

Clare: And it's the Health and Safety Council. Right. And what's the message, please?

Caller: I'm calling about the First Aid course Ms Thomson's arranging with us. I'd like to confirm the week beginning 13 May but I'm not ...

Clare: Sorry, did you say the thirteenth or thirtieth?

Caller: The thirteenth, 13.

Clare: OK ... yes ...

Caller: Yes. The date's fine, but we can only take 25 participants, not 29.

Clare: So that's the First Aid course for the week commencing 13 May and you can only take 25 people.

Caller: That's right, yes.

Clare: Right. I'll give her the message.

Caller: Thanks.

Clare: You're welcome. Bye.

Internal communication

Objectives: To practise writing memos and notes
To review making requests and talking about obligation

Materials needed: Cassette - *Pass Cambridge BEC 1*

Unit overview

- ### Memos, notes and notices

Warmer	T quickly elicits differences between memos, notes and notices.
Reading	Ss scan memos etc. for general information and answer questions.
	Ss brainstorm differences between memos, notes and notices.
Language Focus	Ss review the language of requests and obligation/necessity.
Speaking	Ss exchange information about internal communication in their own companies.

- ### Writing memos

Listening	Ss take notes from a telephone conversation.
Language focus	Ss review language of requests in memos.
Writing	Ss write a memo from their notes.

- ### Writing notes

Writing	Ss focus on text reduction strategies in note-writing, crossing out words in a note then grouping the types of words omitted.
	Ss focus on general conciseness by removing redundancy from two notes.
Listening	Ss take notes from a telephone conversation.
Writing	Ss write a note based on a telephone conversation.

- ### Self-study

Writing	Ss turn a memo into a personal note.
	Ss write a short note from written stimuli.
Exam practice	*Memo writing (Writing Test Part 2).*

Internal communication

Memos, notes and notices

1 **Warmer (books closed):** T quickly brainstorms the basic differences between memos, notes and notices. Answers can include very basic information about purpose and use but should not go into linguistic/stylistic details, which are focused on in **Ex 3**.

2 **Ex 1:** Ss quickly scan the various forms of communication to get some general information about the company, its markets and activities. Ss are free to interpret the information as they wish (e.g. the name Veronique Leboeuf suggests the company has activities in the French market). There are no definite right/wrong answers to these warm-up questions.

Suggested answers:
Markets: Britain (Manchester Head Office), Italy (Rome conference), Spain (Madrid office), France (Veronique Leboeuf).

Activities: Manufacturer of office supplies and furniture (given in rubric), sells products directly in Europe.

Location: Manchester (Head Office).

3 **Ex 2:** Ss scan through the texts once more and find the relevant information. During feedback, Ss identify the passages in support of their answers. Alternatively, T asks Ss read through the texts once more with a time limit. Then Ss close their books and T asks them to answer the six questions from memory. This would involve a different reading strategy as Ss would read for detailed comprehension in an attempt to process the content of all the notes.

1 30 Oct to 1 Nov   2 A holiday in Florida   3 Thursday 23 July
4 Henry Wallace   5 Henry and Paula (but not Veronique Leboeuf)
6 The name and telephone number of the customer who phoned about the new seating range

4 **Ex 3:** T may wish to put Ss in pairs/groups to pool their knowledge. T encourages Ss to discuss the uses of the three media, the type of information communicated and the potential reader. Many of the differences between the documents will depend on the writer/reader relationship rather than conventions.

Suggested answers:
Memo: Addressed to groups or individuals. More formal status than a note. Formal style, no omission of words, no abbreviations, formal style of address, use of job titles.

Notes: Addressed to an individual. Informal, short, abbreviations (tel no.), contractions (you've), omission of subjects, auxiliaries and articles ([I] Can't find ...), use of first names.

Notices: Not addressed to anyone in particular. Formal style, no contractions, no ellipsis, no abbreviations.

5 **Ex 4:** In feedback, Ss supply the phrases in their full sentences. Although this language may seem easy, it is very useful to focus on it to encourage Ss to use such forms in their notes and memos.

Requests	Obligation/necessity
please (send ...)	*please (go ahead ...)*
could you (give ...)	*you need to (arrive ...)*
could we (meet ...)	*it is essential that (everybody books ...)*
	(salary sheets) should (arrive ...)

6 **Ex 5:** Ss work in pairs and discuss the type of internal communication they use at work. They also express their opinion as to how effective the communication is.

Writing memos

7 **Ex 1:** Before Ss do this exercise, T plays the cassette once for gist and asks Ss what Sarah is calling about. Ss then listen again and take notes in order to obtain the information needed to write the memo in **Ex 2**. T may wish not to provide feedback at this point but to have Ss listen again to check their information after drafting the memo in **Ex 2**.

8 **Ex 2:** Having taken notes in **Ex 1**, Ss now compose a memo to send to Henry's salespeople. Ss write the memo individually or in pairs and may present their draft to the other Ss who can criticise the memo for informational content, formality and length. T reminds Ss that complete fulfilment of the task is essential in the exam: Ss should therefore check that all essential information is included.

Suggested answer: (11 words)
To: All salespeople
From: Henry Wallace
Please note that you need to enclose receipts with expenses claims.

Internal communication

Memos, notes and notices

Reading **1** Danos is a manufacturer of office furniture and supplies. Look at the examples of the company's internal communication below and find the following information:

- the company's markets
- some of the company's activities
- where it is based.

MEMORANDUM

To: All National Sales Managers
From: Henry Wallace
Sales Director
Date: 10 July 1999

INTERNATIONAL SALES CONFERENCE

Our International Sales Conference will take place from 30 October to 1 November in Rome. I will send details of the hotel later. Please go ahead and book your flight to Rome now. Please note that you need to arrive in Rome by 15.00 on the Friday and stay until 16.30 on the Sunday. It is essential that everybody books an APEX flight or equivalent. Please contact me in case of any difficulty.

SALESPERSON OF THE YEAR

The decision for Salesperson of the Year has been almost impossible as there have been so many excellent performances. However, because of her work in turning round a long-term fall in sales, the prize goes to:

**Paula Stuart
(Madrid office)**

Congratulations to Paula, who wins a holiday in Florida.

[Handwritten note:]
Henry
Meeting with Veronique
(about carrera). Could we
meet on the 14th anyway?
Paula.

[Handwritten note:]
Sue,
Can't find name or tel no. of
customer who phoned about
New Seating range. If you've
got it, could you give it to
me ASAP?
Thanks,
Mike

MEMORANDUM

To: Managers
From: Sarah Longman
Accounts Dept
Date: 4 July 1999

Salary sheets for the third quarter should arrive at Manchester Head Office by the following dates:

For August:	Thursday 23 July
For September:	Thursday 21 August
For October:	Tuesday 23 September

NB Please send salary details by GUARANTEED DELIVERY.

DANOS OFFICES

---

2 Answer the questions below.

1 When is the next International Sales Conference?
2 What is the prize for Salesperson of the Year?
3 When do salary details for August have to arrive at Head Office?
4 Who is the Head of the Sales Department?
5 Who is meeting on 14 July?
6 What has Mike lost?

3 Read the documents on the opposite page again. What are the differences between memos, notes and notices?

Functions **4** Look at the memos and notes again. Find phrases to express requests and obligation/necessity. Put them in the groups below.

Requests	Obligation/necessity
please (send ...)	you need to (arrive ...)

Speaking **5** Work in pairs. Find out what kind of written communication your partner uses at work. How efficient is internal communication where he/she works?

Writing memos

Listening 1 **1** Sarah Longman calls Henry Wallace to talk about expenses. Listen and take notes.

Writing memos

It is not necessary to use very formal language when writing memos. We often make requests with simple forms such as **Please ...** and **Could you ...?**

Please inform .... *the secretary by 24 November.*
Could you please inform

Writing **2** Now use your notes to write the memo Henry needs to send his salespeople.

Internal communication

Writing notes

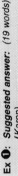

9 T reminds Ss of the importance of text reduction strategies for note-writing. Text length can be reduced in two ways: 1) through grammatical omissions (omission of subject, auxiliaries etc.) or 2) by eliminating redundancy. **Ex 1** deals with the former while **Ex 3** deals with the latter.

10 **Ex 1**: T tells Ss that they must reduce the number of words without leaving out any important information. Ss can change the word order if necessary (e.g. *Is it OK if we meet on Tuesday?* → *Tuesday OK?*). T also tells Ss that they can cross words out but the final note should be grammatically correct. Ss work in pairs and delete all unnecessary words from the note. T can introduce an element of competition by challenging pairs to reduce the note to the least number of words possible.

Suggested answer: (14 words excluding salutations - contractions counted as two words) *Sorry but can't make meeting Thursday because of doctor's appointment. Tuesday OK?*

11 **Ex 2**: T tells Ss to look at their reduced notes and list all the words they deleted from **Ex 1**. Ss then group the words into grammatical types.

Suggested answers:
the, a (articles)
I, it (subject pronouns)
am, is (verb be)
on, at, on (prepositions)
very (modifier)*

* T may refer to this category as *other* rather than use a grammatical term such as *modifier*.

12 **Ex 3**: This exercise focuses on omitting non-essential information. T brings the **Writing tip** to the Ss' attention and brainstorms what might constitute non-essential information in each note. T then points out that Ss can replace existing words with new words in order to reduce the notes. The final draft must be grammatically correct and contain all essential information, but nothing more. Pairs/groups can compete to reduce the notes to their minimal length. Alternatively, the original notes can be written on the board/OHT and Ss can take turns to shorten the message.

Suggested answer: (19 words excluding names)
Sue
Mr Scott in Edinburgh wants someone to discuss requirements for new equipment. Interested?
Can we talk about it today?
Henry

Suggested answer: (15 words excluding names)
Henry
Mike's flying to Finland tomorrow. Please contact him before he goes to discuss pricing strategy.
Sue

13 **Ex 4**: T sets the scene and tells Ss to take notes from the telephone conversation. T plays the cassette twice and elicits feedback afterwards to check comprehension before asking Ss to write the note for Steve Cooper. Ss work individually or in pairs. Ss present their draft to the other Ss for feedback on task completion, length and grammatical accuracy. Ss redraft if necessary, possibly for homework.

Suggested answer: (17 words)
Steve.
Are you available Tuesday lunchtime for a meeting with John and me? Could you let me know? Karen.

Self-study

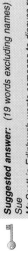

Ex 1: *Suggested answer:* (19 words)
(Karen)
Meeting Tuesday 21 January to discuss training schedule. Please prepare proposals by 18 January and give copies in advance.
(John)

Ex 2: *Suggested answer:* (20 words)
(To: Marketing Dept)
Could all staff please attend a meeting on 21 January at 10.45 in the boardroom to discuss the new brochure.

Ex 3: *Suggested answer:* (18 words)
(To: All staff)
Elizabeth Sharp, the new HR Manager, will be here on Tuesday 16 April. Please introduce yourselves to her.

Essential vocabulary

Paperwork
brochure
diary
memo
note
notice
proposal
receipt
schedule

General
appointment
boardroom
to cancel
to claim
essential
expenses
head office
obligation
prize
quarter
request
requirements
to take place

The words in italics are not on the Cambridge BEC 1 wordlist.

Writing notes

Writing

1 Work in pairs. Make the following note shorter by crossing out all the unnecessary words. Do not change the meaning of the note or leave out any important information.

> John
> I am very sorry but I can't make the meeting on Thursday at 10.30 because of a doctor's appointment. Is it OK if we meet on Tuesday?
> Thank you.
> Karen

2 Informal notes are usually very short and leave out certain types of words. Look at the note again and list the words you left out. Then put the words into groups and write them below.

Articles
the
a
_____

Writing tip:
In short notes do not include any information unless it is absolutely necessary.

3 Rewrite the following notes in about 20 words. Do not change the meaning or leave out any important information.

> Sue
> I received a letter from Mr Scott in Edinburgh this morning. He wants to know if someone can go to Edinburgh to look at his office and to discuss his requirements for new equipment with him. Are you interested? If so, can we talk about it some time this morning?
> Thanks
> Henry

> Henry – I spoke to Mike yesterday. He's flying to Finland tomorrow to visit the sales office. Could you please contact him before he goes in order to discuss the pricing strategy?
> Sue

Listening 2

4 Karen Mitchell receives a phone call from John Woods, the Head of Human Resources. Listen and take notes. Then write a short note for Karen to leave on Steve Cooper's desk.

DANOS OFFICES

Internal communication

---

1 Look at the memo below from John Woods to all Training Officers. Rewrite it as a personal note from John to Karen Mitchell. Use about 20 words but do not leave out any important information.

> To: All Training Officers
>
> From: John Woods
>   Human Resources Manager
>
> Date: 14 January 1999
>
> There will be a meeting on Tuesday 21 January to discuss the training schedule. Please prepare your proposals by 18 January and make sure that everyone has a copy in advance.
>
> Thank you

> _____
> _____
> _____
> John

2 Use the note and diary page below to write a memo to all staff in the Marketing Department. Write about 20 words.

> Alex
> Could you organise a meeting on Tuesday with all the Marketing Department to discuss our new brochure and then send a memo to inform them about it?
> Look at my desk diary for the best time. We'll hold the meeting in the boardroom and I think it'll take about an hour.
> Thanks

Tuesday 8 June	
09.00	Meeting with Paul Ross
	9.30-10.30
10.00	
11.00	
12.00	Lunch with Stuart Fraser
	12-1.30
13.00	

MEMO

To: Marketing Dept

From:
_____
_____
_____
_____

Exam practice

3
- Elizabeth Sharp is going to be the new Human Resources Manager at your company.
- She is going to visit your office to learn more about the company.
- Write a memo to all staff:
  * explaining who she is
  * saying when she will be in the office
  * asking staff to introduce themselves to her.
- Write about **20 words**.

MEMO

To: All staff

From:
_____
_____
_____
_____

Tapescript: Listening 1

Henry	Hello, Henry Wallace speaking.
Sarah	Hello, Henry, it's Sarah Longman from Accounts.
Henry	Oh hello, Sarah. What can I do for you?
Sarah	I'm calling all of the heads of department about expenses. I just wanted to remind you that if someone claims any expenses, they must enclose receipts with the claim.
Henry	OK. I'll send a memo to remind my salespeople.
Sarah	That would be great.
Henry	Thanks for calling.
Sarah	Thanks, Henry. Bye.

Tapescript: Listening 2

Karen	Hello. Karen Mitchell.
John	Hello Karen, it's John.
Karen	Oh hi, John. How are you?
John	I'm fine thanks. Look, I got your note yesterday about the meeting. I'm sorry I didn't get back to you.
Karen	That's OK. But I'm flying out to Paris next week and we need to meet before I leave. Is Thursday all right for you?
John	Not really no. How about Tuesday?
Karen	Fine, I've got to be in the office on Tuesday morning anyway. How about lunchtime?
John	That's fine by me, but we should find out if Steve's available then, as well.
Karen	That's true. I'll leave a note on his desk and see if lunchtime's OK for him.
John	If it's OK with Steve, let me know and we can fix a time.
Karen	I'll write him a note now. Thanks John. Bye.
John	Bye.

Facts and figures

Objectives:	To enable Ss to describe trends
	To practise reading for specific information
	To review adjectives and adverbs

Materials needed: None

Unit overview

● An annual report

| Reading | Ss read extracts from the Millennium Annual Report and answer *'Right, Wrong, Doesn't say'* comprehension questions. |
| Speaking | Ss work in pairs and tell their partner what their own company's annual report will contain. |

● Describing graphs

Reading	Ss match sentences about Millennium with information in graph and bar chart form.
Vocabulary	Ss complete word families: infinitive and past simple verb forms and nouns.
Language focus	Ss review adjectives and adverbs describing degrees of change.
Vocabulary	Ss complete gaps in two short texts about Millennium's performance. Ss focus on prepositions used to describe change.
Speaking	Ss work in pairs and take turns to describe a graph or draw their partner's graph.

● Self-study

Vocabulary	Matching verbs and diagrams (verbs of movement).
Language focus	Gap-fill exercise (prepositions).
Vocabulary	Matching exercise (compound nouns).
Exam practice	*Matching visuals with sentences (Reading Test Part 3).*

An annual report

1 **Warmer (books closed):** T introduces the idea of the annual report (maybe with some examples of some company reports) and elicits from Ss who the report is written for (shareholders), why (to inform shareholders of the financial situation - and hence to reassure/attract) and what type of information it contains (company activities and financial information such as the balance sheet and profit and loss account). T could ask when the Ss' own company report is published and what the last one reported. The discussion could include how the report is vital for promoting a positive image of the company; it is usually an extremely attractive and glossy publication.

2 Before Ss do the comprehension questions in Ex ❶, T asks them some global questions: *What type of software does the company manufacture? Was 1998 a good year? Would you invest in the company? Why/why not?*

3 T asks more questions about the text before Ss read for specific information for the answers to the questions in Ex ❶. T asks Ss to find something which is:
- satisfactory for the company (e.g. further steady growth in Britain)
- disappointing for the company (e.g. the effect of the strong pound on growth in Europe)
- a challenge for the company (e.g. changes in distribution).

4 **Ex ❶:** Ss then read the texts for specific information and answer the *'Right, Wrong, Doesn't say'* questions. T points out Ss should refer to both the text and the visual information. Ss compare answers in pairs before general feedback.

 1 A   2 B   3 B   4 C   5 A   6 A   7 B

In feedback T highlights any vocabulary from the **Essential vocabulary** list for the unit. However, T should encourage Ss not to try to understand every word.

5 **Ex ❷:** T may wish to prompt Ss by asking them to consider such things as positive and negative results, the company's most successful activities, changes and major developments over the year. T asks Ss to report back to the rest of the group to round off the activity and to reinforce the use of the target language.

If Ss work in the same company T can ask each pair to list points they would include in the report and then compare their list with other Ss'.

If Ss are pre-experience and do not have a company to discuss, T has samples of company reports for Ss to scan quickly in pairs. Ss then report back on how their particular company is doing generally.

Describing graphs

6 T asks Ss to look back through the Chairman's statement on page 33 and underline any language connected with rising and falling. Rising verbs: *rise, increase*; nouns: *rise, growth*; falling verbs: *reduce*. T asks Ss if they can add any more.

7 **Ex ❶:** T introduces the activity by telling Ss that the graph and bar chart provide further details about Millennium's performance. Ss need to look at each sentence and first decide which diagram it refers to (the graph shows sales by region and the bar chart shows sales by product range). Ss can then look to see which specific line or bar corresponds to each sentence. T ensures Ss understand *recover, level off, improve, peak*.

 2 F   3 A   4 B   5 E   6 G   7 D   8 H

Facts and figures

An annual report

Reading **1** Look at the extracts from the Millennium Software 1998 Annual Report. Are the sentences on the opposite page 'Right' or 'Wrong'? If there is not enough information to answer, choose 'Doesn't say'.

Chairman's Statement

Last year saw both the continued development of trends within the industry and some unexpected results. The domestic British market saw further steady growth but could be overtaken by US sales next year. As in 1997, sales in the USA rose sharply with the successful release of three new computer games. However, hopes of the European market showing the same rate of growth were affected by a strong pound.

Computer games increased their domination of sales in 1998 with the football game *The Golden Boot: France 98* selling over 100,000 units in World Cup year. Other sports titles are now amongst the company's top brands.

The company also enjoyed a sharp rise in sales of educational products. Our new range of interactive multimedia products, *Schoolware*, launched in late 1997, is now a top-selling brand. Further *Schoolware* titles to be launched this year should ensure continued growth in this market.

Sales figures for 1998 show very clearly the changing face of the company's activities. Millennium Software is now a producer of entertainment and educational products. In order to adapt to these markets, the company will have to expand by increasing its product range and reducing its development times.

Moreover, the company faces new challenges in distribution. Large retail chains with pan-European buying power are becoming increasingly dominant in the distribution of computer software. These superstores now offer competitive prices and a narrow product range based on top-selling titles. With computer shops, they now account for nearly two thirds of sales.

David Matthews

David Matthews, Chairman

4 | **Annual Report 1998**

1998 distribution

Others 5%
Department stores 5%
Independent 7%
Wholesalers 19%
Superstores 39%
Computer shops 25%

Top selling Millennium titles 1998

Title	Units
The Golden Boot	112,000
Road Rage III	63,000
Tournament Golf 98	51,000
Law & Order II	48,000
Virtual Ninja	39,000
Club Manager 98	22,000

Sales per games machine as %

PlayStation	42%
Nintendo N64	28%
PCs	24%
Sega Saturn	6%

---

1 Superstores sell more Millennium software than computer shops.
  A Right   B Wrong   C Doesn't say

2 PCs are the most popular games machine for Millennium games.
  A Right   B Wrong   C Doesn't say

3 Sales increased sharply in the company's home market last year.
  A Right   B Wrong   C Doesn't say

4 *The Golden Boot* sold more copies in France than Britain.
  A Right   B Wrong   C Doesn't say

5 The company is developing its range of multimedia educational software.
  A Right   B Wrong   C Doesn't say

6 In future the company will have to produce new games more quickly.
  A Right   B Wrong   C Doesn't say

7 Superstores sell a wide range of computer software.
  A Right   B Wrong   C Doesn't say

Speaking **2** Work in pairs. What will be in the Chairman's Statement in the next Annual Report of your partner's company?

Describing graphs

Reading **1** Read the sentences below about Millennium Software's performance. Write a letter from the diagrams next to each sentence.

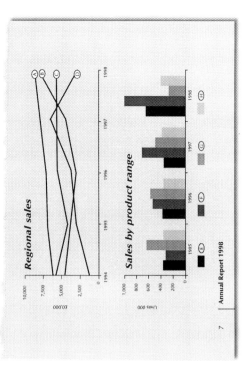

Regional sales

Sales by product range

7 | **Annual Report 1998**

1 After a fall in 1995, sales in Asia recovered and then levelled off. (C)
2 There was very strong growth in sales of computer games from 1995 to 1998.
3 Sales in Britain improved steadily throughout the period from 1994 to 1998.
4 Sales in the USA fell slightly in 1995 and 1996 before a strong recovery in 1997, followed by a sharp rise in 1998.
5 Sales of educational software remained steady until 1997 but increased sharply in 1998.
6 There was a steady decrease in sales of office software from 1995 to 1998.
7 Sales in continental Europe grew from 1994, peaked in 1997 and then dropped sharply.
8 Sales of communications software remained steady throughout the period.

Facts and figures

Self-study

Essential vocabulary

Describing trend	**General**
to increase/increase	annual report
to rise/rise	brand
to grow/growth	income
improve/improvement	product launch
to recover/recovery	range
to peak/peak	retail
to level off	
to remain steady	
to decrease/decrease	
to drop/drop	
to fall/fall	
sharp(ly)	
strong(ly)	
steady/steadily	
slow(ly)	
slight(ly)	

The words in italics are not on the Cambridge BEC 1 wordlist.

---

8 **Ex 2**: Ss compare their answers in pairs before general feedback.

Infinitive	Verb Past simple	Noun
drop	**dropped**	a drop
decrease	**decreased**	a decrease
increase	**increased**	an increase
rise	**rose**	a rise
grow	**grew**	growth
improve	**improved**	*an improvement*
recover	recovered	a recovery
peak	**peaked**	a peak

In feedback T ensures Ss are aware of the word stress for the noun and verb forms of *decrease* and *increase* (the stress is on the first syllable of the noun but the second syllable of the verb).

9 **Ex 3**: T directs Ss to look back at the Chairman's Statement in the Annual Report to find three examples of adjectives and three of adverbs, e.g. **Adjectives**: *steady growth*, **sharp rise**, *competitive prices*; **Adverbs**: *rose* **sharply**, *show* **clearly**, *increasingly dominant*.

T draws Ss' attention to *increasingly dominant* as an example of an adverb describing an adjective. Ss then complete the **Don't forget!** section.

Adjectives and adverbs
• Adjectives give information about **nouns**.
  There was a sharp rise in sales of computer games.
• Adverbs give information about **verbs** or **adjectives**.
  Sales of computer games rose sharply last year.
  Educational software is becoming increasingly important.

10 **Ex 4**: Ss fill the gaps in the descriptions of Millennium's net sales and net income.

Net sales
Net sales remained **steady** *at* £17m *in* 1994 and 1995 then rose **sharply** *in* 1996 to reach £21m. This was followed *by* further growth as sales **peaked** *at* £22m *in* 1997. However, as a strong pound began to affect exports to Europe, net sales fell **slightly** *in* 1998.

Net income
After net income **fell/dropped** *by* £0.25m *in* 1995, there was a strong **recovery/increase/rise** *in* 1996 due to increased sales and reduced costs. This was followed *by* a further **increase/rise** in net income *of* £0.7m *over* the next two years: it grew **steadily** *from* £1.4m *in* 1996 *to* £2.1m *in* 1998.

11 **Ex 5**: Ss underline the prepositions in **Ex 4**. (Answers underlined in above text.) T draws Ss' attention to the use of the prepositions before Ss complete the sentences.
• *at* to describe static situations.
• verb + *by* + change
• noun + *of* + change
• *in* to describe the area affected by change/time period.

1 *in*
2 *from to*
3 *by*
4 *of*

12 **Ex 6**: T ensures Ss do not show their graph to their partner. T rounds off the activity by obtaining one final version of each graph description from across the whole group.

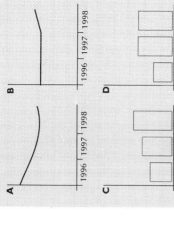

Vocabulary

1 Complete the table below.

Infinitive	Verb Past simple	Noun
fall	fell	a fall
drop	....	a decrease
....	....	....
increase		....
rise		growth
improve		....
....	recovered	
peak	....	....

Grammar

2 Look back at the adjectives and adverbs in the unit. Complete the information below.

Adjectives and adverbs
- Adjectives give information about _____.
  There was a **sharp rise** in sales of computer games.
- Adverbs give information about _____ or _____.
  Sales of computer games **rose sharply** last year.
  Educational software is becoming **increasingly important**.

Unit2B
Unit60

4 Complete the descriptions of Millennium Software's net sales and net income.

Net sales (£m)

1994 1995 1996 1997 1998

Net sales remained (1) _____ at £17m in 1994 and 1995 then rose (2) _____ in 1996 to reach £21m. This was followed by further growth as sales (3) _____ at £22m in 1997. However, as a strong pound began to affect exports to Europe, net sales fell (4) _____ in 1998.

Annual Report 1998

Net income (£m)

1994 1995 1996 1997 1998

After net income (5) _____ by £0.25m in 1995, there was a strong (6) _____ in 1996 due to increased sales and reduced costs. This was followed by a further (7) _____ in net income of £0.7m over the next two years: it grew from £1.4m in 1996 to £2.1m (8) _____ in 1998.

5 Underline the prepositions in Exercise 4. Then complete the following sentences.

1 There was a fall _____ operating costs.
2 Operating costs fell _____ £12m _____ £10m.
3 Operating costs fell _____ £2m.
4 There was a fall _____ £2m.

Operating costs
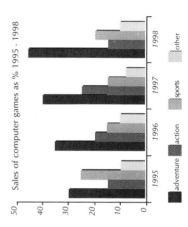
£12m £10m

Speaking

6 Work in pairs. Student A: Look at the Activity sheets on pages 125-126. Student B: Look at the Activity sheets on pages 131-132.

---

1 Use the words below to label the pictures.

peak | remain steady | fall
rise | level off | recover

A ↗ B → C ↘
D → E ↗ F ↗

2 Complete the sentences with one of the following prepositions.

in   at   by   from   of

1 Last year there was a drop _____ net sales _____ 9%.
2 Market share increased _____ 3%, up to 8%.
3 Net sales peaked _____ £22m in 1997.
4 European sales went _____ £4.2m to £3.0m.
5 Sales levelled off _____ £5m in 1998.
6 Costs rose _____ £3.3m. This was a rise _____ 10%.
7 Office software sales fell _____ 10% in 1997.
8 A strong pound meant a fall _____ exports in 1998.

3 Match the following words.

1 retail   brand
2 product   chain
3 net   income
4 top-selling report
5 annual   launch

4 Write a short description of the graph below.

Sales of computer games as % 1995 - 1998

50
40
30
20
10
0
1995 1996 1997 1998

adventure action adventure sports other

---

5 Exam practice

- Look at the charts below. They show the orders for eight different companies over three years.
- Which company does each sentence 1-5 describe?
- For each sentence mark the correct letter **A-H.**
- Do not use any letter more than once.

A 1996 1997 1998
B 1996 1997 1998
C 1996 1997 1998
D 1996 1997 1998
E 1996 1997 1998
F 1996 1997 1998
G 1996 1997 1998
H 1996 1997 1998

1 After a sharp drop in 1996, orders recovered for twelve months and then fell again in 1998.

2 Orders rose sharply in 1997 but peaked at the end of the year and then fell back to their 1996 levels.

3 Orders remained steady between 1996 and 1998.

4 The order books showed strong growth throughout the three year period.

5 After decreasing steadily for two years, orders finally levelled off and began a recovery in 1998.

Performance

Objectives: To enable Ss to talk about company performance
To practise listening for gist and for specific information
To review the present perfect and past simple
To practise talking about reasons and consequences

Materials needed: Cassette – *Pass Cambridge BEC 1*

Unit overview

• Measuring performance

Listening 1	Ss listen to a presentation about a privatised company and complete a bar chart and a graph. Ss then listen again and answer comprehension questions.
Language focus	Ss find examples of various uses of the present perfect and past simple tenses in the tapescript and describe the use of these two tenses. Ss match sentence halves to make sentences in the present perfect or past simple.
Speaking	Ss do a *Find someone who ...* exercise, asking questions about previous experiences.

• Explaining results

Listening 2	Ss listen to questions asked after the presentation and complete notes about the rail company. Ss then listen and complete multiple-choice comprehension questions.
Language focus	Ss review language for giving reasons and stating consequences.
Speaking	Ss ask for and give reasons for changes in their company.

• Self-study

Vocabulary	Jumbled phrases (presentation phrases).
Language focus	Gap-fill presentation (present perfect/past simple).
	Linking phrases to make sentences expressing result or consequence.
Exam practice	*Matching visuals with sentences (Reading Test Part 3).*

Measuring performance

Great Eastern Railways was bought by FirstGroup as part of the privatisation process of UK railways. The company has now changed its name to First Great Eastern. However, on the cassette it is referred to as Great Eastern.

1 **Warmer (books closed):** T introduces the context of the presentation, mentioning that the rail company is privatised and needs to attract investment. T briefly compares with Ss's own situation (i.e. possibly state-owned railways). T asks Ss to suggest criteria they would use to judge a railway company (e.g. *cleanliness, efficiency, ticket price, punctuality, reliability, safety and good service*). T asks Ss whether possible investors would have additional or different criteria (e.g., *high and growing volume of business, low costs and high profits, market potential*).

2 **Ex ❶:** Ss listen to a presentation reporting on performance in the period leading up to privatisation.

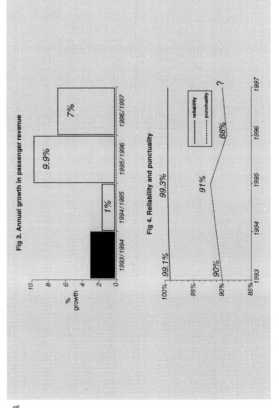

Fig 3. Annual growth in passenger revenue

Fig 4. Reliability and punctuality

Ss compare their information in the two diagrams first with their partner and then as a whole group activity. This provides an opportunity to review the language of trends (covered in Unit 5a).

T may also need to check Ss' understanding of *passenger revenue, rail network, reliability record.*

3 **Ex ❷:** Ss listen for detail.

1 *1997*
2 *FirstGroup*
3 *Reduced costs and more efficient sales practices*
4 *Bad service*
5 *She hasn't received the final figures yet.*

4 T asks Ss to compare the railway company's performance with that of the railway service in their own country (service, punctuality, etc.).

---

5 **Ex ❸:** T links this activity with **Ex ❷** by eliciting from Ss the point that the presentation refers to recent and past activities.

Suggested answers:

- **an action at an unfinished or indefinite time**
  Punctuality has continued to improve this year.

- **a situation that has started in the past and is still continuing**
  ... has only been a private company since it was bought by FirstGroup ... in 1997.
  they have affected the company since 1993 ...
  ... in 1995 where it has remained ...

- **an action that happened at a definite time in the past**
  was bought by FirstGroup... in 1997.
  In the years before privatisation, the company made a lot of changes...
  ... growth slowed from 2.4% in the 1993/94 ...
  ... resulted in growth reaching ... in 1995/96 ...
  ... was followed by 7% in 1996/97
  Reliability improved steadily ... in 1995 ...
  Punctuality ... rose steadily ... in 1995 ...
  ... punctuality improved in 1997 ...

- **a change that affects the present situation**
  ... have made a big difference financially ...
  ... has improved customer satisfaction ...

Present perfect	*Past simple*
unfinished or indefinite time	*definite time in the past*
started in the past and still continuing	
change that affects the present situation	

In feedback T draws Ss' attention to the language used to report the effects of change and elicits some sample sentences for some mini-practice:
Has anything made a big difference to your way of life over the last ten years?
What has improved in the company since you started working for it?
Has your company made any changes which have resulted in improved working conditions?

6 T clarifies the difference between *for* and *since* and refers Ss to the **Don't forget!** section.

7 **Ex ❹:** The main purpose of this exercise is to reinforce the use of the present perfect and past simple. T also reviews some of the trends language practised in Unit 5a.

2 *1997*
3 *when the network was privatised*
4 *between 1993 and 1995*
5 *the last two years*
6 *so far this year*

8 **Ex ❺:** T reminds Ss that questions about what people have done in their life can be good conversation starters. T takes Ss through the example pointing out that the start-up question is followed by further follow-up questions which require fairly specific and full responses, usually in the past simple. Ss each think of three more details for each question before they work round the class finding the people. T does feedback at the end of the activity to consolidate the present perfect and the past simple tenses.

Performance

Measuring performance

Listening 1

1 First Great Eastern is one of 25 private rail companies operating in Britain. The company's Communications Manager, Juliet Sharman, makes a presentation to possible investors. **Listen and complete the information below.**

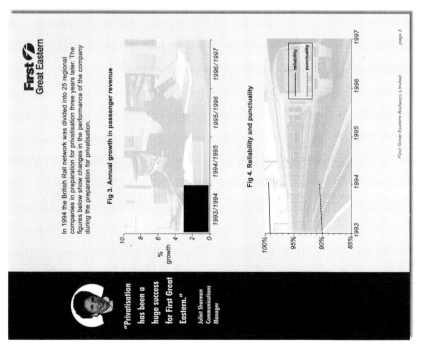

First Great Eastern

"Privatisation has been a huge success for First Great Eastern."

Juliet Sharman
Communications Manager

In 1994 the British Rail network was divided into 25 regional companies in preparation for privatisation three years later. The figures below show changes in the performance of the company during the preparation for privatisation.

Fig 3. Annual growth in passenger revenue

| 1993/1994 | 1994/1995 | 1995/1996 | 1996/1997 |

% growth: 0–10

Fig 4. Reliability and punctuality

reliability
punctuality

85% – 100%, 1993 1994 1995 1996 1997

First Great Eastern Railways Limited   page 8

2 Listen again and answer the questions.

1 When did First Great Eastern become a private company?
2 What is the name of its parent company?
3 How did the company increase revenues in 1995/96?
4 Why have some privatised rail companies been in the newspapers recently?
5 Why has Juliet not given the punctuality figure for 1997?

Grammar **3** **Look at the tapescript on page 136. Find an example of each of the following:**

• an action at an unfinished or indefinite time

• a situation that started in the past and is still continuing

• an action that happened at a definite time in the past

• a change that affects the present situation

Now write descriptions in the correct groups below.

Present perfect	Past simple
unfinished or indefinite time	

For and since

• **For** is used with periods of time such as days, months and years.
  I've worked here for three months now.

• **Since** is used with points in time such as **Monday, July, 1996.**
  We've lived here since 1995.

4 Match the sentence halves about First Great Eastern.

1 Revenue growth was slow — the last two years.
2 The company has been private since before privatisation.
3 FirstGroup bought the company so far this year.
4 Reliability improved steadily 1997.
5 Revenue has increased sharply over between 1993 and 1995.
6 The company has not published any figures when the network was privatised.

Speaking **5** Find people in your group who have done the things below.
Then ask three follow-up questions. Find someone who has ...

• been to a conference this year.
• changed jobs this year.
• worked in a foreign country.
• done some kind of training this year.
• been promoted in the last five years.

Speaking tip:
To keep a conversation going, follow up all yes/no questions with more open questions (when? why? how? etc.).

Explaining results

9 **Ex ❶**: Ss compare their notes with a partner before general feedback.

> *Punctuality: Problems with the railway track, which belongs to another company called Railtrack.*
>
> *Investment plans: Investing £9m in upgrading its stations and leasing new trains.*
>
> *Profits in the future: the Government is going to give less and less money. Because, the biggest costs are fixed. The only way they can improve profits is by increasing passenger volumes.*

10 **Ex ❷**: Ss listen and answer the multiple-choice questions.

1 B   2 C   3 A

In feedback T elicits the reasons for spending £9m and the consequences of having to pay other companies for track and trains. This prepares for the focus on reasons and consequences in the **Don't forget!** section.

11 Ss look at the **Don't forget!** section. T ensures that Ss realise that *therefore* tends to be more formal than *so*. Also *so* (with this meaning) tends to be used as a conjunction within a sentence rather than at the beginning of a sentence. T elicits further examples of reasons and consequences from Ss, related to their own situation (*inflation, exchange rates, rise in salaries, price cuts etc.*).

12 **Ex ❸**: T gives Ss a few minutes to write down five changes or results.

T models with one or two Ss the sort of questions Ss will need to ask their partner e.g. *Could you tell me about …*. Ss will also need to ask follow-up questions.

Self-study

Ex ❶:
2 *I'd like to begin with a look at*
3 *As you can see*
4 *The graph clearly shows*
5 *I'd like you to look at*
6 *I'd like to draw your attention to*

Ex ❷:
1 *has been*
2 *has already achieved*
3 *have worked*
4 *has performed*
5 *had*
6 *were*
7 *did not look*
8 *made*
9 *were not*
10 *has improved*

Ex ❸:
2 *New trains have **resulted in/led to** more reliable service.*
3 *The number of delays increased **because of/due to** track problems.*
4 *We can't raise prices. **That's why/Therefore**, we have to increase volumes.*
5 *Customer satisfaction has improved **due to/because of** better facilities.*
6 *Reduced ticket prices **resulted in/led to** an increase in passenger volumes.*

Ex ❹: 1 C   2 D   3 G   4 A   5 H

Essential vocabulary

Giving reasons
because of
due to
to lead to
to result in
that's why
therefore

Presentations
as you can see
bar chart
to draw attention to
figure (Fig 3)
graph
the graph clearly shows
to make a presentation

General
customer satisfaction
customer service
delay
to lease
penalty
performance
privatisation
to promote
punctuality
to reduce
reliability
revenue
track
to upgrade
volume

The words in italics are not on the Cambridge BEC 1 wordlist.

Explaining results

Listening 2

1 Juliet Sharman finishes her presentation and the investors ask her questions. Listen and complete the notes below.

handwritten notes:
- Punctuality in 1996?
- Investment plans?
- Profits in the future?

First Great Eastern

Liverpool Street Station, London

2 Listen again and choose the correct option to complete the sentences.

1 The railway track that First Great Eastern uses belongs to
A the company.
B another private company.
C the Government.

2 The company is spending £9m in order to
A improve the condition of the track.
B build new stations and improve punctuality.
C improve customer service and reliability.

3 The company's biggest costs are paying
A other companies for the track and trains.
B the Government so it can operate services.
C for new stations and facilities.

> **Reasons and consequences**
> - We can talk about reasons with the following:
> *Reliability fell **because of/due to** problems with the track.*
> ***That's why** we're improving our service.*
> - We can talk about consequences with the following:
> *Our costs are fixed **so** we have to increase passenger volumes.*
> *There will be less financial support. **Therefore**, we have to increase revenue.*
> *The investment will **lead to/result in** better customer service.*

Speaking 3 Work in pairs. Write five results or changes that have happened in your company on a piece of paper. Give the paper to your partner. Find out the reasons for the results and changes.

---

1 Re-arrange the words to make presentation phrases.

1 you'll / the / notice
You'll notice the ...

2 I'd / at / with / a / like / begin / look / to

3 as / can / you / see

4 the / clearly / shows / graph

5 I'd / at / like / to / you / look

6 I'd / to / your / like / to / draw / attention

2 Complete the presentation. Put the verbs in brackets into the present perfect or past simple.

Good afternoon everyone. Welcome to the presentation of the company's half year sales results. As you can see, this year (1 be) _____ very successful so far and the company (2 already/achieve) _____ many of its targets for the year. Our sales people (3 work) _____ very hard and the department (4 perform) _____ very well. The success is especially pleasing when you think back to the problems we (5 have) _____ last summer. Sales (6 be) _____ down by 10% and things (7 not/look) _____ good at all. We (8 make) _____ some difficult decisions last year, which a lot of people (9 not/be) _____ happy with. However, since then we're happy to say that performance (10 improve) _____ sharply.

3 Write sentences linking the following ideas.

1 the £9m investment → better customer service
The £9m investment led to better customer service.

2 new trains → more reliable service

3 the number of delays increased ← track problems

4 we can't raise prices → we have to increase volumes

5 customer satisfaction has improved ← better facilities

6 reduced ticket prices → an increase in passenger volumes

Exam practice

4
- Look at the pie charts below. They show sales figures for three different companies X, Y and Z for eight different products **A-H**.
- Which chart does each sentence **1-5** describe?
- For each sentence, mark the correct letter **A-H**.
- Do not use any letter more than once.

A — X 10%, Z 24%, Y 66%

B — X 35%, Z 35%, Y 30%

C — X 35%, Z 30%, Y 35%

D — X 10%, Z 10%, Y 80%

E — X 35%, Z 45%, Y 20%

F — X 60%, Z 20%, Y 20%

G — X 33.3%, Z 33.3%, Y 33.3%

H — X 20%, Z 50%, Y 30%

1 Sales for Z were not as high as for X and Y.

2 Together, X and Z have less than a third of the market.

3 The market is evenly divided between the three companies.

4 Y has two thirds of the market for this product.

5 For this product Z has as much of the market as X and Y together.

Tapescript: Listening 1

Good afternoon. My name is Juliet Sharman and I'm here to talk about Great Eastern's performance. As you all know, Great Eastern has only been a private company since it was bought by FirstGroup as part of the privatisation of the national railway network in 1997. In the years before privatisation, the company made a lot of changes to prepare it for the free market. I'd like to tell you a bit about those changes and show you how they've affected the company's performance since 1993. To do this, I'd like to draw your attention to figures three and four on page eight of your information brochures.

I'd like to begin with a look at the bar chart, which shows annual growth in passenger revenue from 1993 to 1997. As you can see, growth slowed from 2.4% in 1993/94 down to just 1% in 94/95. However, reduced costs and more efficient sales practices resulted in growth reaching 9.9% in 1995/96. This was followed by 7% in 1996/97. The bar chart clearly shows that the changes have made a big difference financially and have improved customer satisfaction, as we'll see.

I'm sure you've all read newspaper stories about bad service on the privatised rail network, so I'd like you to look at figure four, which shows Great Eastern's reliability and punctuality figures. As you can see from this graph, the company has an excellent reliability record. Reliability improved steadily from 99.1% in 1993 to 99.3% in 1995, where it has remained. Punctuality also rose steadily, going from 90% in 1993 to 91% in 1995. You'll notice the drop to 88% in 1996, which I'll explain later. Although we haven't received the final figures yet, I can tell you that punctuality improved in 1997 and has continued to improve this year as a result of further investment.

Tapescript: Listening 2

Juliet   So, that's the end of my presentation. Does anyone have any questions?

Investor 1   Yes. Earlier you mentioned the drop in punctuality in 1996. What was the problem?

Juliet   Sorry, I said I'd explain that, didn't I? Well, it was mainly because of problems with the railway track. As you know, we have to lease both the track and our trains from other companies. The track belongs to a company called Railtrack. Although we receive penalty payments from them for any delays due to the track, it doesn't help our reliability figures. We don't like the situation but we can't change it. Next question, please.

Investor 2   Could you tell us a bit about the company's future investment plans?

Juliet   Of course. At the moment Great Eastern is investing £9m in upgrading its stations. This includes facilities, information systems and security. We're also investing in new trains, which will lead to improved reliability levels. The gentleman at the back, please ...

Investor 3   With the Government reducing its financial support to the company each year, how do you hope to improve profits in the future?

Juliet   That's a good question. The Government is going to give us less and less money over the next few years. And, as I said, we have to lease both the track and our trains, so our biggest costs are fixed. The only way the company can improve profits is by increasing passenger volumes. That's why we're spending so much on improving customer satisfaction. Next question, please.

Exam focus: Reading

Objectives: To familiarise Ss with the content of the Reading Test
                   To provide useful tips
                   To practise the Reading Test

Materials needed: None

Unit overview

- **The Reading Test**

  T gives an overview of the Reading Test.

- **How to succeed**

  Ss read tips for doing the Reading Test.

- **Exam practice** (not a complete test)

  Part One: Multiple-choice.

  Part Two: Matching.

  Part Three: Matching (graphs and charts).

  Part Five: Multiple-choice and matching.

  Part Six: Multiple-choice gap-filling.

The Reading Test

If T is unfamiliar with the Reading Test, he/she should look at the following:

- BEC 1: Teachers' Information Pack
- UCLES BEC 1 Sample Papers
- Linguarama Cambridge BEC 1 Practice Tests 1 and 2.

1 **Warmer:** T asks Ss to work in pairs and find as many types of reading task as possible that they have done so far in the exam-style exercises in the **Self-study** sections of the units. T relates feedback to the overview table about the Reading Test and explains key features.

Part 1: Multiple-choice
Ss read a short item then select the sentence which most closely matches the meaning of the original **(Unit 4b)**.

Part 2: Matching
Ss identify sentences to match the correct item in a lexical group (job titles, department names etc.). There are always more items than sentences **(Unit 1b)**.

Part 3: Matching
Ss match sentences with the correct visuals (graphs, pie charts etc.). There are always more visuals than sentences **(Units 5a and 5b)**.

Part 4: 'Right, Wrong, Doesn't say'
Not tested in **Self-study** so far. However, this type of exercise is in the body of the core units **(Unit 2b, page 19; Unit 5a, page 30)**.

Part 5: Multiple-choice and matching
Ss do two different types of comprehension exercise. The first type, multiple-choice has not been tested in the **Self-study** units so far. However, see **Unit 1b, page 3** and **Unit 2a, page 14**. For the second type, Ss match five sentences with the correct items from a list of eight in order to make correct statements **(Unit 1b)**.

Part 6: Multiple-choice gap-filling
This is the **only** part of Cambridge BEC 1 which specifically tests candidates' knowledge of grammar and vocabulary **(Units 1a and 2b)**.

2 T discusses timing and stresses the importance of assigning 45 minutes for reading out of the total 70 minutes (leaving 25 minutes for writing). T reminds Ss that reading accounts for 45% of the written papers and is the reason for the high amount of reading practice in the book.

How to succeed

3 T takes Ss through the tips and explains them in more detail.

Exam practice

4 T tells Ss that they will now do a complete Reading Test except for Part Four. (There are space and time constraints; moreover, 'Right, Wrong, Doesn't say' questions appear frequently in the core units.) Ss will have the opportunity of doing full practice tests using the UCLES Sample Papers or the Linguarama Practice Tests later in the course.

Part One

5 T reminds Ss of the content of this part of the Reading Test and Ss read the tips. Ss do Questions 1-5 and in feedback discuss what language helped them to choose their answers (e.g. 1 not until, 2 try again, 3 brand, 4 distribution, 5 purchase).

One of the tips referred to the fact that it is often necessary to be careful about negative forms; Ss may have had problems with not available until in Question 1.

1 C	2 A	3 B	4 B	5 A

Part Two

6 In feedback Ss report which words helped them choose the answers (6 company's income and expenses, 7 new executives, 8 smaller companies/Stella owns, 9 company owns and owes, 10 company/checked financial reports).

6 G	7 D	8 C	9 H	10 F

Exam focus: Reading

The Reading Test

The Cambridge BEC I Reading Test has six questions. Questions 1-5 test general comprehension. Question 6 specifically tests your knowledge of grammar and vocabulary.

Part	Input	Task
1	5 short notes, messages, adverts, timetables etc.	Multiple-choice
2	Notice, list, plan etc.	Matching
3	Graphs, charts, tables	Matching
4	Letter, advert, report etc. (150 - 200 words)	Right, Wrong, Doesn't say
5	Newspaper article, advert etc. (250 - 350 words)	Multiple-choice & matching
6	Newspaper article, advert etc. (125 - 150 words)	Multiple-choice gap-filling

Length: The Reading questions should take about 45 minutes of the Reading & Writing Test.

How to succeed

Here are some important tips for doing the Reading Test.

- Read all instructions **carefully**.
- Read through the whole text once before looking at the questions.
- Read through all the questions before answering Question 1.
- Read Question 1 again and then look quickly through the text for the answer.
- Underline the answer in the text - it will make checking quicker.
- The questions are in the same order as the answers. If you are confident that an answer is right, begin looking for the next answer from that point in the text, not from the beginning.
- Leave difficult questions and return to them later if you have time.
- Only write **one** answer for each question.
- **Never** leave a question unanswered. If you are running out of time or really have no idea, guess.
- Use any time you have left to check your answers.

Exam practice

On the next three pages you can practise five of the six parts of the Reading Test. Look at the specific tips for each part of the test before you answer the questions.

Part One

Reading tips
1 Read all three options before answering.
2 Be careful of negative forms.

Questions 1-5
- Look at questions 1-5.
- In each question, which phrase or sentence is correct?
- For each question, mark the correct letter **A, B or C.**

1
I am sorry but the parts will not be available until 25 January.

The parts can be delivered
- **A** immediately.
- **B** before 25 January.
- **C** after 25 January.

2
Mr Ranson called while you were on the phone - he'll try again this afternoon.

Mr Ranson
- **A** promised to call back.
- **B** left a message.
- **C** was put through.

3
Congratulations to Vanessa Clark on her promotion to Brand Manager.

Vanessa Clark works in
- **A** production.
- **B** marketing.
- **C** finance.

4
Sales were good but distribution problems led to a slight drop in profits.

The company had problems with
- **A** producing enough goods.
- **B** delivering enough goods.
- **C** selling enough goods.

5
☐ Tick if you wish to make an immediate purchase.

You have to tell the company if you want
- **A** to buy the product.
- **B** more information.
- **C** a product demonstration.

Exam focus: Reading

Part Two

Reading tips
1 Read all the information before answering.
2 Do the easy questions quickly and then see which possible answers are left.

Questions 6-10
- Look at the list below. It shows the contents of a company's Annual Report.
- Decide in which part of the report (A-H) you would find the information (6-10).
- For each question, mark the correct letter (A-H).

Stella Group Plc

Annual Report

- **A** Chairman's Statement
- **B** National Sales Reports
- **C** Review of Subsidiaries
- **D** Changes in Key Personnel
- **E** Group Organigram
- **F** Auditor's Report
- **G** Profit and Loss Account
- **H** Balance Sheet

---

6 A statement of the company's income and expenses.

7 The names of new executives and board members.

8 A look at the performance of smaller companies that Stella owns.

9 A list of what the company owns and owes.

10 A statement by the company that checked the financial reports.

Part Three

7   Part Three tests comprehension of descriptions of graphs, bar charts and pie charts. T takes Ss through the tips. T elicits a description of each visual before Ss do the exercise in order to review vocabulary describing trends and to encourage Ss to predict vocabulary.

11 G	12 C	13 E	14 A	15 D

Part Four is not tested in this unit.

Part Five

8   Ss read the tips. In discussion, T might also like to elicit from Ss general tips about reading a longer text (e.g. don't panic if you don't know every word, aim to get the general meaning at the first reading, use words you know to help you understand parts you don't know etc.).

16 C	17 B	18 C	19 A	20 C	21 B	22 E	23 H

Part Six

9   T reads the tips with Ss and asks them to provide examples of types of words that might fill the gaps. T refers students to the list of grammatical categories on page 22 of the **Exam focus: Vocabulary** unit. In feedback T ensures Ss are aware of the range of typical language the gaps might contain (e.g. pronouns, nouns, adjectives, adverbs, verbs, connectors, articles, relative pronouns). T encourages Ss to try to complete the gaps before looking at the three options.

24 A	25 A	26 B	27 B	28 C	29 B	30 C	31 A	32 A	33 C

Part Three

Reading tips

1 Look at the graphs and try to predict vocabulary describing direction (*rise, fall*) and the strength of movement (*steadily, sharply*).
2 Read all the sentences before answering.
3 Be careful of words such as *but, despite* etc.

Questions 11-15

- Look at the graphs and charts below. They show unemployment in eight different countries.
- Which country does each sentence (11-15) describe?
- For each sentence mark the correct letter (A-H).
- Do not use any letter more than once.

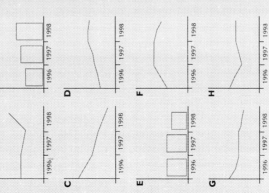

11 The steady drop in unemployment levelled off in 1997 before falling once more the following year.

12 Unemployment fell steadily throughout the period.

13 The rate of unemployment remained steady for two years and then fell in 1998.

14 Despite a slight fall in the previous year, the number of unemployed rose sharply in 1998.

15 After rising steadily for two years, unemployment began to decrease in 1998.

Part Five

Reading tips

1 Read through **all** the text first.
2 Read all questions 16-19 before answering.
3 Begin with question 16 and work through the text.
4 Now read all questions 20-23.
5 Scan the text for the answers.
6 **Never** leave a question unanswered.
7 When you have finished, check all your answers.

Questions 16-23

- Read the Chairman's Statement below and answer questions **16-23** on the opposite page.

Chairman's Statement

The company continued to grow and increase its product range in 1998. The most important new developments included a range of children's drinks and low calorie diet drinks, which both proved very popular.

The company is best known for its range of refreshing fruit drinks and, not surprisingly, these were our biggest sellers once more. There were two new additions to the range, *Squish!* and *Liquid Sunshine*, both of which have a Caribbean flavour. The first sales figures suggest that our expensive TV advertising campaign was very successful and that these products will be as popular as the rest of the fruit drink range.

Continued growth in the keep-fit market meant that our energy drinks did well in 1998. Sales of one of them, *Booster!*, were second only to fruit drinks in April. The strength of this particular market also explains the success of our new diet drinks.

There were, however, big differences in the performance of our older products. The company's oldest product, mineral water, continued to enjoy a healthy share of a very profitable mass market. It seems our customers are still happy to stay with the brand despite the increasing number of competitors' products. Unfortunately, the same cannot be said of our *Ice-T* and *Chocomania* drinks. Sales increased in the summer after we re-launched both products but customers soon bought other brands and total annual sales for both product ranges were disappointing.

The company also said goodbye to its own brand of cola in 1998. After two unsuccessful years of trying to enter the huge cola market, 1998 was another very poor year. The company finally accepted that it had made a wrong decision and stopped production in September.

Exam focus: Reading

Part Six

Reading tips

1 Read through **all** the text first.
2 What type of word could fill each gap?
3 Write possible answers in the gaps in pencil on the exam paper. Then look to see if these words are among the answers.
4 Look again at the gaps you are not happy with.
5 **Never** leave a gap unanswered.
6 When you have finished, **read** the complete text.

Questions 24-33

- Read the newspaper article below about a new alliance in the packaging industry.
- Choose the correct word from **A, B or C** below.
- For each question, mark the correct letter **A, B or C.**

The Big Number

The county's demand for telephones, mobile phones, faxes and the Internet is growing at an increasingly fast rate. In fact, it is growing (24) ..... quickly that our telephone numbering system needs re-organising (25) ..... some major changes will have to be made. These changes, (26) .....will make the system simpler and easier to use. It is (27) ..... an important task that all the UK phone companies are working together to make (28) ..... changes.

The changes will (29) ..... only make hundreds of millions of new numbers, but they will (30) ..... bring order and flexibility to the system for years to come.

(31) ..... main changes will happen between now and the year 2001, so there will be (32) ..... of time to prepare. You will find details of the number changes on our website, (33) ..... you can visit on www.numberchange.org, or call our freephone helpline on 0808 224 2000.

Questions 16-19

- For questions 16-19, choose the correct answer.
- Mark one letter (A, B or C) for the correct answer.

16 The new fruit drinks cost a lot of money to
A develop.
B produce.
C launch.

17 The best selling drinks in April were
A energy drinks.
B fruit drinks.
C diet drinks.

18 The company's brand of mineral water has a
A small share of a small market.
B large share of a small market.
C large share of a large market.

19 Sales for Ice-T and Chocomania
A rose and then fell again.
B increased steadily.
C were disappointing all year.

Questions 20-23

- For questions 20-23, use the information in the text to match each sentence with one of the company's products (A-H).
- For each question, mark one letter (A-H).
- Do not use any letter more than once.

20 The company has introduced two new products to its range of .....

21 Growth in the keep-fit market was good for sales of energy drinks and .....

22 The company's longest selling brand is .....

23 The company's worst performing product was .....

A	Children's drinks
B	Diet drinks
C	Fruit drinks
D	Energy drinks
E	Mineral water
F	Ice-T
G	Chocomania
H	Cola

24 A so   B that   C too
25 A and   B with   C before
26 A despite   B however   C although
27 A much   B such   C so
28 A this   B there   C these
29 A if   B not   C but
30 A furthermore   B additionally   C also
31 A The   B Those   C Their
32 A plenty   B many   C lot
33 A when   B who   C which

Exam focus: Reading

Product description

Objectives:	To enable Ss to describe products in general terms
	To practise listening for specific information
	To review language for talking about dimensions and comparatives and superlatives
	To practise question formation

Materials needed: Cassette - *Pass Cambridge BEC 1*

Unit overview

● Presenting a product

Warmer	T elicits vocabulary related to *board game*.
Listening 1	Ss listen to a presentation of new board games and identify pictures. Ss listen for more detail and identify what notes refer to. T reviews language related to dimensions.
Language focus	Ss form questions about the games.
Speaking	Ss work in pairs and describe a board game they like.

● Describing a product

Listening 2	Ss listen to the same sales manager talking to a retailer and identify which games are of interest. Ss then listen again and answer comprehension questions.
Language focus	Ss review comparatives and superlatives.
Speaking	Ss work in pairs. They list and rank points they considered when buying something they both bought.

● Self-study

Vocabulary	Word-building and question formation exercise.
Language focus	Comparatives and superlatives exercise.
Writing	Ss write about a product they have recently bought.
Exam practice	*Multiple-choice gap-fill (Reading Test Part 6).*

Presenting a product

1   **Warmer (books closed):** T writes *board game* on the board. T asks Ss to work in pairs and think of five words or phrases connected with the idea of *board game*. T elicits Ss' responses and uses this as a chance to pre-teach necessary vocabulary for the unit, i.e. *board, dice, timer, cards, pieces* and *counters.*

2   **Ex ❶:** Ss listen and identify the two games which Robert describes.

> Mindtwist (standard version):   Picture 1 (£17.99)
> Mindtwist Travel: Picture 4 (£10.99)

3   **Ex ❷:** Ss listen to the cassette in more detail and decide what the numbered descriptions refer to.

> 1 general knowledge   type of game
> 2 size, weight and cost   differences between Mindtwist *standard and travel versions*
> 3 wood   what the pieces are made of (material) in the standard version
> 4 23 x 23 cm   size/measurements of the Mindtwist Travel board
> 5 300 grammes   total weight of Mindtwist Travel
> 6 £10.99   price of Mindtwist Travel

4   T builds up Ss' vocabulary to describe dimensions. T may wish to write the following words on the board: *size, weight, cost, material.* T plays the cassette again and Ss write down any related vocabulary they hear, e.g.

size	weight	cost	material
smaller	*light-weight*	*will retail at £17.99*	*wooden*
measures	*300 grammes*		*made of coloured plastic*
23cm square			

T ensures that Ss know verbs related to these words: *to measure, to weigh, to cost, to be made of.* T also ensures that Ss know key adjectives:

size: *big, small, long, short*
weight: *heavy, light*
cost: *expensive, cheap, high, low.*

T also ensures that Ss know the nouns *length, height and width.* T should tell Ss that the positive adjective is generally used in questions (e.g. *How big is it?* not *How small is it?*). This point arises in **Ex ❶** of **Self-study.**

5   **Ex ❸:** T elicits complete questions for the first few answers in **Ex ❷**. If Ss are confident at forming questions, T asks them to work in pairs and form the remaining questions. Ss are expected to demonstrate their ability to form questions in Part 2 of the Speaking Test (information gap activity). If Ss have problems with question-forming, T will need to provide extra support to prepare them for the examination.

> **Suggested answers:**
> 2 *What are the differences between the standard and the travel version?*
> 3 *What are the playing pieces made of in the standard version?*
> 4 *How big is the board in the travel version?*
>   *What is the size of the board in the travel version?*
> 5 *How heavy is the travel version?*
>   *What is the weight of the board in the travel version?*
> 6 *How much will the travel version cost?*
>   *What is the price of the travel version?*

6   **Ex ❹:** Ss work in pairs describing games that they like. In order to give this activity more structure and review language which has arisen during the lesson, T may wish to write some prompts on the board, e.g., *type of game, size, weight, material, price, how to play, comments.* T could conclude by asking Ss to play *Twenty Questions*, with the other Ss asking *yes/no* questions to guess the name of the game.

Describing a product

7   Before Ss listen to the cassette, T prepares them by asking how they think Columbine sells its games: directly to the public? through catalogues? through retailers? etc.

8   **Ex ❶:** Ss listen for gist on the first listening, simply to get an idea of the games Sophie is interested in.

> *Sophie orders both versions of Mindtwist. She is most interested in the travel version.*

9   **Ex ❷:** Ss listen again and answer more detailed questions.

> 1 *Board games are selling better than ever before.*
> 2 *Mindtwist is Columbine's newest board game. It is available in standard and travel versions.*
> 3 *None.*
> 4 *Their instructions.*
> 5 *She isn't sure it will sell as well as the board games. Not everybody is interested in antiques.*
> 6 *It's reasonable.*
> 7 *If she buys both versions, she can get a discount of 5%.*

Product description

Presenting a product

Listening 1 **1** Robert Saunders, the Sales Manager at Columbine Games, talks about two new products. Listen to his presentation. Which products does he talk about? How much do they cost?

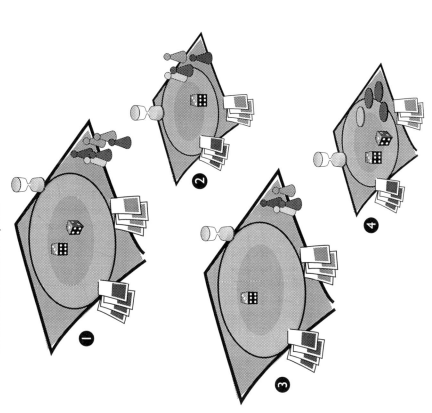

2 Listen to the presentation again. The speakers refer to the following things. What are they talking about?

1 General knowledge
2 Size, weight and cost
3 Wood
4 23 x 23 cm
5 300 grammes
6 £10.99

Grammar **3** Write questions for the answers in Exercise 2.

1 _What type of game is Mindtwist?_

2 _____

3 _____

4 _____

5 _____

6 _____

Speaking **4** Work in pairs. Describe a board game that you like.

Describing a product

Listening 2 **1** Robert Saunders talks to Sophie Powell, a retailer, about some of Columbine's products. Which games is Sophie interested in?

- Mindtwist
- Mindtwist Travel
- Collect

2 Listen again. Answer the questions below.

1 Why is Sophie interested in board games?
2 What is special about Mindtwist?
3 How many travel size general knowledge games does Sophie stock?
4 What does Sophie not like about some of Columbine's board games?
5 Why is Sophie not interested in Collect?
6 What does Sophie think about the price of Mindtwist Travel?
7 How can Sophie get a discount on Mindtwist?

Product description

10 T refers back to the answers to Questions 1 and 5 in **Ex ❷** and reviews the form of comparatives and superlatives. T then refers Ss to the **Don't forget!** section. T particularly reminds Ss of the irregular forms: *good/better/the best* and *bad/worse/the worst*.

11 **Ex ❸**: T asks Ss to correct the sentences about Columbine's games. As students focus on correctness of meaning, they will be using the comparative and superlative forms referred to earlier. T may point out that *fewer* in the first sentence is used with countable nouns. *Less* is only used with uncountable nouns.

3 *The instructions on Columbine games have become easier than before.*
4 *Collect is the smallest of the products that Robert shows Sophie.*
  Collect is not as big as the other games.
5 *Sophie's customers will be more interested in Mindtwist than Collect.*
  Sophie's customers will be less interested in collect than Mindtwist
  Sophie's customers won't be as interested in Collect as Mindtwist.
6 *Mindtwist Travel is less expensive than the standard version.*
  Mindtwist Travel costs less than the standard version.
  Mindtwist Travel isn't as expensive as the standard version.

12 **Ex ❹**: Ss work in pairs and think of something they have both bought. They discuss the criteria they used in selecting it and write them down. They then order all of the criteria mentioned in terms of importance for themselves. Once they have done this, T gives them a little more time to prepare to report back to the rest of the class.

For example, Juan and Roberto are working in pairs discussing criteria for choosing a car. Juan talks about price, reliability and service from the garage. Roberto talks about price, image and performance. They then order these five criteria and report back to the other Ss.

Self-study

Ex ❶: 2 short   *How long is the board?*
3 cheap   *How much does the game cost?*
4 size   *How big is Collect?*
5 easy   *How difficult are the instructions?*

Ex ❷: **Suggested answers:**
2 *The Extra is 2 kilos **heavier than the Super.***
3 *The Extra is more **expensive than the other display panels.***
4 *The Super is not as **heavy/big/expensive as the Extra.***
5 *The Standard is the least **expensive of the display panels.***
6 *The Standard is the **lightest/cheapest/smallest of the display panels.***

Ex ❹: 1 B   2 A   3 A   4 B   5 A   6 C   7 C   8 A   9 B   10 C

Essential vocabulary

Describing products
length (long/short)
to be made of ...
to measure
size (big/small)
to weigh
weight (heavy/light)

General
board game
complicated
difficult
discount
general knowledge
instructions
reasonable
retailer
to stock
version

The words in italics are not on the Cambridge BEC 1 wordlist.

Comparison

- The comparative is formed by adding **-er** to short words and **more/less** to longer words.
  This game is smaller than the other games on the market.
  Mindtwist is more interesting than the other games.

- We use **as ... as** with two things that are the same and also with negatives.
  Collect is as new as Mindtwist.
  It isn't as big as the other game.

- The superlative of short words is formed with **-est**. With longer words we add **the most/the least.**
  These games are the latest in Columbine's range.
  This is the least interesting of the games.

! good - **better** - **the best**
! bad - **worse** - **the worst**

Unit 30

3 Correct the information about Columbine games in the sentences below.

1 Sophie is selling ~~fewer~~ board games than before. more
2 Mindtwist Travel is ~~heavier than~~ the standard game. not as heavy as
3 The instructions on Columbine games have become more difficult than before.
4 Collect is the biggest of the products that Robert shows Sophie.
5 Sophie's customers will be more interested in Collect than Mindtwist.
6 Mindtwist Travel costs the same as the standard version.

Speaking **4** Work in pairs. Think of something you have both bought. Make a list of the points you considered when you bought it. Discuss the importance of the points and put them in order. Then prepare to report back to the rest of the group.

Product name ....

Points considered	Me	My partner
price		

Product description

---

1 Complete the groups of words below. Then use one word from each group to form a question.

1 weight / heavy, light
How heavy is the travel version of the game? _____

2 length / long _____

3 cost / expensive _____

4 / big, small _____

5 difficulty / difficult _____

2 Look at the catalogue information comparing three display panels and complete the sentences below.

Portable Folding Display Panels

Product name	Number of panels	Weight	Dimensions	Price
Standard	4 panels	10 kilos	1.8 x 1.2m	£498.00
Super	6 panels	15 kilos	1.8 x 1.6m	£545.00
Extra	8 panels	17 kilos	1.8 x 2.4m	£660.00

1 The Extra has more __panels than the Super.__
2 The Extra is 2 kilos _____
3 The Extra is more _____
4 The Super is not as _____
5 The Standard is the least _____
6 The Standard is the _____

Product description

---

3 Write about a product you have recently bought.
- Where was it made?
- What is it made of?
- Why did you buy it instead of a similar product?

Exam practice
- Read the text below about a fax machine.
- Choose the correct word from **A**, **B** or **C** to fill each gap.

Lomax KR 700 Plain Paper Fax/Digital Answerphone

The KR 700 is the latest addition to our range of fax machines. It is a **(1)** _____ advanced version of the KR 600 with an answerphone facility and **(2)** _____ other special features. One of these special features means that you **(3)** _____ perform one operation while the machine is **(4)** _____ another one. There are several dialling techniques **(5)** _____ allow you to send faxes easily, quickly and cheaply. It takes **(6)** _____ fifteen seconds to fax an A4 page. **(7)** _____, the laser printing gives you high quality pictures.
The answerphone **(8)** _____ fourteen minutes' recording time, which is a bonus for any business. **(9)** _____ it is such a flexible machine, it is compact. It will fit into the **(10)** _____ space in the office or at home.

	A	B	C
1	most	more	best
2	many	any	more
3	can	must	should
4	perform	performing	performed
5	which	what	who
6	all	less	just
7	Extra	Addition	Furthermore
8	has	have	having
9	However	Although	Also
10	small	smaller	smallest

Tapescript: Listening 1

Morning everybody. Now, as you know, this morning we're going to talk about our latest products in our range of games. Before we talk about the selling points of each game, I'd just like to describe them briefly. I'll begin with this general knowledge game called Mindtwist, which comes in two versions: a standard size and a travel size.

As you can see, the differences are size, weight and, of course, cost. The standard version has a normal size board, two packs of cards, six wooden playing pieces, a timer and two dice. The travel size, Mindtwist Travel, is obviously smaller: it has a thin, light-weight, magnetic board which measures just 23cm square. The cards are smaller and the four playing pieces are magnetic counters which are made of coloured plastic. The total weight is only 300 grammes. The standard version will retail at £17.99 and the travel size at £10.99.

And now I'd like to show you another new game called Collect. This is a card game for three to six players …

Tapescript: Listening 2

Robert	So Sophie, how are our products selling?
Sophie	Board games are the big seller at the moment. They're selling better than ever before?
Robert	Good, so you might be interested in having a bigger range of our board games then.
Sophie	Yes, if there's anything different.
Robert	We've got Mindtwist. It's our newest board game. The game itself comes in two versions: standard and travel. The games are basically the same but the travel version's lighter and smaller. There are also fewer playing pieces.
Sophie	I stock several general knowledge games already, but I don't have a travel size. I might be interested in that.
Robert	Right. This is it. You can see it's nice and compact.
Sophie	Mmm, it looks interesting. Are the instructions easy to follow? Some of your games have very complicated instructions.
Robert	Yes, other customers have told us that as well. So we've made the instructions easier. But I have another travel size game, called Collect. It's even easier to play. Let me show you. It's a card game based on the television programme Collectables. You know, antiques.
Sophie	Oh yes.
Robert	And it isn't as big as the board game either.
Sophie	Hmm, well, it sounds different, but I'm not sure it'll sell as well as the board games. Not everybody's interested in antiques. Anyway, what's the recommended retail price for the Mindtwist travel version?
Robert	£10.99.
Sophie	That sounds reasonable. And what would you be willing to sell it to us for?
Robert	£9.99.
Sophie	Would there be a discount on large orders?
Robert	Not on Mindtwist on its own, no. But if you were to buy both versions of Mindtwist, I could give you 5% on both games.
Sophie	OK. I'll take them both, but I'll order just a few to start with.
Robert	Good. I'll get an order form.

Product development

Objectives:	To enable Ss to talk about product development
	To practise reading and listening for specific information
	To review sequencing words (*first, after that etc.*)
	To review the present continuous and *going to* for future arrangements and intentions

Materials needed: Cassette - *Pass Cambridge BEC 1*
Cards - **Set A 9 cards:** *Pass Cambridge BEC 1 Unit 7b/1A-9A* One set per pair/group
Set B 6 cards: *Pass Cambridge BEC 1 Unit 7b/1B-6B* One set per pair/group

Unit overview

● Product testing

Speaking	Ss do a quiz about drug development in the USA.
Reading	Ss read an article to find answers to the quiz. Ss re-read the article and complete a table about the stages of the development process.
Language focus	Ss review language for sequencing (*first, then, next*, etc.).
Writing	Ss put cards describing the drug development process in order then write a text linking the stages.
Speaking	Ss talk in pairs about the development of one of their company's products or services.

● Marketing a product

Listening	Ss listen to a marketing manager talking about plans for the launch of a new arthritis drug and answer comprehension questions. Ss listen again and order the stages in the process.
Language focus	Ss review the present continuous for future arrangements and *going to* for intentions.
Speaking	Ss talk in pairs about their company's plans. Ss then ask and answer questions about personal plans (using cards).

● Self-study

Vocabulary	Gap-fill exercise (sequencers).
Language focus	Gap-fill exercise (present continuous for future arrangements and *going to*).
Vocabulary	Multiple-choice gap-fill exercise.
Exam practice	*Multiple-choice comprehension exercise (Reading Test Part 1).*

Product testing

1 **Warmer (books closed):** T writes *drug development* on the board and asks Ss to work in pairs and think of five words connected with the subject (*test, monitor, launch, develop, animals*).

2 **Ex ❶:** Ss work in pairs and do a quiz about drug development. The aim is to interest Ss in the topic and to provide a reason for reading the article in **Ex ❷**.

3 **Ex ❷:** Ss read the article to find the answers to the quiz.

| 1 B | 2 C | 3 A | 4 A | 5 A | 6 B | 7 C |

4 **Ex ❸:** Ss read the article again and complete the table.

	Laboratory	People		
		Stage 1	Stage 2	Stage 3
Test period:	2½ years	About 1 year	About 2 years	About 3 years
Tested on:	Animals	Fewer than 100 healthy people	100-300 people who suffer from the disease	1,000-3,000 people in hospitals and clinics
Reason for testing:	To show how the drug works and its level of safety.	To test safety.	To see how well the drug works.	To monitor the patient for the success of the drug and side-effects.

5 **Ex ❹:** Ss underline any sequencing words and phrases in the text.

Paragraph 2: There are four stages of .... First of all ... Then ....
Paragraph 3: The first stage ... After that, ... The final stage ... While ...
Paragraph 4: When ... ...
Paragraph 5: When ... ... finally ...

6 T then refers Ss to the **Don't forget!** section. T should stress the usefulness of preparing the listener by making a global comment about the stages that follow, (e.g. *There are four stages of testing a new drug*). T should also ensure that Ss are confident with the use of the sequencers as they will be important for **Ex ❺** and **❻**.

T will need to point out that *while* is used to link two simultaneous actions within one sentence. *When* can be used in the same way. It is also used to link one action which happens after another (followed by either the present simple or the present perfect). In the article the present perfect is used with *when* to emphasise that one action is completed before the next happens (e.g. *When the authorities have approved the new drug, the doctors can ...*).

7 **Ex ❺:** Ss work in pairs or groups. T gives each pair/group a set of cards describing drug development. Ss put them in the correct order, without looking at the article they have just read. T then asks them to write a description of the drug development process, using sequencers for clarity. T tells Ss they can omit/alter certain words or change active to passive so as not to be wordy or repetitive.

Suggested answer:
There are a number of stages in the drug development process. First of all, the company tests the new drug on animals. After that, the company tests the drug on healthy people to check safety. The drug is then tested on a small number of patients to see how well it works. Finally, the drug is tested on a larger number of patients. While the company is testing the drug, it keeps a record of test results for the authorities. When the company has finished tests on humans, it applies to the authorities for approval. When the authorities approve the drug, the company can finally launch it.

8 **Ex ❻:** Ss work in pairs and talk about the development of a product or service in their company. They should be encouraged to use some sequencers for clarity. However, the main aim of this exercise is to transfer what they have learned to their own situation and to develop fluency.

Product development

Product testing

Speaking **1** How much do you know about the development of drugs in the pharmaceutical industry in the USA? Work in pairs and do the quiz below.

1 How many years of testing are there before a drug reaches the market?
A 6 B 12 C 18

2 About how much does it cost to develop a new drug in the USA?
A $160 million B $260 million C $360 million

3 What percentage of drugs tested on humans reaches the market?
A 20 B 40 C 60

4 How many stages of testing on humans are there in the USA?
A 3 B 4 C 9

5 How many people, on average, take part in testing drugs?
A 1,000 - 5,000 B 5,000 - 10,000 C 10,000 - 15,000

6 How long do the authorities take to approve a New Drug Application?
A 6 months B 2.5 years C 5 years

7 How much will be spent on drug development in five years' time?
A About $4 bn B About $12 bn C About $25 bn

Reading **2** Read the article below to find the answers to the quiz.

Drug development in the USA

The development of new drugs is essential if we are to stop the spread of diseases. However, it takes an average of twelve years to develop a drug and it costs a company about $359 million. Only five out of every 5,000 drugs that start the testing process are tested on humans. Only one in five of those actually reaches the market.

There are four stages of testing a new drug. First of all, a company carries out tests for about two and a half years in the laboratory and on animals. This is to show how the drug works against a particular disease and to show its level of safety. Then testing on humans can begin.

The first stage of human testing tests the safety of the drug on fewer than one hundred healthy people and lasts about a year. After that, the drug is tested for about two years on 100 - 300 people who suffer from the disease to see how well the drug works. The final stage lasts about three years: the drug is usually tested on 1,000 - 3,000 patients in hospitals and clinics. While they are carrying out these tests, doctors monitor the patient closely and keep a record of the success of the drug and any side-effects.

Science Now

23

Science Now, March 1999

When a company has completed the three stages of tests on humans, the company makes a New Drug Application to the authorities, which is often 1,000 pages or more. The authorities should take a maximum of six months to review a New Drug Application but they usually take longer; the average review time is 29.9 months.

When the authorities have approved the New Drug Application, doctors can finally give it to their patients. The company still keeps a quality control record of the drug, including any side-effects.

Discovering and developing safe and successful new drugs is a long, difficult and expensive process. The research-based pharmaceutical industry is investing $12.6 billion in research and development this year and that investment will probably double in five years.

3 Read the article again and complete the table below.

	Laboratory	People		
		Stage 1	Stage 2	Stage 3
Test period:				
Tested on:				
Reason for testing:				

Vocabulary **4** Underline the sequencing words and phrases in the text.

Sequencing

When we are describing a sequence or process, it is important to be clear about the order.
- We can talk about the stages involved:
  There are four stages of testing a new drug.
  The first/second/third/final stage is ...
- We can also use simple sequencing words:
  first/first of all   when
  then/next/after that   while
  finally

Writing **5** Work in pairs or groups. Your teacher will give you some cards describing drug development. Put the stages in order. Then write a description of the process.

Speaking **6** Work in pairs. Talk about the development of one of your company's products or services.

Marketing a product

9 **Ex ❶**: Before listening, T elicits how drugs are normally distributed (*on prescription, over the counter* etc.). Ss listen to the cassette and answer the questions.

> 1 *Arthran.*
> 2 *For anyone who suffers from arthritis.*
> 3 *It will be available in hospitals or on prescription from doctors.*
> 4 *Tiredness.*
> 5 *There will be general information posters on display in doctors' waiting rooms and information leaflets for patients.*

10 **Ex ❷**: It must be stressed that Ss will have great difficulty if they try to put the actions into the correct order immediately. T should tell them to listen and note down any dates they hear next to the appropriate actions. After that, they should be able to order the actions quite easily.

> 1 *send information packs to doctors (end of April)*
> 2 *visit doctors to talk about the product (beginning of May)*
> 3 *give posters to doctors (a week before the launch)*
> 4 *launch the drug (in 5 weeks' time - on 18 May)*
> 5 *give information leaflets to patients (just after the launch on 18 May)*

11 T asks Ss which tense was mostly used on the cassette to talk about Arthran's plans for the launch of the drug. (Answer: mostly the present continuous). T leads into a discussion of the use of the present continuous for future arrangements.

T also refers to the use of *going to* to talk about intentions. (It was also used on the cassette, e.g. *Of course,* **we're going to give** *doctors and patients all the necessary information.*)

T refers Ss to the **Don't forget!** section. T mentions that sometimes the distinction between arrangements and intentions is rather fine; sometimes native speakers might disagree about which form to use.

T then asks Ss to summarise the plans for the launch of Arthran using the information in **Ex ❷**. (Ss will need to use the present continuous and some of the sequencers from the first part of the unit.)

12 **Ex ❸**: Ss work in pairs and tell each other about their company's plans.

13 **Ex ❹**: Ss work in pairs with the cards face down in a pile in front of them. They take turns to pick up a card and ask their partner a question about plans related to the topic on the card.

Self-study

Ex ❶:
	2 *After that/then*	3 *are starting*		
	3 *then/after that*			
	4 *when*			
	5 *while*	5 *Are you going to use/Are you using*		

Ex ❷:
	2 *are you going to do/are you doing*	3		
	4 *are using*			

Ex ❸: 1 A   2 C   3 B   4 A   5 B

Ex ❹: 1 B   2 B   3 A   4 B   5 C

Essential vocabulary

Product development	Drugs	General
to approve	chemist	*advertising campaign*
authorities	*disease*	information pack
average (on average)	healthy	leaflet
development	*over-the-counter*	poster
to monitor	patient	
to reach (the market)	*prescription*	
research & development (R & D)	safe	
stage	safety	
to take (+ time)	*side-effects*	
to test		

The words in italics are not on the Cambridge BEC 1 wordlist.

Marketing a product

Listening

1 A medical journalist asks a marketing manager about a new drug for arthritis. Listen and answer the questions.

1 What is the drug called?
2 Who is the drug for?
3 Where will patients be able to get the drug?
4 What are the possible side effects?
5 How will patients get information about the drug?

2 Listen again and note down any dates you hear. Then put the actions below into the correct order.

☐ give general information posters to doctors

☐ visit doctors to talk about the product

☐ launch the drug

☐ give information leaflets to patients

☐ send information packs to doctors   *(end of April)*

Future arrangements and intentions

- We use **the present continuous** (often with a time phrase) to talk about arrangements in the future.
  We're visiting doctors at the beginning of May.
  *When **are** you **launching** the new product?*
- We can use **going to** to talk about our intentions.
  *We **are going to** work closely with doctors.*
  *We **aren't going to** have any direct contact with patients.*

Speaking

3 Work in pairs. Find out if your partner's company has plans for any of the following.

a new product launch   a new advertising campaign
new training courses   new projects

4 Work in pairs. Your teacher will give you some cards. Ask your partner questions about his/her plans for the future.

Product development

Exam practice

4
- Look at questions 1-5.
- In each question, which phrase or sentence is correct?
- For each question, mark the correct letter **A, B or C.**

1
While we are developing the product, we will write regular reports to ensure that you are informed of its progress.

A We're going to write reports before we develop the product.
B We're going to write reports at the same time as we develop the product.
C We're going to write reports after we develop the product.

2
MEMO
To: Peter
From: Tom
The publicity leaflets for the new model will not be back from the printers until Friday 11 July.

A We might have the leaflets before 11 July.
B We won't have the leaflets before 11 July.
C We are sure to have the leaflets before 11 July.

3
Launch schedule
24/5 - Press conference.
31/5 - TV advertising starts. Distribute posters.
7/6 - Deliver leaflets. Radio advertising starts.
14/6 - Free competition starts on the radio.

How many written forms of publicity are there?

A two
B three
C four

4 We are carrying out market research in the north and the Midlands from 22nd-26th.

A We have done the research in the north and the Midlands.
B We haven't done the research in the north and the Midlands yet.
C We have decided not to do research in the north and the Midlands.

5
John
Still waiting for approval from the authorities. Hope to get it next week so that we can finalise the launch date.
Pete

A They have finalised a date for the launch.
B They hope to launch the product next week.
C They cannot yet finalise a date for the launch.

---

1 Complete the text below with sequencing words.

The process for testing new drugs involves many stages. (1) __First of all,__ they are tested in a laboratory and on animals. (2) _____ the company applies to the authorities to start tests on people. There are three stages of testing on humans. The company completes the third stage of tests on humans and (3) _____ it applies to the authorities for a licence to start using the drug. (4) _____ the company has its licence, it supplies doctors and hospitals with the new drug. The company continues monitoring the drug (5) _____ patients are using it.

2 Complete the conversation below about the launch of a new product. Put each verb into the correct form (present continuous or going to).

Philip   Have you heard about the new product in our range?
Jane   Yes. When (1 *you/launch*) __are you launching__ it?
Philip   On 11 September.
Jane   How much advertising (2 *you/do*) _____ before then?
Philip   Oh, quite a lot. First, we (3 *start*) _____ an advertising campaign on television on 10 September. Then we (4 *use*) _____ newspaper advertisements the following week.
Jane   (5 *you/use*) _____ posters too?
Philip   Yes, on the street and at stations.

3 Complete the sentences with the correct word.

1 Our company is _____ a new product in spring.
   A launching   B bringing   C giving
2 It _____ several years to develop one of our products.
   A lasts   B needs   C takes
3 I'm afraid that product isn't _____ until next week.
   A free   B available   C public
4 We'll have to _____ sales of this new product for several months.
   A monitor   B look   C see
5 What _____ do you need?
   A informers   B information   C informs

Product development

Tapescript: Listening

J = Journalist
MM = Marketing Manager

J   So, you're launching a new product for arthritis - Arthran. Who is Arthran for exactly?
MM   Anybody who suffers from the condition.
J   And how soon is this product going to be on the market?
MM   Well, we're launching it in five weeks' time, on 25 May, but obviously we're starting the publicity campaign before then.
J   And is it going to be available from the chemist's as well as doctors?
MM   No, it's a powerful drug and will only be available in hospitals or on prescription from doctors - not over the counter.
J   I see. And what are the side effects?
MM   The main one is tiredness. Doctors need to advise their patients not to drive while they're taking this drug. Of course, we're going to give doctors and patients all the necessary information about the drug and how to use it.
J   And how are you going to do that?
MM   Well, at the beginning of May we're visiting doctors in hospitals and surgeries. But we're sending them detailed information packs at the end of April so they can read all about the drug and prepare for our visits.
J   And what information is there for patients?
MM   Well, about a week before the launch, we're going to give general information posters to doctors for them to display in their waiting rooms.
J   What's the purpose of those?
MM   To make patients aware of the new drug so they'll ask their doctors about it. And we're also producing information leaflets at the moment for patients who'll take the drug. They'll be available just after the launch on 25 May.

Business equipment

Objectives:	To enable Ss to talk about business equipment
	To practise reading for specific information
	To practise listening for gist and specific information
	To review language for giving instructions and practise form-filling

Materials needed: Cassette - *Pass Cambridge BEC 1*

Unit overview

● Office equipment

Vocabulary	Ss sort items of office equipment according to whether they are essential, useful, not important.
Reading	Ss scan two advertisements for photocopiers. Ss read the advertisements again and answer multiple-choice questions.
Speaking	Ss discuss which of the two photocopiers would be best for three different people.
Writing	Ss complete a form to obtain more information about one of the photocopiers.

● Giving instructions

Listening	Ss listen to a conversation to identify the problem with a new shredder.
	Ss listen again to complete instructions on using the shredder.
Language focus	Ss review language for giving instructions.
Speaking	Ss play a board game to consolidate business-equipment-related vocabulary. (**Activity sheet** page 128)
	Ss take turns to give instructions for and identify pieces of equipment.

● Self-study

Vocabulary	Sorting exercise (matching verbs with machines).
	Word-building exercise (equipment-related vocabulary).
Writing	Ss give written advice on problems with equipment.
	Ss write operating instructions for a piece of equipment.
Exam practice	*Multiple-choice reading comprehension exercise (Reading Test Part 1).*

Office equipment

1 **Ex ❶**: Ss sort vocabulary relating to office equipment. Ss discuss their categories in pairs before a general feedback session.

2 **Ex ❷**: Ss scan the two photocopier advertisements in order to answer the two questions. The advertisements are authentic with correspondingly rich language. T should therefore remind students that they do not need to understand every word; they should simply focus on the answers to the questions.

- *The Agfa*
- *The Xerox*
  (The offer is available until the end of March 1998.)

3 **Ex ❸**: Ss read the advertisements in more detail in order to answer the multiple-choice questions.

1 A   2 A   3 C   4 B   5 C   6 B   7 B   8 A

4 **Ex ❹**: Ss read the descriptions of the three people and decide which photocopier each person should buy.

Suggested answers:
1 *James Clarkson should buy the Xerox. He works from home. A bigger machine may not be practical.*
2 *Eleanor Lewis should buy the Agfa. She works for a large company so the machine may need to make a large number of copies quickly.*
3 *David Hollingsworth should buy the Xerox. He only needs the copier for occasional use at home.*

5 **Ex ❺**: Ss complete the form for more information for James Clarkson from the previous exercise.

Name: *James Clarkson*
Job title: *Architect*
Is interested in: *12 - Xerox XC830*
No. of employees in his company: *1-25*
Activity: *Business and professional services*
Information required for an immediate purchase: ✔

Business equipment

Office equipment

Vocabulary 1 Put the following words into the groups below.

computer shredder envelopes eraser fax machine
pencils scissors photocopier printer stapler

essential for you at work	necessary but you don't use every day	not important

Reading 2 Look quickly at the two advertisements for photocopiers.

- Which machine has more special features?
- Which advertisement includes a special offer? How long is the offer available for?

The Brand New Agfa X220 – launched January '98

The combination of capacity, size and functions, makes the Agfa X220 the best copier for general use. Its duplex capabilities and speed put it in the professional class without being too large or sophisticated. And thanks to its modular design it can be configured to suit practically all situations.

- 25 copies per minute
- up to 30,000 copies per month
- Reduction/Enlargement
- Options
  - Automatic Document Feeder
  - Duplex Document Feeder
  - 10 Bin Sorter
  - 10 Bin Sorter Stapler
  - Duplex
  - 2 x 500 sheet stand

Freephone the Arena Enquiry Desk on

UNBEATABLE COPIER DEALS FROM XEROX

THE DOCUMENT COMPANY XEROX

The Xerox XC830 is the perfect, high performance copier for the small or medium office. With its copy speed of **8 copies per minute** and its **100 sheet paper tray** it can competently handle even the toughest of copying tasks. Using its advanced features it will optimise the **quality of photos and bound documents**, as well as providing **reduction and enlargement of 70 to 141%.** Included with this product is the **3 Year Express Exchange Warranty** unique to Xerox. And if you purchase now you will receive the NEW Xerox Colour Inkjet Printer, the **DocuPrint XJ4C, absolutely free** (RRP £198 including VAT). Offer available only until 31/3/98.

XJ4C Printer free when you buy a XC830 copier

Freephone the Arena Enquiry Desk on 0800 026 6761 or tick box 56 for information

3 Read the advertisements again and look at the sentences below. Choose 'Right', 'Wrong' or 'Doesn't say' for each sentence.

1 The Agfa X220 has a lot of functions and is a convenient size.
A Right B Wrong C Doesn't say

2 Both copiers can make documents bigger and smaller.
A Right B Wrong C Doesn't say

3 Agfa will buy back the photocopier after three years.
A Right B Wrong C Doesn't say

4 The Xerox has a 5 year guarantee.
A Right B Wrong C Doesn't say

5 The copiers can be bought or rented.
A Right B Wrong C Doesn't say

6 The Xerox is a faster copier than the Agfa.
A Right B Wrong C Doesn't say

7 If the customer buys the Xerox, the printer costs only £198.
A Right B Wrong C Doesn't say

8 The Agfa can staple documents together.
A Right B Wrong C Doesn't say

Speaking 4 Work in pairs. The following people want to buy a photocopier immediately. Which of the two photocopiers should each person buy?

1 **James Clarkson** is a self-employed architect who works from home. He has one employee: a part-time secretary. He mainly needs to copy contracts before sending them to clients.

2 **Eleanor Lewis** is the Head of the Accounts Department at Pyramid, a large company. Her department keeps copies of invoices it receives for payment and also needs copies of a lot of the paperwork.

3 **David Hollingsworth** works as an account manager for Global Insurance. Although he sometimes works in the office, most of the time he visits clients or works from home. He does not have a photocopier at home at the moment but would like to be able to use one occasionally.

Writing 5 James Clarkson decides to get more information about the Xerox XC830 photocopier. Complete the request form below for him.

For further information about products featured in this catalogue, please complete the address panel and put a tick in the relevant boxes below.

Name: _____ Company name: _Clarkson Design_

Job title: _____ Tel: _01483 946211_ Fax: _01483 946213_

Address: _Rose House, 94 Welham Park, GUILDFORD, Surrey GU6 2LK_

1 □ Agfa X220 Copier
2 □ Brit Vic Vending Machines
3 □ BT Video Conferencing System
4 □ Canon BJC-4200 & Powershot 350

5 □ Canon Personal Copiers
6 □ Hewlett Packard Laserjet 4000
7 □ Hewlett Packard Scanjet 6100C
8 □ Lotus Intranet Software

9 □ Mitsubishi MT-30 Mobile Phone
10 □ Philips Speechmike
11 □ Sharp Notevision Projector
12 □ Xerox XC830

How many employees are there in your company?
1-25 □ 26-50 □ 51-100 □ 101-200 □ Over 200 □

Company activity:
□ AGRICULTURE
□ BANKING/FINANCE/INSURANCE
□ BUSINESS AND PROFESSIONAL SERVICES
□ CENTRAL AND LOCAL GOVERNMENT
□ CONSTRUCTION
□ EDUCATION AND TRAINING
□ HOTELS AND CATERING
□ LEGAL/ACCOUNTING
□ MANUFACTURING
□ REAL ESTATE
□ RESEARCH AND DEVELOPMENT
□ OTHER

Tick if you require this information for an immediate purchase □
Or for a purchase within 3-6 months □ 6-9 months □ 9-12 months □ 12+ months □

Business equipment

Giving instructions

6 **Ex ❶**: Ss listen to a conversation about a new shredder in order to decide what the problem is and how Anna and Becky solve it.

Anna cannot find the operating instructions for the shredder and doesn't know how to operate the machine.
Becky explains the instructions to Anna.

7 **Ex ❷**: Ss listen again in more detail in order to complete the notes.

Instructions for use of shredder

How to use
1 To switch on, press the green button.
2 Put the paper in.
3 To switch off, press the red button.

Possible problems   **What to do**
● The machine jams   **Press the red button. Remove the excess**
                                           paper and start again.
● The motor overheats   **The machine switches off automatically.**
                                           Leave it for 15-30 minutes before you
                                           switch on again.

Caution!
● **Do not put your fingers into the shredder.**
● **Be careful with long hair and loose clothing.**

Call Customer Service on 01961 733 574 if there are any other problems.

8 T draws attention to the use of the imperative for giving instructions. T pays particular attention to negative instructions with *never* and *don't*.

9 **Ex ❸**: Ss work in a group of four to play the game. To make counters T photocopies and cuts out the line drawings of the machines on the game **Activity sheet** on page 128. Each player should now have a counter with the name of a piece of equipment: *photocopier, fax machine, printer* or *shredder*. Ss throw two coins to start and move as shown on the game. Each student follows the instructions on the square he/she lands on and continues to move **only** if the instructions are appropriate to his/her machine. If they are not appropriate, the player ignores them and play moves to the player on his/her right. Play continues until someone finishes the game and wins. The purpose of the game is to recycle vocabulary in order to prepare for the following exercise.

10 **Ex ❹**: One S gives instructions for one of the pieces of equipment illustrated, without saying which one it is. His/her partner guesses which object it is. Ss then change roles.

Self-study

Ex ❶: *Suggested answers:*

fax machine	printer	photocopier	shredder
dial	jam	jam	jam
jam	press	enlarge	press
press	print	reduce	insert
print	insert	press	shred
insert	switch on	insert	switch on
switch on	overheat	switch on	overheat
overheat		overheat	send
send		copy	
copy		print	

Ex ❷:

Noun	Verb
insertion	**insert**
operation	**operate**
reduction	reduce
copy	**copy**
printer	**print**
removal	**remove**

Ex ❸: *Suggested answers:*
2 Open the paper tray and insert more paper.
3 Press the red button. Remove the excess paper. Start again with less paper.
4 Open the door of the machine. Remove any jammed paper.
5 Switch it off. Leave it to cool. Try again.
6 Check there are staples in the machine. If there aren't, insert some.

Ex ❺:
● Good afternoon, Copier Service Centre. Can I help you?
▶ *Yes, the photocopier in our office isn't working. Could someone come here and look at it?*
● What's the problem exactly?
▶ *Well, it keeps overheating and the paper keeps jamming. It jammed again today but I couldn't remove the paper - so now it doesn't work at all.*
● And when did you buy the copier?
▶ *Last year - but there's a 3-year warranty.*
● Right. Could you give me your details and I'll send someone to deal with it tomorrow.
▶ *Thank you. My name's Jill Fellowes and the name of the company is …*

Ex ❻: 1 C   2 A   3 C   4 C   5 C   6 B

Essential vocabulary

Office equipment
to copy
to dial
to enlarge/enlargement
envelope
eraser
fax machine
guarantee
to jam

operating instructions
to overheat
photocopier
to print
printer
reduction
to remove/removal
scissors (pair of)

shredder
stapler
to switch on/off
warranty

General
to be careful
convenient
feature
special offer
to rent

The words in italics are not on the Cambridge BEC 1 wordlist.

Giving instructions

Listening 1 The Accounts Department at Pyramid has bought a new shredder. The secretary, Anna, has a problem. She telephones Becky in the Purchasing Department. What is the problem? Listen to their conversation. What do they do about it?

2 Listen again and take notes. Then complete Anna's notice.

Instructions for use of shredder

How to use
- To switch on, press the green button.
- Put the paper in.
- To switch off, press the red button.

Possible problems   **What to do**
- The machine jams
- The motor overheats

Caution!
-
-

Call Customer Service on 01961 733 574 if there are any other problems.

Giving instructions
- The easiest way to give instructions in English is to use the imperative.
  Switch on the machine.
- Sometimes you need to give negative instructions.
  Never insert your fingers into the shredder.
  Don't use the machine without reading the instructions first.

Speaking 3 Look at the Business Equipment Game on page 128. Your teacher will give you instructions.

4 Work in pairs. Student A: Choose one of the pictures below. Give instructions. Student B: What piece of equipment is it?

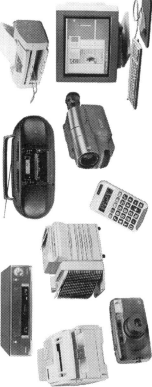

---

5 Jill Fellowes telephones the Copier Service Centre about problems with the photocopier in her office. Half of some words are missing. Complete her conversation.

● Good afternoon, Copier Service Centre. Can I help_ you?
▶ Ye_, the photoc_____ in ou___ office is ___ working. Cou___ someone co___ here and lo___ at i_?
● What's th_ problem exac____?
▶ Well, it keeps overhe_____ and the pap___ keeps jamm___. It jam___ again tod___ but I couldn't rem___ the pap___ - so no_ it does___ work a_ all.
● An_ when di_ you bu_ the cop____?
▶ Last ye___ - but there's a 3-year warr_____.
● Right. Cou___ you gi_ me yo_ details an_ I'll se___ someone t_ deal wi___ it tomo____.
▶ Thank you. My name's Jill Fellowes and the name of the company is ...

1 Put the following verbs into the groups below. You can use some verbs more than once.

dial   jam   enlarge   reduce   press   print
insert   shred   switch on   overheat   send   copy

Fax machine	Printer	Photocopier	Shredder
dial			

2 Complete the table below.

Noun	Verb
enlargement	enlarge
insertion	
operation	
	reduce
copy	
printer	
removal	

Exam practice

● Look at questions 1-6.
● In each question, which piece of equipment does the sentence refer to?
● For each question, mark the correct letter **A**, **B** or **C**.

1 If your machine doesn't receive, contact the supplier.
A printer   B shredder   C fax machine

2 The cutter will jam if you insert too much paper.
A shredder   B photocopier   C printer

3 If you reduce the article, you can use A4.
A shredder   B fax machine   C photocopier

4 It's not sending because you've inserted the paper in the wrong place.
A photocopier   B shredder   C fax machine

5 It's a small machine but you can pre-programme up to 50 numbers.
A shredder   B printer   C fax machine

6 Remove the paper from the feeder and put it on the glass - it might work then.
A shredder   B photocopier   C printer

3 Read the problems below. What instructions would you give each person? Write your answers.

1 The pre-programmed number for our bank doesn't work. *Check the bank's fax number. Perhaps it's not correct.*

2 The photocopier has run out of paper.

3 The cutter on the shredder has jammed.

4 Some paper is jammed in the photocopier.

5 The photocopier is overheating.

6 The stapler on the photocopier isn't working.

4 Write operating instructions for one of the pieces of equipment in Exercise 4 on page 55.

Tapescript: Listening

Becky	*Purchasing.*
Anna	*Hi Becky. It's Anna from Accounts here.*
Becky	*Hi.*
Anna	*Becky, you know that shredder we've just bought?*
Becky	*Yes?*
Anna	*Well, everyone keeps asking how to use it and I can't find the operating instructions.*
Becky	*Ah! Now I think they may still be here. Hold on a second … Yes, I've got them here, Anna. What do you want to know?*
Anna	*Well, what to do if it doesn't work. You know, things like that.*
Becky	*Well. It says here that the machine jams if you insert too much paper into it. If that happens, press the red button, remove the excess paper and start again with less paper.*
Anna	*Right. Are there any other possible problems?*
Becky	*The motor overheats sometimes. If that happens, it switches off automatically. Just leave it for 15 to 30 minutes before you switch it on again.*
Anna	*OK, I've got all that. Is there anything else I should know?*
Becky	*Yes, there are a few things to be careful about - like never put your fingers in the shredder.*
Anna	*That's a bit obvious, isn't it?*
Becky	*And be careful with long hair and loose articles of clothing like ties. And that's it.*
Anna	*Thanks, Becky. I'll put a notice with the instructions on the wall next to the shredder.*
Becky	*Good idea.*

Correspondence

Objectives:	To raise awareness of and practise writing formal correspondence
	To practise reading for specific information
Materials needed:	None

- **Sending a quotation**

  Warmer | T brainstorms different types of business letter.

  Reading | Ss read three types of correspondence and match them with descriptions before answering comprehension questions.

  Speaking | Ss discuss differences between letters, faxes and e-mails then exchange information about their correspondence.

- **Letters of acceptance**

  Reading | Ss order extracts from a business letter and match the extracts with descriptions of the paragraphs.

  Language focus | Ss match functions with letter phrases.

  Writing | Ss write a letter querying an invoice.

- **Self-study**

  Vocabulary | Explanation of abbreviations.

  | Matching exercise (letter openings and closures).

  | Spoken vs. written functional phrases.

  Writing | Ss correct a grammatically correct but informal letter of enquiry.

  Exam practice | *Party invitation notice (Writing Test Part 2).*

  | *Letter replying to an enquiry (Writing Test Part 3).*

Sending a quotation

Unit 85 of *Linguarama English Reference Guide 2* refers to letter writing.

1 **Warmer:** T quickly brainstorms different types of formal business letter such as complaint, enquiry, etc. T could also brainstorm alternative types of inter-company correspondence (e.g. fax, e-mail, memo) and discuss when Ss would use a formal letter and when they would use these alternatives. One of the deciding factors is the relationship between the writer and reader.

2 **Ex ❶:** Ss quickly scan the three forms of correspondence to find the necessary information. The aim of the exercise is to introduce some samples of writing and to make the point that the type of correspondence we use and the language we use depends on a number of factors, including relationship. During feedback, Ss explain how they reached their conclusions and list some of the deciding factors.

1 *Julian Hughes (fax) - has already organised courses for Norwest. Dave (e-mail) may also have done so.*
2 *Rebecca Brooks (letter) - has not worked with Norwest before.*
3 *Dave (e-mail) - is a personal friend of Alan's.*

3 **Ex ❷:** Ss read through the questions and scan the correspondence for the relevant information. It is not necessary for them to understand every word/abbreviation. During feedback Ss explain their answers, referring to the correspondence.

1 *Synergy Management Consultants (7.5 hours)*
2 *Watson & Railton*
3 *ATC Consulting (£525 includes VAT, whereas Watson & Railton's £499 does not)*
4 *Synergy Management Consultants*
5 *Watson & Railton (or in-company)*

4 **Ex ❸:** Ss work in pairs and read the correspondence for detailed comprehension, noting any differences between the three replies. The differences fall into several categories such as salutations, use of language and familiarity. The linguistic differences include use of conventional phrases and also vocabulary such as *venue/location, delegates/no. of people*. T points out that *attach* can be used only with letters but *attach* can be used with both letters and e-mails. The salutations are especially important and, although referred to in the **Self-study** section, need highlighting.

1 *Julian Hughes (fax): Uses Alan's first name, signs off with his own first name, no reference line, some informal language (**Many thanks**), some abbreviations (**I've attached**) and some less formal vocabulary (**no. of people**).*
2 *Rebecca Brooks (letter): Uses formal salutations (**Dear Mr Pickering, Yours sincerely**), reference line, formal phrases (**your enquiry of 16 April**), formal vocabulary (**venue, delegates**) and uses no contractions at all.*
3 *Dave (e-mail): Uses first names, no reference line, informal time reference (**yesterday**), contractions (**Here's, I've**), informal vocabulary (**quote, wanted, give me a call**), ellipsis (**hope you can read it OK**), and informal salutations (**Best wishes**).*

5 **Ex ❹:** Ss work in pairs and exchange information about their own correspondence.

Letters of acceptance

6 **Ex ❶:** As an alternative to doing the exercise from the book, T could photocopy the extracts, cut them into separate pieces and give them to Ss as a jigsaw. T points out that the jigsaw letter is a reply to the correspondence from the previous page. During feedback Ss explain why they chose their particular order.

1 *I am writing with reference to …*   2 *I am happy to confirm …*
3 *As some of our managers …*   4 *I look forward …*

7 **Ex ❷:** Ss read the four functions and match them with the relevant paragraph from the jigsaw letter. During feedback Ss identify the exact language supporting their answers. This will highlight the functional phrases in the letter and lead into the next exercise.

Making reference   Paragraph 1 - *I am writing with reference to …*
Giving the reason for writing   Paragraph 2 - *I am pleased to confirm …*
Making a request   Paragraph 3 - *Would it be possible to …?*
                    I would be grateful if you could …
Signalling the end of the letter Paragraph 4 - *I look forward to …*

Correspondence

Sending a quotation

Reading **1** Alan Pickering works for Norwest Plant Hire. He is organising a training course for managers in his company. He writes to three companies to ask for quotations. Look at the replies and say who:

- has already organised courses for Norwest
- has not worked with Norwest before
- is a personal friend of Alan's.

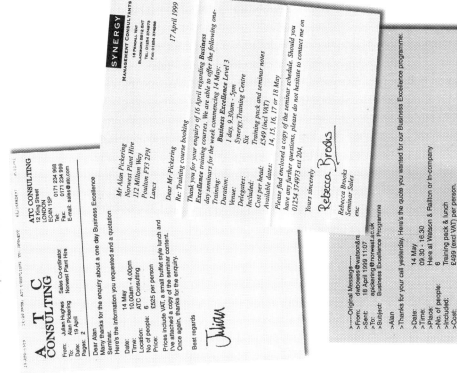

A T C CONSULTING

12 King Street
LONDON
EC4N 1SP
Tel: 0171 234 968
Fax: 0171 234 999
E-mail: sales@atc.com

From: Julian Hughes   Sales Coordinator
To: Alan Pickering   Norwest Plant Hire
Date: 19 April
Pages: 2

Dear Alan
Many thanks for the enquiry about a one day Business Excellence Seminar.
Here's the information you requested and a quotation

Date: 14 May
Time: 10.00am - 4.00pm
Location: ATC Consulting
No of people: 6
Price: £525 per person

Prices include VAT, a small buffet style lunch and
I've attached a copy of the seminar content.
Once again, thanks for the enquiry.

Best regards

Julian

SYNERGY
MANAGEMENT CONSULTANTS

16 Pendall Way
Blackburn BB12 8HT
Tel: 01254 374973
Fax: 01254 374988

17 April 1999

Mr Alan Pickering
Norwest Plant Hire
112 Milton Way
Poulton FY3 2PN
Lancs

Dear Mr Pickering

Re: Training course booking

Thank you for your enquiry of 16 April regarding Business Excellence training courses. We are able to offer the following one-day seminars for the week commencing 14 May:

Training: Business Excellence Level 3
Duration: 1 day, 9.30am - 5pm
Venue: Synergy Training Centre
Delegates: Six
Included: Training pack and seminar notes
Cost per head: £49 (incl VAT)
Available dates: 14, 15, 16, 17 or 18 May

Please find enclosed a copy of the seminar schedule. Should you have any further questions, please do not hesitate to contact me on 01254 374973 ext 204.

Yours sincerely

Rebecca Brooks
Rebecca Brooks
Seminar Sales
enc

-----Original Message-----
>From: dwbowes@watson.re
>Sent: 18 April 1999 11:07
>To: apickering@norwest.ac.uk
>Subject: Business Excellence Programme

>Alan
>Thanks for your call yesterday. Here's the quote you wanted for our Business Excellence programme:

>Date: 14 May
>Time: 09.30 - 16.30
>Place: Here at Watson & Railton or in-company
>No. of people: 6
>Included: Training pack & lunch
>Cost: £499 (excl VAT) per person.

>If you have any questions, give me a call. I've attached a WORD file with the course schedule -
>hope you can open it OK.
>Best wishes
>Dave

---

2 Answer the following questions.

1 Which is the longest seminar?
2 Which company's offer includes a training pack and food?
3 Which of the quotations is the cheapest?
4 Which company offers more than one possible date?
5 Which of the companies could do the seminar at Norwest?

3 What differences are there between the fax, letter and e-mail?

Speaking **4** Work in pairs. What percentage of letters, faxes and e-mails does your partner receive and write? Are any of them in English?

Letters of acceptance

Reading **1** Alan decides to accept the Synergy offer and writes a letter of acceptance. Put the paragraphs of his letter into the correct order.

NORWEST

112 Milton Way
Poulton FY3 2PN
Lancashire
01254 882497

Rebecca Brooks
Synergy Management Consultants
16 Pendall Way
Blackburn
BB12 8HT

26 April 1999

Re: Your quotation of 17 April

Dear Ms Brooks

I am pleased to confirm the booking on the Business Excellence Level 3 seminar for six people on Tuesday 14 May.

I look forward to hearing from you in the near future.

As some of our managers are travelling from a distance, would it be possible to start the seminar at 10.00am instead of 9.30am as stated in your quotation? I would be grateful if you could send me information about the seminar and directions for travelling by car.

I am writing with reference to your quotation of 17 April regarding the one-day Business Excellence seminar at your premises in Blackburn.

2 Match the functions with the paragraphs above. Underline the phrases that helped you.

making a request   making reference

giving the reason for writing   signalling the end of a letter

8 **Ex 3**: The matching exercise introduces some more functional phrases. Ss match phrases with functions and then T leads feedback. Ss can also match the functions with phrases in the jigsaw letter where applicable.

2 I am writing to ....
3 I am pleased to ....
4 I am afraid that ....
5 We would be grateful if you could ....
6 I enclose ...
7 If you require any further information, please do not hesitate to contact us.
8 I look forward to receiving your reply.

9 **Ex 4**: The unit finishes with a writing task similar to Part Three of the Cambridge BEC 1 Writing Test. First of all, the class brainstorms the contents of the required letter. Then T puts Ss in pairs and asks them to follow the procedure under the bullets in the exercise. Ss submit the first draft for editing by the class. If time permits, Ss submit a second version for group feedback; otherwise, this can be set for homework. T may wish Ss to write their drafts on OHT so that the rest of the class can give feedback easily. T may also focus on conciseness (in the exam the body of a formal letter is expected to be about 50-60 words).

Suggested answer: (61 words excluding salutation and closure)

Re: Training course invoice 2948

Dear Mrs Brooks

Thank you for your letter and invoice of 25 May 1999.

I am afraid we are unable to accept the invoice as only six participants attended the seminar, not eight. Moreover, training packs were included in the price.

I would be grateful if you could send me a correct invoice for the training course. I look forward to receiving your reply.

Yours sincerely

Alan Pickering

Self-study

Ex 1: 2 enclosed 3 Department 4 note well *(from the Latin: nota bene)*
5 regarding 6 week 7 excluding
8 including 9 extension

Ex 2: 1 Dear Ms Rees   Yours sincerely   2 Dear Paul   Regards
3 Dear Sir/Madam Yours faithfully   4 Gentlemen   Yours truly*
* Gentlemen is the US equivalent of Dear Sirs (UK). Yours truly is used in the US but rarely in the UK.

Ex 3: 1 A spoken B written or spoken   2 A spoken   B written
3 A spoken B written   4 A written or spoken B spoken
5 A written B written or spoken   6 A spoken   B written or spoken

Ex 4: *Suggested answer: (50 words excluding salutation and closure)*
(Dear Ms Daley)

I am writing to enquire about your latest photocopiers. We are renting a photocopier from you but we would now like to buy one.

I would be very grateful if you could send us a brochure and some product literature. Would it also be possible to send us a price list?

I look forward to hearing from you.

(Yours sincerely)

Ex 5: *Suggested answer: (45 words)*
Thank you for your enquiry of 1 May 1999.

I enclose a brochure and a price list. The brochure includes details about special offers for customers who are renting a copier at the moment.

If you have any questions, please do not hesitate to contact me.

Ex 6: *Suggested answer: (23 words)*
Party
As you know, Friday is Simon's last day at Sonitech. You are all invited to a farewell party in Reception at 5.30.

Essential vocabulary

Formal letter phrases
Thank you for your letter of ...
With reference to ...
I am writing to ...
I am pleased to ...
I am afraid that ...
I would be grateful if you could ...
I enclose ...
If you require any further information, please do not hesitate to contact us.
I look forward to hearing from you.

Yours sincerely
Yours faithfully
Best wishes/regards

Abbreviations
ASAP *(as soon as possible)*
Dept (Department)
enc (enclosed)
excl (excluding)
inc (including)

ext *(extension number)*
NB (note well)
re *(regarding)*
wk (week)

General
enquiry
quotation
seminar

The words in italics are not on the Cambridge BEC 1 wordlist.

Exam practice

5 Read the letter in Exercise 4 again.
- Write a reply to Marco Francone:
  * thanking him for his enquiry
  * enclosing a brochure and price list
  * telling him about a new special offer
  * asking him to contact you if he has any questions.
- Write about **50-60 words**.

Dear Mr Francone

_____

_____

_____

_____

_____

Yours sincerely

Exam practice

6 Simon Howe is leaving the company next week. You decide to have a farewell party for him.
- Write a notice to all your colleagues:
  * informing them about the party
  * saying when and where the party is
  * inviting them to the party.
- Write about **20 words**.

_____

_____

_____

Correspondence

Vocabulary

1 What do the following abbreviations mean?

1 ASAP   _as soon as possible_
2 enc   _____
3 Dept   _____
4 NB   _____
5 re   _____
6 wk   _____
7 excl   _____
8 incl   _____
9 ext   _____

2 Match the following opening and closing phrases.

1 Dear Ms Rees	Regards
2 Dear Paul	Yours truly
3 Dear Sir/Madam	Yours sincerely
4 Gentlemen	Yours faithfully

3 Are the following usually spoken (S) or written (W)?

1 A We got the goods yesterday.
   B We received the goods yesterday.
2 A I want to ask about your new product.
   B I would like to enquire about your new product.
3 A We're sorry that the order was late.
   B We are afraid that the order was delayed.
4 A Could you please confirm the date?
   B Let me know if the date is OK.
5 A If you require any further assistance, ...
   B If you need any more help, ...
6 A I can't wait to see you.
   B I look forward to seeing you.

4 A colleague has written a formal letter and asked you to check it. There are no grammatical mistakes in the letter but some of the style is not formal enough. Find and change the informal phrases.

Dear Ms Daley

I am writing because we want some information about your latest photocopiers. We are renting a photocopier from you but now we want to buy one.

I'd be really happy if you sent us a brochure and some product literature. Please send us a price list as well.

Thanks a lot. We can't wait to hear from you.

Regards

Marco Francone

Correspondence

Vocabulary **3** Match the functions with the phrases.

1 Making reference	I am afraid that ...
2 Giving the reason for writing	With reference to your letter of ...
3 Giving good news	We would be grateful if you could ...
4 Giving bad news	I look forward to receiving your reply.
5 Making a request	I am pleased to ...
6 Enclosing something	I am writing to ...
7 Offering assistance	I enclose ...
8 Referring to future contact	If you require any further information, please do not hesitate to contact us.

Writing **4** Alan Pickering receives the invoice from Synergy after the training course. There are some items which he thinks are wrong. Use the invoice and his handwritten notes to write a reply to Synergy.

Before you write:
- plan the number of paragraphs you need
- make notes under the paragraph headings
- think of typical letter phrases that you can use.

SYNERGY
MANAGEMENT CONSULTANTS
16 PENDALL WAY
BLACKBURN BB12 8HT
TEL: 01254 374873
FAX: 01254 374988

24 May 1999

Mr Alan Pickering
Human Resource Manager
Norwest Plant Hire
112 Milton Way
Poulton FY3 2PN
Lancs

Re: Training course invoice

Dear Mr Pickering

Thank you for your letter of 17 May. I am very pleased that you enjoyed the course and found it useful for your managers.

I enclose the invoice which you requested in your letter.

A 2% reduction is offered on payments within 10 days.

I would like to thank you for booking your training course with our organisation and we look forward to seeing you again in the future.

Yours sincerely

Rebecca Brooks

Rebecca Brooks
Seminar Sales

enc

SYNERGY
MANAGEMENT CONSULTANTS

INVOICE

16 PENDALL WAY
BLACKBURN
BB12 8HT
TEL: 01254 374873
FAX: 01254 374988

Mr Alan Pickering
NORWEST PLANT HIRE
112 Milton Way
Poulton
FY2 2PN
Lancs

Invoice date: 24 MAY 1999
Invoice number: 2348

TRAINING COURSE 14 MAY 1999
COURSE: 1 day Business Excellence
             level 3
DELEGATES: 3
EXTRAS: Training Packs @ £2.50 per person

Total Cost: £4,422 (incl VAT)

offered on payments

Sally,
could you write to Rebecca
Brooks and question these items on the invoice?
I've circled them.
Thanks

Bankers: Lloyds Bank PLC 24 High Street Blackburn BB2 5AB
Account number: 40080954
Bank sort code: 34 65 87
Registered office: Synergy Management Consultants 16 Pendall Way
Blackburn BB12 8HT
Registered number: 760462

Unit 8b   59   Correspondence

Exam focus: Writing

Objectives:	To familiarise Ss with the content of the Writing Test
	To provide useful tips
	To practise the Writing Test

Materials needed: None

Unit overview

- **The Writing Test**

  T elicits Ss' knowledge of the Writing Test and gives an overview.

- **How to succeed**

  T brainstorms what Ss think the examiner is looking for and takes Ss through tips regarding task completion and language.

- **Memos and notes**

  Ss focus on Part Two of the Writing Test and rank four candidates' answers. T emphasises the importance of task completion. Ss read tips then write a memo.

- **Letters and longer memos**

  Ss focus on Part Three of the Writing Test. They focus on how to plan their answer then write a letter.

- **Exam practice**

  Part One: Form-filling.

  Part Two: Note.

  Part Three: Longer memo.

> If T is unfamiliar with the Writing Test, he/she should look at the following:
> - BEC 1: Teachers' Information Pack
> - UCLES BEC 1 Sample Papers
> - Linguarama Cambridge BEC 1 Practice Tests 1 and 2.
>
> Writing tasks are assessed according to fulfilment of task and quality of language. Full marking criteria are in the Answer keys with the Linguarama Practice Tests. Rather than worrying about detailed assessment, T should ask the following questions and reward or penalise accordingly:
>
> **Task:** Are all parts of the task fulfilled?
> **Language:** Is it easy to follow?

1 **Warmer (books closed):** T asks Ss what they know about the Writing Test (length, types of task etc.). T puts Ss' answers on the board and asks Ss what they find most difficult about the writing tasks they have encountered in *Pass Cambridge BEC 1* so far. Ss may mention keeping to the word limit. Unit 4b contains helpful tips about how to cut down written information. T may wish to elicit these from Ss as a reminder (leave out: articles, subject pronouns, the verb *be*, prepositions and modifiers).

2 Ss read the overview of the Writing Test. T answers any questions Ss may have regarding its format and administration.

T points out that the Reading and Writing Tests are combined in one examination paper totalling 70 minutes. Ss must leave enough time for the Writing Test (25 minutes at least).

T illustrates the different parts of the Writing Test by directing Ss to the **Exam practice** page of the unit and briefly describing the format and requirements of each of the three parts. (*The Linguarama Teachers' Information Pack* gives full notes for T's reference.)

Ss have not yet been asked to complete a Part One Writing task in *Pass Cambridge BEC 1* as they are relatively straightforward. T therefore may wish at this point to tell Ss about Part One (form-filling); in particular T may wish to stress that the 'writing' element is minimal (Ss simply read the input material and then transfer information).

T also reminds Ss that answers are transferred to an Answer Sheet and shows them one (available in the Linguarama centre). T tells Ss they will have to write Part One answers in capital letters (otherwise the marking machine will be unable to process the answers). Capital letters should not be used for Parts Two and Three. T suggests that Ss should always check the instructions regarding capitals for all three parts.

How to succeed

3 **(Books closed):** T asks Ss what they think the examiner is looking for in the Writing Test. Ss' responses will probably include: grammatical accuracy, spelling, range of business vocabulary, organisation and appropriate language. T quickly brainstorms good advice (e.g. use grammar you are confident about rather than taking risks, demonstrate your range of vocabulary by not repeating a word when an alternative is available, use sequencers to organise your thoughts clearly etc.).

4 T takes Ss through the tips on *Task* and *Language*. T stresses that the candidate must complete the task in full.

Memos and notes

5 **Ex 1:** Ss work in pairs. T asks Ss to read the task carefully first and then look at the four candidates' answers. Ss first note the task and language errors. They then order them from best to worst.

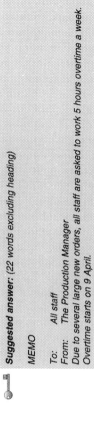

1 *Candidate D*   2 *Candidate A*   3 *Candidate B*   4 *Candidate C*

Task
Candidate A: *Completes two parts of the task but does not give exact dates or times.*
Candidate B: *Completes two parts of the task but does not give exact dates or times.*
Candidate C: *Completes one part of the task but does not give exact dates or times.*
Too long, well over the word limit.
Candidate D: *Completes all three parts of the task.*

Language
Candidate A: *Very good language.*
Candidate B: *First part good language, although possibly lifted verbatim from the rubric. Second part poor. Lack of functional expressions for making a request (**Please you book**) and incorrect word order (**for me**).*
Candidate C: *Very wordy and poor language. Spelling mistakes (**troubel** and **gratefull**), wrong tense (**I am needing**) and vocabulary (**fly**). Possibly also odd register: I am sorry ... I am very grateful for your help.*
Candidate D: *Very clear, despite one mistake (**leeving**).*

In feedback T stresses that grammatical accuracy is not enough for a pass. All three parts of the task must be completed. T tells Ss that Candidate D would probably receive full marks despite a minor mistake in the answer.

T also makes the point in feedback that Candidate C was well over the word limit (45 words). Ss need not keep strictly to the word limit but no more than approximately a third over or under is permissible.

6 **Ex 2:** Before Ss write a memo themselves, T asks them to read through the tips. T points out that one point in the task usually requires Ss to use their imagination; in this case, they will have to decide what starting date to stipulate.

Ss do the task individually and then compare their version with their partner. T monitors.

Suggested answer: *(22 words excluding heading)*

MEMO

To: All staff
From: The Production Manager
Due to several large new orders, all staff are asked to work 5 hours overtime a week. Overtime starts on 9 April.

7 In feedback T checks that Ss have completed all three parts of the task. T also reminds Ss that over-length answers are penalised: Ss should not provide additional information unless specifically instructed to do so.

Exam focus: Writing

The Writing Test

The BEC I Writing Test has three questions.

Part	Input	Task
1	Short memos, letters, notices	Form-filling
2	Instructions only	Write a memo or note (about 20 words)
3	Memo, letter, notice advertisement	Write a letter or memo (about 50-60 words)

Length: About 25 minutes of the Reading and Writing Test should be used for Writing.

How to succeed

Your ability to complete the task successfully is just as important as the accuracy of your grammar and vocabulary.

Task

- Successful task completion means following all **instructions**.
- Pay attention to the word limit. If you do not write enough words, you have probably not completed the task fully. If you write too many, you have probably included unnecessary information.
- Check whether the instructions tell you to use capital letters or not on the Answer Sheet.
- Even if you write a grammatically perfect answer, it may still get low marks if you do not include all the necessary information.

Language

- Task completion is so important that you can still get top marks even with small grammar and spelling mistakes.
- However, accuracy is important so use language that you feel confident about.
- Try not to repeat the same words. Show a range of vocabulary.
- Organise your ideas clearly
  - addition (also, as well, furthermore etc.)
  - contrast (but, although, however etc.)
  - sequence (first of all, then, after that etc.).
- Make sure the language is appropriate to the type of writing. (Short forms, e.g. I'm, are acceptable in notes but not in formal letters.)
- Check your writing when you have finished.

Memos and notes

1 Read the examination tips on the opposite page and look at the Part Two task below. Underline the task and language errors. Then put them in order from best to worst.

Question 46

- You are attending a conference on 14-18 May in Budapest. You need to make your travel arrangements.
- Write a memo to Jessica Carston, your secretary:
  - * giving her the dates
  - * saying when you want to fly
  - * asking her to book a flight.
- Write **about 20 words**.

Could you book a flight for me to Budapest? I want to go on the 14th and come back on the 18th.
Thank you.

Candidate A

I am attending a conference on 14-18 May in Budapest. Please you book for me a flight

Candidate B

I am sorry to trouble you Jessica but I am attending a conference in Budapest and I am needing to book a fly in the morning early. Could you please do it for me? I am very gratefull for your help.

Candidate C

Could you please book a return flight? I need to arrive Budapest 14 May before lunch and leaving 18 May after 4pm

Candidate D

2 Read these tips and do the exam question below.

1 Read all instructions **carefully**. Do you need to write a memo or a note?
2 Check you have completed all three parts of the task. Use the instructions as a checklist.
3 Check the length of your first draft and edit if necessary.
4 Think about ways of making notes shorter. Which words can you leave out?
5 Proof-read your answer before transferring it. Check grammar, vocabulary and style.

Question 46

- Your department has just received several large new orders. The company has decided to ask everyone in the department to work five extra hours per week.
- Write a memo to all staff in the department:
  - * explaining the situation
  - * saying when overtime will begin
  - * asking the staff to work overtime.
- Write **about 20 words**.

Exam focus: Writing

Exam focus: Writing

Letters and longer memos

8. Part Three differs from Part Two in that candidates are expected to write a formal letter or longer memo and are not expected to be so concise (word limit 50-60 words). Ss should pay attention to tone and style, making sure that their letter or memo is suitably formal. Paragraphing is also an important consideration. However, T should tell Ss that Cambridge BEC 1 does not require formal letter layout. The question paper provides an opening address and closing salutation, which do not count towards the total number of words. T tells Ss that they are expected to know some basic standard letter phrases and abbreviations. T may wish to remind them of the unit on letter writing in the *Linguarama English Reference Guide 2* (Unit 85).

9. Ss read the task. T then directs them to the tips with the suggested stages they should go through in order to write the letter. T stresses the importance of the final point: checking the final version to ensure the task has been completed in full.

10. Ss work individually or in pairs to complete the task. Before they exchange versions with other pairs in the group, T reminds them to double check for task completion.

> *Suggested answer: (57 words excluding salutation and closure)*
>
> *(Dear Ms Yates)*
>
> *Thank you for your letter of 12 July and the brochure.*
>
> *I would like to receive a visit from one of your salespeople. I suggest the morning of 4 August at 10 am. Could you telephone me to confirm this?*
>
> *I am interested in a new shredder and possibly a photocopier.*
>
> *I look forward to hearing from you.*
>
> *(Yours sincerely)*

11. In feedback T may need to remind Ss of language for arranging a meeting. *I suggest* is suitably neutral and concise. T may wish to teach other phrases such as *Would 4 August be convenient?*

12. T directs Ss to the **Self-study** section and suggests they do the three parts of the Writing Test at home under timed conditions (25 minutes total).

Self-study

Part One
Questions 1-5

1. EZY
2. LEISUREWEAR
3. B
4. EWA JUSKOVIAK
5. 48122440970

The answers should be in capital letters.

Part Two
Question 6
Suggested answer: (22 words)

(Chris)

I'm working at home tomorrow because I have to prepare a report for Thursday's meeting. My home phone number is 0181 767 0289.

Part Three
Question 7
Suggested answer: (55 words excluding header)

(MEMO)

(To: Moira Jansen)
(From: Tina Jones)

I've seen an advertisement for a new photocopier, the TX200 Officepro. It prints excellent quality colour pictures and scans A4 colour documents. It's faster and smaller than our current machine, which is now three years old.

I think we should buy it. It costs only £1,000 plus VAT. They can deliver in two weeks.

Letters and longer memos

❶ Read the Part Three task and follow the instructions below.

Question 47

● Read this letter from Rebecca Yates, the Sales Manager at one of your suppliers.

12 July 1999

Mr Paul Wright
Purchasing Manager

Dear Mr Wright

As part of our customer service, we are pleased to enclose our latest brochure, showing our exciting new products and unbelievable prices.

We would like the opportunity to visit your company in order to inform you personally of the latest product developments and discuss ways of making our service even more suited to your needs.

If you would like to take advantage of a visit from a member of our sales team, could you please inform us of a suitable date and time? Could you also tell us which products would be of particular interest to you?

Yours sincerely

Rebecca Yates
Sales Manager

● Write a reply to Ms Yates:
  * thanking her for the brochure
  * accepting the offer of a visit from a salesperson
  * suggesting a date and time
  * saying which products you would be interested in.
● Write **50-60 words**.

1 Plan the structure of your answer. How many paragraphs will there be? What is their purpose?
2 Think of phrases and key vocabulary to put in the paragraphs.
3 Check that your plan fully completes all four parts of the task. Then write a first draft.
4 Check the first draft:
  - *Does it fully complete the task?*
  - *Is the information clearly organised?*
  - *Is there any unnecessary information?*
  - *How many words are there?*
5 Make changes to the first draft.
6 Check the final version:
  - *Does it fully complete the task?*
  - *Are the grammar, spelling, punctuation and style correct?*

Part Two

Question 6
● You have decided to work at home tomorrow.
● Write a note for your colleague:
  * saying you won't be in the office tomorrow
  * saying why you are going to work from home
  * giving your home telephone number.
● Write **about 20 words**.
● **Do not write in capital letters.**

Part Three

Question 7
● Your department needs a new photocopier and you have seen this advertisement in a magazine.

TX2000 OfficePro
Three machines in one!

The new **TX2000 OfficePro** is all you need to print, copy or scan all your colour office documents. With the **OfficePro** you can print up to 4 high quality colour pages a minute, copy up to 3 near-photo quality A4 images a minute and scan full colour A4 documents.

Easy to use and compact, the new **OfficePro** is the ideal solution for the small office that needs to produce high quality documents.

● Write a memo to your boss:
  * mentioning the advertisement
  * describing some features of the TX2000
  * saying why the department should buy it
  * giving the price and delivery time.
● Write **50-60 words**.
● **Do not write in capital letters.**

Part One

Questions 1-5
● Read the memo and business card.
● Complete the form below.
● Write each word, phrase or number in **CAPITAL LETTERS**.

To: Lyndsey Dalgano
From: Mustah Singh

Date: 14.02.99

Lyndsey

Could you add this company to our directory of suppliers? I've enclosed a business card for the contact person, Ewa Juskoviak.

We'd better list the company as a category B supplier to begin with - until we get to know them better.

Thanks very much

EZY
Leisurewear

Ewa Juskoviak
Sales Executive

ul. Masarska 24
31-535 Kraków
Poland
Tel: +48 12 244 0970
Fax: +48 12 244 0979

DIRECTORY OF SUPPLIERS

Company name: (1) ....
Goods supplied: (2) ....
Category: (3) ....
Contact name: (4) ....
Phone number: (5) ....

Business hotels

<table>
<tr><td>**Objectives:**</td><td>To enable Ss to talk about hotel facilities for business people
To practise reading and listening for specific information
To enable Ss to ask for/give directions</td></tr>
<tr><td>**Materials needed:**</td><td>Cassette - *Pass Cambridge BEC 1*
Cards - 12 cards: *Pass Cambridge BEC 1*, Unit 10a/1-12 One set per pair/group</td></tr>
</table>

Unit overview

● Hotel facilities

Warmer | T elicits typical hotel facilities (books closed).

Reading | Ss open their books and look at the facilities described in the hotel advertisements before matching the hotels with people.

Speaking | Ss ask each other which hotel they would prefer.

● The business traveller

Speaking | Ss decide which five facilities are the most important for the business traveller.

Listening 1 | Ss listen to a hotel manager and compare their answers with his before listening again and answering multiple-choice comprehension questions.

Language focus | Ss read the tapescript and identify verbs and adjectives followed by the infinitive.

Speaking | Ss work in pairs and ask their partner about the best hotel he/she has stayed in and whether it would be suitable for a business traveller.

● Asking the way

Listening 2 | Ss take notes on how to get to the centre of London from a hotel. Ss listen again and draw routes on a map of London.

Writing | Ss write directions to famous landmarks in London.

Speaking | Ss give each other spoken directions to landmarks in London.

● Self-study

Vocabulary | Matching exercise (hotel adjectives and nouns).

Word fields (parts of a hotel and hotel facilities).

Exam practice | *Formal letter writing (Writing Paper Part 3).*

Hotel facilities

1   **Warmer (books closed):** T asks Ss to list typical hotel facilities.

2   T asks Ss to open their books and read the information about the three hotels. T asks Ss where the information might come from. Ss compare their list of facilities with those mentioned in the texts.

3   **Ex ❶:** T focuses Ss' attention on the three descriptions and asks Ss to choose one of the three hotels for each character. During feedback Ss justify their decisions by referring to the facilities offered by each hotel. T can further exploit the text by asking Ss to work out how much it would cost for the characters to stay at the hotels for different durations and at different times. This would focus Ss on lexical items such as *single room supplement*.

Suggested answers:

Marco and Francesca Bianchi:	*Hyde Park Gardens or Royal London Hotel (facilities for both of them; depends on how much they want to spend)*
Maurice Breton:	*Royal London Hotel (communication facilities)*
Linda de Hamm:	*St Steven's Hotel (the single supplement is only midweek)*

4   **Ex ❷:** Ss find out from each other which of the three hotels they would prefer and why. T reminds Ss of language for giving reasons (*that's why, so, therefore, due to, because of* etc.). T also points out that in the Speaking Test Ss will be asked to justify their opinions.

The business traveller

5   **Ex ❶:** T elicits experiences of hotels which Ss have stayed at in London to introduces the Holiday Inn at Nelson Dock, London. T draws Ss' attention to the photographs and asks them what facilities are pictured. Ss then work in pairs to choose the five most important facilities for business guests from the list. T elicits answers and reasons for choices. Ss then listen to the cassette and tick the items that Kevin Smith says are important for the business traveller. Kevin Smith mentions eight things which are important. T asks Ss if his list covers the five things they identified.

sauna	*modem socket✓*	*good room lighting✓*
pool	*secretarial service✓*	*bar✓*	*video conferencing*
TV	*quick check-in✓*	*fax✓*	*distance from airport✓*
		room service✓

6   **Ex ❷:** Ss have already heard the cassette. They now read the multiple-choice questions carefully before listening to the cassette again and marking the correct letter. T might wish to get Ss to check their own answers by reading the tapescript and presenting evidence to justify their answers.

1 C	2 B	3 B	4 C	5 A

7   **Ex ❸:** Ss work individually or in pairs. T asks them to read the tapescript and underline all the infinitives. They then identify examples of verbs and adjectives which are followed by the infinitive. (The remaining word followed by an infinitive is the noun *time (to)*; however, T does not dwell on it here.) T elicits any other verbs and adjectives Ss know that are followed by the infinitive (e.g. **Verbs:** *would like to/hope to/expect to,* **Adjectives:** *interesting to/difficult to/useful to).*

Verb + infinitive	Adjective + infinitive
want to/don't want to	*annoying to*
tend to	*important to*
	helpful to
	easy to

8   **Ex ❹:** The speaking activity personalises the subject of hotel facilities as Ss exchange experiences of hotels. T elicits feedback.

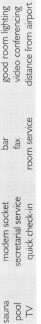

The business traveller

Listening 1 1 Kevin Smith, the Deputy Manager of the Holiday Inn at Nelson Dock, talks about what is important for the business traveller. Before you listen, decide which five things below are most important. Then listen and compare your answers.

sauna	modem socket	bar	good room lighting
pool	secretarial service	fax	video conferencing
TV	quick check-in	room service	distance from airport

2 Listen again and choose the correct option to complete the sentences.

1 Many guests like to eat in their rooms
   A so they can watch TV while they eat.
   B because it is cheaper than the restaurant.
   C so they can do more work.

2 Good lighting means
   A low lighting so guests can relax.
   B bright desk lighting so guests can work.
   C bright lighting for the whole room.

3 The business centre at the hotel
   A is a self-service facility for copying and faxing.
   B organises the food during a conference.
   C recruits temporary secretaries during conferences.

4 The hotel provides
   A a free taxi service to the centre of London.
   B a cheap bus service to the centre of London.
   C a free bus service to the centre of London.

5 Corporate guests
   A do not usually exercise during their stay.
   B like to go swimming during their stay.
   C like to use the fitness room during their stay.

Grammar 3 Look at the tapescript. Find examples of verbs and adjectives followed by the infinitive. Write them below.

Verb + infinitive	Adjective + infinitive
want to	

Speaking 4 Work in pairs. Ask your partner about the best hotel he/she has stayed in. Would your partner recommend it to a business traveller? Why/Why not?

Business hotels

66

Business hotels

Hotel facilities

Reading 1 Which of the three hotels should the following people stay at and why?

L O N D O N

Grosvenor Square Royal London Hotel ★★★★★

Centrally located, the elegant Royal London is in Mayfair, near shops, parks, theatres and other attractions. The hotel has express check-in, 204 standard rooms and 42 work rooms with desks and communication facilities. The hotel also has a large lounge, health club and well-equipped fitness centre.

Standard double room £265 per night

The Strand St Steven's Hotel ★★★

In the heart of theatreland, close to Covent Garden and only metres from Charing Cross, St Steven's is the ideal place for a London break. The hotel offers comfortable, well-equipped rooms and an efficient and friendly service. There is a restaurant, bar and free swimming pool access. The price includes a buffet breakfast.

Price per person per night £56
Mid-week single supplement £56

Portman Square Hyde Park Gardens Hotel ★★★★

A quiet hotel a short walk from Oxford Street and West End theatres, the Hyde Park Gardens has the famous Maritime Restaurant, an informal dining room and a full fitness centre. It also offers a large buffet breakfast, afternoon tea in the lobby and a Sunday Jazz Brunch.

Price per person per night £97
Mid-week single supplement £97

Marco and Francesca Bianchi

Marco is the Managing Director of a large Italian company. He has a meeting with an important supplier in London. His wife is coming to London with him.

Maurice Breton

Maurice is an advertising executive attending an international advertising conference in London. He wants to stay for just one night. He needs to e-mail a report back to his company before he leaves London.

Linda de Hamm

Linda has an interview on Friday for a job as a PA in London. She wants to stay for the weekend and do some shopping while she is in the city.

Speaking 2 Work in pairs. Which of the three hotels would your partner choose. Why?

Asking the way

9 **Ex ❶:** Ss look at the map and read the gapped notes. T plays the cassette and Ss complete the notes. T can either elicit answers or go straight on to **Ex ❷**.

   1 20   2 seven/7   3 40   4 15
   5 free   6 30   7 15   8 £1.80

10 **Ex ❷:** Ss listen to the directions again and mark the two routes on the map.

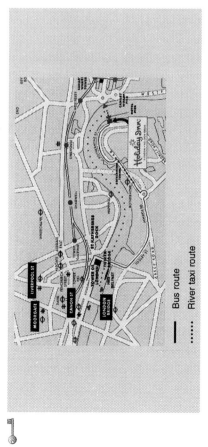

——— Bus route

······· River taxi route

11 **Ex ❸:** Ss read the information about the two guests and look at the map. They then write a short note giving the guests directions. Ss should refer to the phrases at the bottom of the page. If time is available, Ss could repeat the exercise orally in pairs, choosing their own destinations.

12 T ensures that Ss are relatively confident at giving spoken directions. T may wish to use the visuals at the bottom of the page to do some quick controlled practice with Ss.

13 **Ex ❹:** Ss work in pairs. They start at HMS Belfast and direct each other around London using the prompt cards. The dialogues should be complete exchanges beginning with student A politely asking for directions (*Excuse me. Could you tell me the way to ...?*) and saying thank you to conclude the exchange. T could also ask Ss to write short notes giving directions. The notes could be collected in and read out to the class, who would then have to follow the notes and say where the listener is being directed to.

Self-study

Ex ❶:
  1 rooms *(informal, well-equipped, comfortable)*
  2 service *(efficient, friendly)*
  3 buildings *(elegant, centrally-located, quiet)*

Ex ❷:
  2 modem socket   3 fitness centre   4 courtesy bus   5 single supplement
  6 express check-in   7 rush hour   8 health club

Ex ❸:
  1 hotel parts *(lounge, health club, fitness centre, restaurant, swimming pool, dining-room, bar)*
  2 facilities in rooms *(desk, communication facilities)*

Ex ❹: **Suggested answer** *(56 words excluding salutation and closure)*

  (Dear Mr Chung)

  I am writing to confirm the availability of four double rooms for 12 - 14 July. The rooms are all equipped with communication facilities and cost $400 per night, including a buffet breakfast.

  Please find enclosed a brochure with information about the hotel and its business facilities.

  If you require any further information, please do not hesitate to contact us.

  (Yours sincerely)

Essential vocabulary

Hotel
business centre
catering
check-in
communication facilities
courtesy bus
fitness centre
guest
health club
room service
supplement
swimming pool

Directions
along
to cross
near
next to
opposite
past
straight on

General
centrally located
comfortable
desk
lighting
modem socket
rush hour
well-equipped

The words in italics are not on the Cambridge BEC 1 wordlist.

Asking the way

Listening 2

1 Montse Garcerón is staying at the Holiday Inn at Nelson Dock. She asks about travelling into central London. Listen and complete her notes.

St Holiday Inn

Bus

Leaves every (1) _____ minutes between (2) _____ and nine in the morning. After that every (3) _____ minutes.

Takes: (4) _____ mins to Tower Hill Underground Station.

Costs: (5) _____

River taxi

Leaves every (6) _____ mins during the rush hour. After that, runs to a timetable.

Takes: (7) _____ minutes.

Costs: (8) _____ each way.

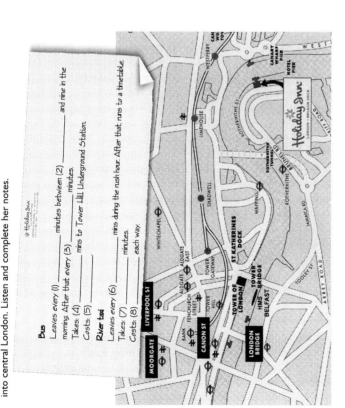

2 Listen again and draw the routes for the bus and the river taxi on the map.

Writing

3 You are the receptionist at the Holiday Inn, Nelson Dock. Write quick directions for the following guests.

• Mr Kiriakov wants to visit HMS Belfast. It is 9.30 am.

• Mrs Sanz wants to visit Canary Wharf Tower and then the Tower of London. It is 8.30 am.

Speaking

4 Work in pairs. Your teacher will give you some cards. Look at the map of London on page 134 and give your partner directions to the places on the cards. You both start from HMS Belfast. Use the words below.

Take the	first left/right.	Go	straight on ...		It's	next to ...
	bus to ...		past ...			near to ...
	train to ...		along ... Street.			opposite ...
						on the left/right of ...

Turn left/right at ...

4

• You work for the Park Hotel in New York.
• Read this letter from a company enquiring about room vacancies.

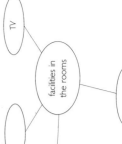

KL Computers
95 Science Park Drive #02-03
The Curie
Singapore 118258

The Park Hotel
134 Central Park South
New York 10019
USA

16 June 1999

Dear Sir/Madam

I am writing to enquire about room vacancies for 12-14 July. We would need four double rooms, preferably with some kind of communication facilities for computers.

I would be very grateful if you could send me a quotation for the above rooms with information about the business facilities that the hotel offers.

Yours faithfully

Charles Chung

Charles Chung
Personal Assistant to Kim Lee

• Write a reply to Mr Chung:
  * confirming the availability of the rooms
  * confirming the dates
  * quoting the price
  * giving information about business facilities.
• Write **50-60 words**.

1 Complete the diagrams with adjectives from the advertisements on page 65.

large
(rooms)

(service)

(hotel)

2 Match the words below.

1	room	supplement
2	modem	service
3	fitness	check-in
4	courtesy	socket
5	single	centre
6	express	club
7	rush	bus
8	health	hour

3 Complete the diagram with vocabulary from the unit.

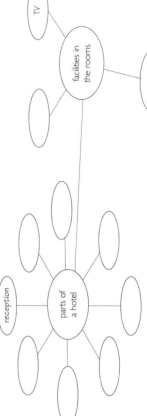

(reception)

(parts of a hotel)

(TV)

(facilities in the rooms)

Tapescript: Listening 1

Interviewer So, what special needs do business travellers have?

Kevin One of the most important things is a quick check-in and check-out. After a long trip it's annoying to have to wait at the hotel reception for five minutes. Room service is also very important. Guests often stay in their rooms working and don't have the time to go out to a restaurant, so they want their meals to be served in their rooms.

Interviewer And what facilities are there in the rooms?

Kevin Well, nowadays communication facilities are essential, so things like a modem socket, where guests can plug their modems in, and a fax are very important.

Interviewer Yes, of course.

Kevin The lighting is also very important. We've just spent a lot of money upgrading the lighting in our rooms. As I said, guests often spend their evenings preparing work, so they need good lighting at their desks.

Interviewer And what about facilities in the hotel in general?

Kevin The bars are important. Corporate guests tend to spend more time in the hotel bars than tourists. It's very important to provide a business centre, too.

Interviewer What services does the business centre provide?

Kevin Basic secretarial services such as photocopying and typing. It also co-ordinates conferences and any catering which is included in them. Clients always find it helpful to have these kind of things organised for them.

Interviewer Right, and what about distance to the airport and city centre? Is that important?

Kevin Yes. We're in the east of London so we're near City Airport. A lot of our guests have meetings in this area, so they don't want to be near Heathrow airport or right in the city centre. But it is easy to get to the centre of London from here. It only takes about 15 minutes with our courtesy bus. And there's a river taxi, as well.

Interviewer Are your corporate guests interested in using your fitness centre or swimming pool!?

Kevin Not really. They're more popular with tourists. Our corporate guests are more interested in getting in and out of the hotel as quickly as possible and working while they're here.

Tapescript: Listening 2

Reception Good morning. Can I help you?

Montse Yes. Could you tell me the best way of getting into the centre of London, please?

Reception Well, there is a courtesy bus, which leaves every 20 minutes during the rush hour, or the river taxi service to London Bridge.

Montse And when is the rush hour?

Reception It's between seven and nine in the morning and five and seven in the evening.

Montse And after nine in the morning?

Reception After nine the courtesy bus service runs every 40 minutes.

Montse Ah ha. And how long does it take?

Reception The bus takes about 15 minutes, depending on the traffic.

Montse And which way does it go?

Reception Here, I'll show you on the map. From the hotel it goes along the river bank and then on to Brunel Road. It crosses the river at Tower Bridge and then stops just after Tower Bridge at Tower Hill Underground Station.

Montse And what about the river taxi, does that change after rush hour?

Reception Yes, it's a half hourly service during rush hour and after that it runs to a timetable. It takes about 15 minutes. It's a really nice trip. You go across to Canary Wharf Pier first, then you go along the river, under Tower Bridge and you stop at a pier just before London Bridge. The only thing is, it costs £1.80 each way.

Montse OK. Thanks very much. Bye.

Reception You're welcome.

Commuting

Objectives: To enable Ss to talk about traffic and transport
To practise reading and listening for specific information
To review the language of prediction

Materials needed: Cassette - *Pass Cambridge BEC 1*
Cards - 12 cards: *Pass Cambridge BEC 1 Unit 10b/1-12* One set per pair/group

Unit overview

• Reducing traffic

Warmer	T elicits Ss' ways of getting to work, the problems of driving and ways of improving the situation.
Listening	Ss listen to six speakers and match them with headlines. Ss then listen to the speakers again and note whether they agree with each traffic scheme and their reasons.
Speaking	Ss discuss the transport schemes mentioned in the headlines.

• Transport policy

Reading	Ss read a newspaper article and complete a table about transport schemes and their effects. Ss then read the article again and answer multiple-choice comprehension questions.
Language focus	Ss review the use of *will* and *going to* for predictions.
Speaking	Ss make predictions about the future of transport. They then play a board game about commuting to work. **(Activity sheet** page 129)

• Self-study

Vocabulary	Crossword (transport vocabulary).
	Sentence completion (*traffic* vs *transport*).
	Ss write about transport schemes in their city.
Exam practice	*Multiple-choice comprehension exercise (Reading Test Part 1).*

Reducing traffic

1 **Warmer (books closed):** T writes the word *commuter* on the board, elicits its meaning and leads into a discussion of Ss' ways of getting to work, the problems of driving to work and ways of improving the traffic situation.

2 **Ex ❶:** Ss read the seven headlines about different transport schemes. T elicits which are in operation in Ss' city/town. T points out to Ss that there are seven headlines but only six speakers, so one headline will have no number. T plays the cassette and Ss number the headlines in the order in which they are commented upon.

🗝 Speaker 2   *Green tax could push up fuel prices by 60%*
     Speaker 3   *Edinburgh reduces city centre traffic with pedestrian zones*
     Speaker 4   *Leicester launches new pay-as-you-drive scheme*
     Speaker 5   *Government to tax parking at work*
     Speaker 6   *New smart cards to make buses and trains cheaper*

3 **Ex ❷:** Ss listen to the cassette again and note down only whether the speakers agree or disagree. T warns Ss that some speakers may not give a clear opinion if they are not sure. Ss then listen again and take notes on the speakers' reasons. T reminds Ss that it is a note-taking exercise and that grammatically complete sentences are not required.

🗝

Speaker	Agrees/disagrees	Reasons
2	disagrees	*price makes no difference, will increase companies' costs, put jobs at risk*
3	agrees	*can't relax when shopping, shopping should be fun and not stressful*
4	not sure	*people might leave their car at home more often, no public transport so driving more expensive for speaker*
5	disagrees	*getting to work twice as long and expensive on public transport*
6	agrees	*hates not having right money on buses, likes the idea of smart card and cheaper buses*

4 **Ex ❸:** Ss work in pairs and exchange their opinions on the traffic reduction schemes mentioned in the headlines on the previous page. T encourages Ss to take notes and report back their partner's answers. The feedback could be developed into a class discussion on the subject of transport policies for the future, if time permits. Ss could also discuss government transport policies in their own country, which would lead into the following text.

Transport policy

5 Before doing **Ex ❶**, Ss scan the article to see which of the transport schemes from page 69 are mentioned.

6 **Ex ❶:** Ss scan the article once more and complete the table by listing the transport schemes mentioned in the article and their effects. Ss quote from the text in support of their answers.

🗝

Transport schemes	Effects
Increase tax on petrol	*Will affect people who live in the country but do little to reduce inner city traffic*
Pay-as-you-drive on motorways	*Will push cars on to smaller roads*
Smart cards and electronic monitoring of roads	*Will lead to more efficient use of transport systems but will not reduce the number of cars or persuade people to leave their cars at home*

Unit 10b

Commuting

Reducing traffic

Listening 1 Six people talk about the topics in the newspaper headlines below. Listen to the speakers and number the headlines.

23

Green tax could push up fuel prices by up to 60%

Government to tax parking at work
By Jane Suttie

Leicester launches new pay-as-you-drive scheme

New smart card to make buses and trains cheaper

Edinburgh reduces city centre traffic with pedestrian zones

Leeds city centre gets fast lane for people sharing cars
By Ian Robinson

New bus lanes motorways

2 Listen again. Does each speaker agree or disagree with the particular transport scheme? Why?

	Agrees/disagrees	Reason
Speaker 1	Disagrees	Traffic will be twice as bad, more accidents, people will be stuck in traffic jams, late for work
Speaker 2		
Speaker 3		
Speaker 4		
Speaker 5		
Speaker 6		

Commuting

Speaking 3 Work in pairs. Look at the newspaper headlines on the opposite page. Which are the two best schemes? Why?

Transport policy

Reading 1 Read the newspaper article about Government transport policy and complete the table.

THE GAZETTE MONDAY JUNE 23 1999 **TRANSF**

How much are we prepared to pay for our cars?

Bridget Connolly reports on the search for an effective and popular transport policy.

Everyone agrees that there are simply too many cars on the road but who will be the first to stop using theirs? Although everyone hates being stuck in traffic, no-one sees their car as part of the growing problem. However, with traffic growth of up to 84 per cent expected by 2031 and the ever-increasing cost of accidents and delays already at $160bn in Europe, there is a growing need to change our 'car culture' and develop alternative forms of transport as quickly as possible.

One answer is to make cars more expensive by increasing taxes on petrol. However, tax increases will affect the people who live in the country more than city drivers and do little to reduce inner city traffic. The Government is also looking at pay-as-you-drive schemes on motorways but this will push

cars on to smaller 'free' roads, which will make the problem worse.

A successful transport policy is not just a question of making the car too expensive but of offering car drivers a real alternative. Many motorists dislike driving to work but say public transport services are too slow, offer poor quality and are far too expensive. If new transport policies are to succeed, public transport needs to be quick, reliable and affordable.

Transport planners are also developing ways of managing the existing road network more efficiently. New technology such as smart cards and electronic monitoring of roads will lead to a more efficient use of transport systems. However, technology will not reduce the number of cars on the road or solve the real problem of how to persuade car drivers to leave their beloved car at home more often.

Changes in travel in Britain 1955-1995

Kilometres travelled per year (billions)

1955
1965
1975
1985
1995

Cars   Buses & coaches   Rail

Transport schemes	Effects
Increase tax on petrol	

Unit 10b

70

7 **Ex ②**: Ss read through all the questions carefully before scanning the text once more for the answers. As the Ss have already scanned the text twice, T can impose a time limit on the task to encourage scanning strategies. T offers no support until after feedback on answers. During feedback Ss quote from the text to support answers. T then answers any questions about vocabulary from the text.

| 1 B | 2 B | 3 C* | 4 A | 5 C | 6 B |

* Although there is reference to a 60% rise in the headlines in **Ex ❶** on page 69, this is not part of the text the Ss are asked to read.

8 T elicits the verb form used in the newspaper article to make predictions (*will*). T uses this to lead into a focus on the use of *will* and *going to* in predictions. T draws Ss' attention to the **Don't forget!** section. Although Ss will probably be familiar with both forms, they will also have difficulties in distinguishing between them. The **Don't forget!** section avoids giving concrete rules about using *will* and *going to* for predictions, simply stating that both can be used. T reminds Ss about the difference between the weak form (*I'll*) used for spoken predictions and the strong form (*will*) used for written predictions and formal presentations.

Language Note

According to Close (*A Teachers' Grammar*, LTP), the essential factor in the use of *going to* for predictions is a focus on some **present** factor which the speaker feels certain will lead to a future event. In other words, the speaker feels that he/she has evidence of what is about to happen.

However, the choice of form will depend on many factors such as formality, speaker, situation and the nature of the evidence upon which the prediction is made. In certain genres such as those listed, *will* is preferred.

9 **Ex ❸**: Ss work in pairs and discuss the issues listed in the box. T may wish to encourage Ss to take notes and present their answers to the class for general discussion.

10 **Ex ❹**: Ss play the Commuter Game in groups of 2-4. Each player has a counter. Instead of using dice, Ss use two coins. (See the instructions to the game on page 129.) If a S lands on a red or green light, another S draws an appropriate colour card and reads out the instructions or dilemma. In the case of dilemmas, the S chooses one of the two options offered by the card. If the S chooses to break the law, he/she tosses a coin to see whether the police catch him/her. Heads: the S is caught and returns to the start of the game. Tails: the S gets away with it and continues as normal. The first player to reach work wins.

Self-study

Ex ❶:

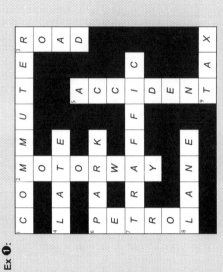

Ex ❷: 2 Public **transport** is very good in the city where I live.
3 The Government's new **transport** policy won't change anything.
4 Sorry I'm late. I was stuck in **traffic** for hours.
5 There's always a **traffic** jam on the motorway in the morning.
6 City centre **traffic** was reduced by the park and ride scheme.
7 There isn't any alternative **transport** where I live.
8 With **traffic** growth of over 2% a year, we need more roads.

Ex ❹: 1 C   2 A   3 B   4 B   5 A

Essential vocabulary

Transport	**General**
accident	*to affect*
commuter	*effect*
fuel	affordable
lane	government
motorway	note
pay-as-you-drive	change
park and ride	pavement
pedestrian zone	policy
petrol	*to share*
public transport	*smart card*
stuck in traffic	tax
traffic jam	
traffic lights	

The words in italics are not on the Cambridge BEC 1 wordlist.

2 Are the sentences below 'Right' or 'Wrong'? If there is not enough information to answer, choose 'Doesn't say'.

1 Cars are the only form of transport that has grown since 1985.

   A Right   B Wrong   C Doesn't say

2 Delays and accidents will cost Europe $160bn in 2031.

   A Right   B Wrong   C Doesn't say

3 The Government is going to double the tax on petrol.

   A Right   B Wrong   C Doesn't say

4 Pay-as-you-drive schemes will reduce the amount of traffic on motorways.

   A Right   B Wrong   C Doesn't say

5 The Government is planning to build more roads in the future.

   A Right   B Wrong   C Doesn't say

6 The use of new technology will reduce the amount of traffic.

   A Right   B Wrong   C Doesn't say

Making predictions

We can use both **going to** and **will** to make predictions about the future.

- We make spoken predictions with **going to** or **'ll**.
  Petrol prices aren't going to make any difference.
  The traffic'll be twice as bad.

- **Will** is used in newspaper articles, formal letters and formal speeches.
  The Government will increase tax on petrol next year.
  The meeting will take place on Tuesday 2 May.

Speaking **3** Work in pairs. How will transport change in your country in the future? Think about the following issues.

the use of company cars   the cost of public transport   the cost of driving
          the quality of public transport   the use of alternative transport

4 Look at the Commuter Game on page 129. Your teacher will give you instructions on how to play the game.

71   Commuting

---

1 Complete the crossword.

[crossword grid]

Across

1 Someone who travels into a city or town to work.
4 The opposite of early.
6 Put your car in a place where it can stay.
7 All cars and buses on the roads.
8 In Britain you drive in the left one.
9 Money you have to give to the Government.

Down

2 A fast road with three lanes in each direction.
3 The long piece of hard ground you drive on.
5 Something that happens when one car hits another.
6 Fuel for cars.

2 Complete the following sentences by adding the word *traffic* or *transport* in the correct place.

traffic
1 Every set of lights was on red this morning.
2 Public is very good in the city where I live.
3 The Government's new policy won't change anything.
4 Sorry I'm late. I was stuck in for hours.
5 There's always a jam on the motorway in the morning.
6 City centre was reduced by the park-and-ride scheme.
7 There isn't any alternative where I live.
8 With growth of over 2% a year, we need more roads.

3 Write about transport in your city. What are the problems? How is the Government dealing with these problems?

Commuting

---

4 Exam practice

- Look at the newspaper headlines in questions 1-5.
- In each question, which phrase or sentence is correct?
- For each question, mark the correct letter **A, B or C.**

1

> **Motorway technology improves flow of rush hour traffic**

A There are fewer accidents during rush hour.
B There is less traffic during rush hour.
C There are fewer traffic jams during rush hour.

2

> **Delays expected on commuter train services**

A People travelling to work by train may be late.
B There are problems with high speed trains.
C Due to problems, all trains will be late.

3

> **Public transport fares to increase**

A There will be more bus and train services.
B It will be more expensive to travel by bus and train.
C Customer service will improve on buses and trains.

4

> **Punctuality improves on bus services**

A The quality of service is improving on buses.
B More buses are now running on time.
C Buses are becoming cheaper to use.

5

> **Pedestrian zones reduce city centre pollution**

A Traffic reductions have improved city centre air quality.
B Larger roads have reduced city centre traffic jams.
C Cycle areas have improved the flow of city centre traffic.

Tapescript: Listening

Speaker 1 I think it's a stupid idea. The motorways are already too full and now they're going to stop cars using one of the lanes. It's crazy. The traffic'll be twice as bad and there'll be a lot more accidents as well. People will spend hours and hours stuck in traffic jams and be late for work all the time.

Speaker 2 OK, I know cars are bad for the environment and all that, but big increases in petrol prices aren't going to make any difference. What about industry? Higher petrol prices are only going to increase companies' costs and put jobs at risk.

Speaker 3 It's about time! When I go shopping there are thousands of people all on a narrow little pavement trying to walk along. It's impossible to relax. Car drivers should use park and ride schemes and leave their cars out of the city centre. Shopping should be fun and not stressful.

Speaker 4 It's difficult to say, really. Paying every time you use a road might be a good idea. I suppose some people might leave their cars at home a bit more often, which would be good. But there isn't any public transport where I live, so it would be more expensive for me personally.

Speaker 5 How am I going to get to work if I can't leave my car there? It takes twice as long to get to work on the bus and it costs twice as much, as well. So, of course I'm not going to use public transport.

Speaker 6 I think it's a good idea. I hate it when you don't have the right money on the buses. They don't accept notes so you need a pocket full of change all the time. I like the idea of a plastic card - especially if it makes them cheaper to use as well. Nobody liked phone cards at first, did they? And now, look: everyone uses them.

Arranging a conference

Unit overview

● An enquiry

Vocabulary	Ss order cards showing how to arrange a conference.
Listening 1	Ss listen to a telephone call about arranging a marketing conference and answer true/false questions before filling in a form.
Speaking	Ss discuss what the conference organiser's job involves.
Reading	Ss scan advertisements about three conference venues for specific information.
Speaking	Ss work in pairs and select a venue for the marketing conference.

● Confirming arrangements

Listening 2	Ss listen to a telephone call in which conference arrangements are checked and complete notes.
Language focus	Ss review language for checking and confirming information.
Speaking	Ss exchange information and complete a conference programme. (**Activity sheet** A and B pages 126 and 132)
Writing	Ss work in pairs to plan and then write a letter of confirmation.

● Self-study

Vocabulary	Collocation exercise (conference verbs and nouns).
	Gap-fill exercise (conference vocabulary).
Language focus	Question writing (linked to conference nouns).
	Keyword exercise (*conference*).
Writing	Making the letter from the previous section more concise.
Exam practice	*Memo writing (Writing Test Part 2).*

Arranging a conference

An enquiry

1 **Warmer (books closed):** T introduces the subject of conferences and elicits briefly whether students have attended or organised conferences and their general opinion of them.

2 **Ex ❶:** T hands out a set of cards to each pair of students to sort into the correct order for organising a conference. T elicits feedback and clarifies any vocabulary points. This vocabulary will be recycled in **Ex ❶** of the **Self-study** section.

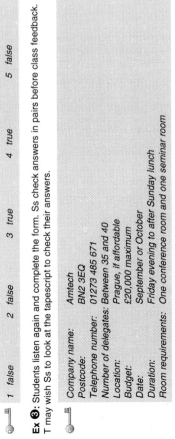

> *Suggested answer:*
> T accepts any logical order; there is no one right answer.
> 1 *Decide on the budget*
> 2 *Decide on the duration*
> 3 *Arrange a date*
> 4 *Choose a location*
> 5 *Invite the delegates*
> 6 *Finalise the programme details*
> 7 *Organise the equipment required (e.g., overhead projector etc.)*

3 **Ex ❷:** T sets the scene before playing the cassette. Students complete the true/false exercise.

> 1 *false* 2 *false* 3 *true* 4 *true* 5 *false*

4 **Ex ❸:** Students listen again and complete the form. Ss check answers in pairs before class feedback. T may wish Ss to look at the tapescript to check their answers.

> *Company name:* Amtech
> *Postcode:* BN2 3EQ
> *Telephone number:* 01273 485 671
> *Number of delegates:* Between 35 and 40
> *Location:* Prague, if affordable
> *Budget:* £20,000 maximum
> *Date:* September or October
> *Duration:* Friday evening to after Sunday lunch
> *Room requirements:* One conference room and one seminar room

5 **Ex ❹:** Ss draw up a list of what they think Rachel's job involves. T then asks them if they would like to do such a job.

6 **Ex ❺:** Before Ss read the proposals, T elicits the type of information Ss would need for deciding on a venue for a conference (price? near the centre/airport? attractive location? modern or old-style charm? etc.) Ss then read the three descriptions and complete the scanning exercise. T points out that the answers may include more than one hotel.

> 1 *The Plaza and The Grand Hotel*
> 2 *The Grand Hotel and the Karoliny Conference Centre*
> 3 *The Plaza*
> 4 *The Grand Hotel*
> 5 *The Karoliny Conference Centre*
> 6 *The Plaza and the Karoliny Conference Centre*
> 7 *The Karoliny Conference Centre*

In feedback, T clarifies any vocabulary points.

7 **Ex ❻:** Ss work out which hotel would be cheapest for Daniel's conference. They then decide if any other considerations would outweigh this factor.

> *Cheapest: The Plaza*

	Plaza	Grand Hotel	Karoliny
2 nights x 40 delegates = 80 nights	*£7,200*	*£8,560*	*£12,000*
2 dinners x 40 delegates = 80 dinners	*£1,600*	*£1,680*	*£2,000*
2 lunches x 40 delegates = 80 lunches	*£1,200*	*£1,280*	*£1,480*
Conference room for 2 days	*£610*	*£690*	*£1,520*
Seminar room for 2 days	*£360*	*£380*	*£400*
Technical equipment for 2 days	*£400*	*£680*	*Included in price*
Total	*£10,970*	*£13,170*	*£17,400*

Arranging a conference

An enquiry

Vocabulary **1** Work in pairs. Your teacher will give you some cards about organising a conference. Put them in order.

Listening 1 **2** Daniel Black calls Rachel Day at Europa Events to discuss a conference. Listen to their conversation. Are the following sentences true or false?

1 Daniel is calling to confirm arrangements for a conference.
2 The company has made a final decision on the location.
3 The company wants to have the conference in autumn.
4 The delegates will have two nights at the hotel.
5 Rachel is going to ring Daniel back with a proposal.

3 Listen again and complete the form below.

europa events

Briefing Form

Company name

Contact name
Daniel Black

Company address
Westbourne Business Park
Brighton

Postcode

Telephone number

Number of delegates

Location

Budget

Date

Duration

Room requirements

Europa Events LTD, 112 Market Road, LONDON, SW4 8HN

Speaking **4** Work in pairs. What do you think Rachel Day's job involves?

Reading **5** Read the information below about conference packages. Which hotel:

- offers easy access to Prague city centre?
- is suitable for smaller conferences with fewer than 30 people?
- is suitable for a company which requires several different rooms for workshops?
- is in a quiet location?
- has its conference facilities in a separate building?
- offers the best facilities for business people?
- does not charge extra for the use of projectors, videos, etc?

europa events

The Plaza, PRAGUE (Min. 40 delegates)

Situated in the heart of Prague, the Plaza is convenient for business travellers from all over Europe. The hotel itself provides the best accommodation and first class facilities for the business traveller. The whole of the fourth floor is dedicated to conference facilities: there are two large conference rooms and four smaller seminar rooms, a business centre, a rest area and a small restaurant.

Grand Hotel Vltava, PRAGUE (Max. 45 delegates)

This historic building in a peaceful setting overlooking the river provides the perfect venue for your conference. In their free time, delegates can enjoy the sights of Prague, many of which are within walking distance. For your convenience we offer a range of conference packages, which we can, of course, extend to meet your requirements.

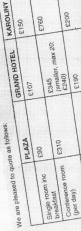

Karoliny Conference Centre, PRAGUE (Min. 20 delegates)

This 60 bedroom hotel is located 30 minutes from the airport by car and just 20 minutes from the centre of Prague by train. We have a well-equipped conference centre next to the hotel itself and the bedrooms have communication facilities for the business user.

We are pleased to quote as follows:

	PLAZA	GRAND HOTEL	KAROLINY
Single room inc breakfast	£90	£107	£150
Conference room (per day)	£310	£345 (smaller, max 20: £240)	£760
Seminar room (per day)	£180 (smaller, max 10: £130)	£190	£200
Technical equipment (per day)	£200	£340	Included in price
	+15+	+16+	
	+20+	+21+	£25+
Lunch per person	£15+		£18.50+
Dinner per person	£20+		

Speaking **6** Work in pairs. Which hotel would be cheapest for Daniel Black's conference? Would you choose this hotel for him?

Arranging a conference

Confirming arrangements

8 **Ex 1**: Before the listening exercise, T asks Ss to read through Rachel's notes and checks Ss know what type of information they are listening for.

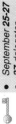

- September **25-27**
- **37 delegates**
- Accommodation for **two nights**
- One conference room and **one seminar room**
- Delegates pay for **phone bills**
- Drinks **go on master account**
- Europa Events to confirm **in writing by the end of the week**

Ss check their answers in pairs before T gives feedback. T may wish to refer them to the tapescript.

9 T replays the cassette for Ss and focuses on language for checking before referring Ss to the **Don't forget!** section. T elicits Rachel's *I'll confirm...* to link in with the section on confirming. T also explains that in **Ex 3** Ss will be asked to write a letter of confirmation.

10 **Ex 2**: Before Ss look at the **Activity sheets** on pages 126 and 132, T introduces the notion of the conference programme and brainstorms the type of information included. Ss then work in pairs to complete the programme. T rounds off the activity by asking for any comments on the programme (e.g., *Are there any details missing, Is the timing all right?*). T will need to explain *plenary* (i.e. to describe a session where all the delegates are together); this is for Ss' passive recognition rather than active use.

11 **Ex 3**: T elicits the answers to the prompt questions and encourages Ss to plan the letter before writing. After Ss have drafted their letter, T may wish to have pairs of Ss exchange drafts to compare versions. T may wish then to make general points about the letter.

Suggested answer:

Dear Mr Black

With reference to our recent telephone conversation, I am writing to confirm the arrangements for the Amtech Marketing Conference.

The conference will take place at the Karoliny Conference Centre in Prague from 25 to 27 September. The 37 delegates will arrive for dinner on the Friday and leave after lunch on Sunday. There will be a conference room and a seminar room for the conference.

The Europa Events representative will welcome delegates on 25 September. Delegates will pay their phone bills; their drinks will go to the Amtech master account.

I enclose the conference programme and will confirm the name of the Europa Events contact person in a few days. If you have any other questions, please do not hesitate to contact me.

Yours sincerely

Self-study

Ex 1:
2 *decide on a budget/details/a proposal*
3 *ask for a quotation/details*
4 *make a proposal*
5 *invite delegates*
6 *finalise details/a budget/a proposal*

Ex 2:
1 *proposal* 2 *location* 3 *arranging*
4 *requirements* 5 *quotation* 6 *confirmation*

Ex 3: *Suggested answers:*
2 *Do you have a preferred location?*
3 *Could you tell me what your budget is, please?*
4 *When do you want to hold the conference?*
5 *How long would you like it to last?*
6 *How many rooms will you need?*

Ex 4: *Suggested answers:*

to organise a conference	conference **organiser**
to hold a conference	conference **programme**
	conference **package**
	conference **centre**
	conference **booking**

Ex 5: *Suggested answer: (58 words excluding salutation and closing phrase)*

(Dear Mr Black)

I am writing to confirm the Amtech marketing conference arrangements.

The location is the Karoliny Conference Centre, Prague. The 37 delegates will arrive for Friday dinner on 25 September and depart after Sunday lunch on 27 September. We will provide a conference and seminar room.

I enclose the conference programme. I will confirm the name of the Europa Events contact person as soon as possible.

(Yours sincerely)

Ex 6: *Suggested answer: (21 words)*
The Marketing Conference is from 25 to 27 September at the Karoliny Conference Centre, Prague. Please confirm that you can attend.

Essential vocabulary

Conference words
- to arrange (a conference)
- *to hold (a conference)*
- to ask for (a quotation)
- to decide on (a budget)
- to finalise (details)
- to invite (delegates)
- to make a (proposal)

- conference booking
- conference centre
- conference organiser
- conference package
- conference programme
- conference room

General
- *access*
- accommodation
- to confirm
- *duration*
- *location*
- *projector*
- suitable
- *workshop*

The words in italics are not on the Cambridge BEC 1 wordlist.

Look back through the unit (including the tapescripts).
How many words connected with conference can you
find? Now write words which go **before** and **after**
conference.

to arrange .... room
.... **(a) conference**
....

5 You are Rachel Day. Make your letter to Daniel Black
more concise. Write only the essential information.
Write **50-60 words**.

Exam practice

- You are Daniel Black. You have organised a
  marketing conference for your company at the
  Karoliny Conference Centre, Prague.
- Write a memo to the delegates:
  * saying where the conference will be
  * saying when the conference will be
  * asking everyone to confirm if they can
    attend.
- **Write about 20 words.**

6

```
MEMO

From:   Daniel Black
To:     Marketing Personnel

_____

_____

_____

_____

_____

_____
```

---

1 Match each verb with a noun.

1 arrange ———— a quotation
2 decide on ———— a conference
3 ask for ———— delegates
4 make ———— a budget
5 invite ———— details
6 finalise ———— a proposal

2 Complete the sentences with the correct form of the
words below.

> quote require locate arrange propose confirm

1 When I have all the details of your requirements, I'll
   make a ——————— in writing.
2 The conference is in a quiet ———————.
3 Rachel Day is ——————— a conference for
   us in October.
4 Please let me know if any delegates have any special
   food ———————, for example, if they are
   vegetarians.
5 They have given us a ——————— of
   £50,000 for the organisation of our sales conference.
6 I'll send you a letter of ——————— next
   week.

3 You are a conference organiser. A client wants to
organise a conference. Write questions to ask the
client about the following.

1 delegates   *How many delegates will*
                there be?
2 location
3 budget
4 time of year
5 duration
6 rooms

Confirming arrangements

Listening 2   **1** Rachel telephones Daniel to check some details about the conference. Listen to their
conversation and take notes.

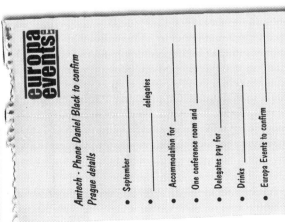

europa events

Amtech - Phone Daniel Black to confirm
Prague details

- September ———————
- ——————— delegates
- Accommodation for ———————
- One conference room and ———————
- Delegates pay for ———————
- Drinks ———————
- Europa Events to confirm ———————

Checking and confirming

- We often have to check information on the telephone.
  I'd like to check some details.
  So, ... Is that correct?
  Sorry, did you say ...?
- We often confirm arrangements with a letter or fax.
  I am writing to confirm ...
  We are happy to confirm ...

Unit 66
2

Speaking   **2** Work in pairs. Student A: Look at the Activity sheet on page 126. Student B: Look at
the Activity sheet on page 132.

Writing   **3** Work in pairs. Write Rachel's letter to Daniel to confirm the conference booking.
Enclose the programme from Exercise 2. Plan the letter before you begin to write.

- What information do you need to include?
- How many paragraphs do you need?
- What information will you write in each paragraph?
- What phrases will you use in each paragraph?

Tapescript: Listening 1

Rachel Good morning, Europa Events. Can I help you?

Daniel Good morning. My name's Daniel Black from Amtech. Could you give me a quotation for the organisation of a marketing conference, please?

Rachel Yes, of course. I'll need to take some details first. So, it's Daniel Black from Amtech. Can you spell the company name, please?

Daniel Yes, it's A-M-T-E-C-H.

Rachel And what's the address?

Daniel Westbourne Business Park, Brighton, BN2 3EQ and the phone number's 01273 485 671.

Rachel 01273 485 671. And it's a marketing conference. How many delegates will there be?

Daniel Between thirty-five and forty.

Rachel Do you have a preferred location?

Daniel Yeah. Well, we're thinking of Prague, if it's affordable.

Rachel That's always the big question, isn't it? Could you tell me what your budget is, please?

Daniel £20,000 maximum.

Rachel OK. And when do you want to hold the conference?

Daniel In September or October.

Rachel How long would you like it to last?

Daniel A weekend. We'd like the delegates to arrive for dinner on the Friday evening and leave after lunch on the Sunday.

Rachel Will you want to have the delegates in one room for the whole conference or will you need seminar rooms?

Daniel Well, we plan to break into two discussion groups during the day, so we'll need one seminar room in addition to the main conference room.

Rachel Right, Mr Black. That's all I need to ask you for the moment. I'll look at your requirements and make a written proposal before the end of the week.

Daniel Fine. Thanks very much.

Tapescript: Listening 2

Daniel Good morning, Daniel Black.

Rachel Hello. This is Rachel Day from Europa Events.

Daniel Hello. How are you?

Rachel Fine thanks. I'm phoning about the marketing conference. I'd like to check some details before I send you the letter of confirmation.

Daniel Sure, go ahead.

Rachel So, the conference will be held on September 25 to 27 for 37 delegates and all of the delegates will require accommodation for two nights. You will have the use of one conference room plus a smaller seminar room. Is that correct?

Daniel Yes, that sounds right.

Rachel Now there's just one thing I'm not sure about. Did you say that you want the delegates to pay their own bar and phone bills before they depart?

Daniel No, just their phone bills.

Rachel So all drinks should go on the master account?

Daniel That's right, yes.

Rachel Fine. That's all I need to know thanks.

Daniel And are you going to be in the hotel at the time of the conference?

Rachel No, it won't be me as I'll be at another conference then. One of my colleagues will be waiting for you at the hotel when you arrive. I'll be able to give you the name of your contact person in a few days.

Daniel Great, thanks.

Rachel So, I'll confirm the whole thing in writing. You should receive the letter before the end of the week.

At a conference

Objectives:
To enable Ss to talk about a conference (facts and evaluation)
To practise listening for specific information
To practise reading for gist and specific information
To review time clauses referring to the future

Materials needed:
Cassette – *Pass Cambridge BEC 1*
Cards – **10 cards: *Pass Cambridge BEC 1* Unit 11b/1-10** One set per pair/group

Unit overview

● Welcome to the conference

Listening 1	Ss listen to the opening speech of a conference and complete the conference programme. Ss then listen again and answer comprehension questions.
Language focus	Ss read the tapescript and underline present simple verb forms referring to the future in time clauses. Ss then complete the **Don't forget!** section. Ss make complete sentences about the programme using prompts on cards and time conjunctions (*after, before, as soon as*, etc.).
Speaking	Ss work in pairs and decide how they would organise a sightseeing tour of their own city/town as part of a weekend conference.

● The conference report

Reading	Ss read extracts from the conference report and match them with the relevant programme item.
Vocabulary	Ss read the extracts again and underline adjectives. They then provide opposites for these adjectives.
Listening 2	Ss listen to a delegate giving feedback on the conference and fill in her feedback form.
Speaking	Ss work in pairs and discuss what makes a good conference.

● Self-study

Language focus	Sentence completion (time clauses).
Vocabulary	Opposites of adjectives.
	Opposites of sentences (focus on *hard* and *long*).
Exam practice	*Multiple-choice reading comprehension exercise (Reading Test Part 1).*

Welcome to the conference

1 **Warmer (books closed):** T introduces the notion of a conference and asks what items are usually included in a conference programme. T may then wish to ask Ss to predict what they would expect to see on a programme for a sales conference.

2 **Ex ❶**: Ss listen and then complete the programme.

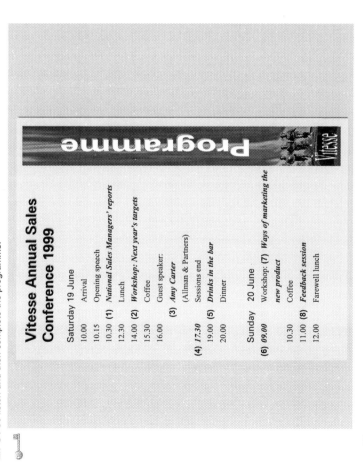

Vitesse Annual Sales Conference 1999

Saturday 19 June

10.00	Arrival
10.15	Opening speech
10.30 **(1)**	*National Sales Managers' reports*
12.30	Lunch
14.00 **(2)**	*Workshop: Next year's targets*
15.30	Coffee
16.00	Guest speaker:
(3)	*Amy Carter*
	(Allman & Partners)
(4) *17.30*	Sessions end
19.00 **(5)**	*Drinks in the bar*
20.00	Dinner

Sunday 20 June

(6) *09.00*	Workshop: **(7)** *Ways of marketing the new product*
10.30	Coffee
11.00 **(8)**	*Feedback session*
12.00	Farewell lunch

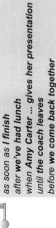

3 **Ex ❷**: Ss listen again and answer the comprehension questions. T may wish to have Ss compare answers in pairs before general feedback.

1 *Six*
2 *Two*
3 *It's useful for everyone to see the overall picture.*
4 *The results of a group-wide survey on the way the company answers the telephone.*
5 *15 minutes (by coach)*
6 *Canada*

4 **Ex ❸**: Ss read the tapescript and extract the verb forms in the time clauses.

as soon as I finish
after we've had lunch
when Amy Carter ... gives her presentation
until the coach leaves
before we come back together

---

5 Ss complete the **Don't forget!** box.

When we express time in the future, before, after, when, as soon as and until are followed by the present simple or present perfect.

6 **Ex ❹**: Ss work in pairs. They take turns to pick up two cards. They then use a time conjunction to make a sentence about the programme.

e.g. *Drinks in the bar/guest speaker/after:*
The delegates will have drinks in the bar after the guest speaker has finished the talk.

7 **Ex ❺**: Ss work in pairs to decide on a sightseeing tour for conference delegates to their city. T may wish to prepare for this pairwork activity with a general class discussion to establish the type of places suitable for delegates (museums, gardens, palaces, shopping streets etc.). When pairs have worked out a suitable programme, T selects one or two samples across the group.

The conference report

8 **Ex ❶**: T may wish to prepare Ss for this activity by discussing who would write up a conference report (the organiser? a staff representative?) and why (to act as an reminder? to act as a record?) to provide information for people who could not attend?). Ss can then read the extracts and decide who wrote this particular report (probably a staff representative).

Ss then read the report extracts and match them with the sessions on the programme.

A *Amy Carter's presentation*
B *Ways of marketing the new product*
C *National Sales Managers' reports*
D *Workshop: Next year's targets*

At a conference

Welcome to the conference

Listening 1 **1** Frank Stanford, the Sales Director of Vitesse Sportswear, makes the opening speech at the company's Annual Sales Conference. Listen and complete the programme.

Programme

Vitesse Annual Sales Conference 1999

Saturday 19 June

10.00	Arrival
10.15	Opening speech
10.30	**(1)** _____
12.30	Lunch
14.00	**(2)** _____
15.30	Coffee
16.00	Guest speaker: _____
(3) _____	(Allman & Partners)
(4) _____	Sessions end
19.00	**(5)** _____
20.00	Dinner

Sunday 20 June

(6) _____	Workshop: **(7)** _____
10.30	Coffee
11.00	**(8)** _____
12.00	Farewell lunch

2 Listen again and answer the questions.

1 How many annual sales conferences has the company already had?
2 How many days do Vitesse conferences normally last?
3 Why are all the delegates together at the first session?
4 What is the guest speaker going to talk about?
5 How far away is the restaurant?
6 Where is Jodie Cox based?

Grammar **3** Read the tapescript and underline the verb forms that follow *as soon as, after, when, until* and *before*. Then complete the information on the opposite page.

Time clauses

● When we express time in the future, *before, after, when, as soon as* and *until* are followed by the _____ or _____.
We'll start the session as soon as he arrives.
We can go for lunch after she's finished her presentation.

(Unit 32)

Speaking **4** Work in pairs. Your teacher will give you some cards. Use the information on the cards, the agenda and the words below to form complete sentences.

before   after   when   as soon as   until

5 Work in pairs. A company is organising a weekend conference in your city. The delegates are arriving at 6pm on Friday and leaving at 8pm on Sunday. Four hours of sightseeing is on the programme. What would you show them and when would be the best time?

The conference report

Reading **1** Two weeks after the conference Vitesse produces a report summarising the conference sessions. Match the extracts from the report with the sessions on the programme.

A An extremely useful presentation that gave us all something to think about. I'm sure everyone will benefit from the helpful tips for dealing with customer calls. We are planning a training pack to improve the way the group deals with incoming calls.

B A highly productive workshop session that resulted in some intelligent ideas for promoting the company's latest product. The launch will mean that we all have an exciting and busy twelve months ahead of us.

C As always, it was interesting to see how the whole company has performed over the last twelve months. All the presentations were brief, professional and extremely well-prepared. The positive figures were certainly a great start to the conference.

D This workshop session gave people the opportunity to discuss the company's sales objectives and strategies. This was a hard but rewarding session with serious and occasionally heated discussion on a range of issues.

Self-study

Ex 1: *Suggested answers:*

2 *we know the number of delegates.*
3 *you arrive at the conference.*
4 *we have had the feedback session.*
5 *the guest speaker arrives.*
6 *I have finished it.*

Ex 2:
2 *badly-prepared*
3 *negative*
4 *useless*
5 *unproductive*
6 *boring/dull*
7 *unrewarding*

Ex 3:
2 *The conference was **easy** to organise.*
3 *She gave a **brief** (or **short**) sales presentation.*
4 *Some of the sessions were too **short**.*
5 *The hotel beds were very **soft**.*
6 *The journey to the restaurant was **short**.*
7 *The speaker was **easy** to understand.*

Ex 4: 1 C   2 A   3 B   4 A   5 C

Essential vocabulary

Conference	Adjectives	General
delegate	brief	to last
feedback	*busy*	to perform
guest speaker	*exciting*	target
report	hard	
session	*heated*	
venue	helpful	
	intelligent	
	interesting	
	positive	
	productive	
	professional	
	rewarding	
	serious	
	useful	
	well-prepared	

The words in italics are not on the Cambridge BEC 1 wordlist.

---

9 **Ex 2**:
1 *Organise a training pack to improve the way the group handles incoming calls.*
2 *In the National Sales Managers' reports (first session).*
3 *Well (positive figures).*
4 *Targets for next year.*

10 **Ex 3**: Ss focus on adjectives evaluating the sessions. T elicits these from Ss before they brainstorm their opposites: *useful, helpful, productive, intelligent, exciting, busy, interesting, brief, professional, well-prepared, positive, hard, rewarding, serious, heated.*

T should draw Ss' attention to the importance of the particular context which requires subjective adjectives of quality. The speaker's opinions are further strengthened by the use of the qualifying adverbs *extremely* and *highly*. T makes the further point that when giving feedback, relatively diplomatic language is used when making negative points (e.g. *occasionally heated*). This prepares Ss for brainstorming the opposites of the adjectives which would also be suitable in the same context.

11 Ss brainstorm opposites of the adjectives. During feedback T should emphasise the opposites which are more useful and downgrade those which Ss are less likely to use actively. T also reminds Ss of ways of storing vocabulary as discussed in Unit 3 **Exam focus: Vocabulary**.

useful	useless (more diplomatic: *not very useful*)
helpful	unhelpful
productive	unproductive
intelligent	stupid (diplomatic: *unintelligent*)
exciting	dull, boring (diplomatic: *unexciting*)
busy	quiet
interesting	boring (diplomatic: *uninteresting*)
brief	long
professional	unprofessional
well-prepared	badly-prepared
positive	negative (diplomatic: *disappointing*)
hard	easy
rewarding	unrewarding
serious	light-hearted
heated	calm

T draws attention to the fact that as *hard* has two meanings, it also has two opposites: *easy* and *soft*. T also points out that *brief* is used for time but not for physical things. Ss will need to know these things for **Ex 3** of **Self-study**.

12 **Ex 4**: T prepares for this by discussing the function of feedback forms and their general usefulness. Ss then listen for Jodie's feedback and complete the form.

Content:	*Interesting sessions and good speakers.*
Organisation:	*A lot better than last year. 30 delegates was just perfect.*
Venue/Accommodation:	*The conference rooms were good and the hotel rooms were clean and comfortable.*
Suggestions:	*Have the next conference in the same hotel. Have the Saturday night dinner in another restaurant.*
Any other comments:	*Saturday night dinner was not good: the food wasn't very good and the service was slow.*

13 **Ex 5**: T may wish to help Ss by asking what criteria they would use to judge a conference. (e.g. *venue, food*). Ss work in pairs and then T elicits general feedback.

2 Answer the questions.

1 What is Vitesse going to do as a result of the guest speaker's session?
2 In which session did the speakers make short presentations?
3 How has the company performed over the last twelve months?
4 What did the delegates find difficult to agree on?

Vocabulary 3 Read the extracts from the report again and underline all the adjectives describing the sessions. What are the opposites of the adjectives?

Listening 2 4 All the Vitesse delegates have to fill in a feedback form. Listen to Jodie Cox talk to a colleague about the conference and fill in the form for her.

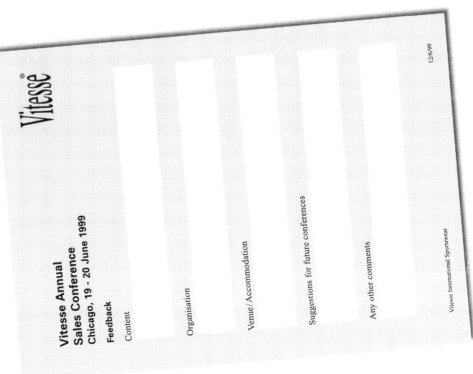

Vitesse®

**Vitesse Annual
Sales Conference
Chicago, 19 - 20 June 1999**

Feedback

Content

Organisation

Venue/Accommodation

Suggestions for future conferences

Any other comments

Vitesse International Sportswear

12/6/99

Speaking 5 Work in pairs. What makes a good conference?

Exam practice

- Look at questions 1-5.
- In each question, which sentence is correct?
- For each question, mark the correct letter **A**, **B** or **C**.

1 | Due to circumstances beyond our control, the conference will be postponed. |

A The conference will take place as planned.
B The conference will not take place.
C The conference will take place at a later date.

2 | Delegates are asked to check out by 10.30am. |

The delegates should leave their rooms
A before half past ten.
B at ten thirty.
C earlier than half past eleven.

3 | Could all speakers please produce summaries of the sessions they gave. |

The speakers should write
A full details of what is in their session.
B a brief report about their session.
C a proposal for their session.

4 | **WORKSHOPS**
Improving margins   **Wagner suite**
Selling on the telephone   **Schumann suite**
Marketing new products   **Bach suite** |

The workshop on increasing profits will be in the
A Wagner suite.
B Schumann suite.
C Bach suite.

5 | Mr Sylvester is used to giving presentations to large audiences. |

Mr Sylvester
A doesn't give presentations to large groups any more.
B often gave presentations to large groups in the past.
C often gives presentations to large groups.

---

1 Complete the following sentences in your own words.

1 We'll send everyone a memo as soon as …
  we make the final arrangements.
2 We can't book the rooms until …
3 I'll give you the programme before …
4 The conference will finish after …
5 We'll start the session as soon as …
6 I'll copy the report for you when …

2 Look at the adjectives below. Write the opposite adjective next to it.

1 helpful   *unhelpful*
2 well-prepared
3 positive
4 useful
5 productive
6 exciting
7 rewarding

3 Write the opposites of the sentences below.

1 She sent me a *long* conference report.
  She sent me a short conference report.
2 The conference was *hard* to organise.
3 She gave a *long* sales presentation.
4 Some of the sessions were too *long*.
5 The hotel beds were very *hard*.
6 The journey to the restaurant was *long*.
7 The speaker was *hard* to understand.

Tapescript: Listening 1

Good morning everybody. Welcome to the 7th annual International Sales Conference. It's great to see so many of you - old faces and new ones! Now we're going to have two very busy days as usual, but I am sure you'll enjoy them. As soon as I finish, which won't be long, I promise you, we'll begin with our first session, which is our Sales Managers giving their National Sales Reports for their own countries.

We'll stay together for that session as I feel it's useful for everybody to see the overall picture. Then, after we've had lunch, we're going to divide into groups to discuss our targets for next year and how to reach them. At four o'clock we'll come back together again when Amy Carter, our guest speaker, gives her presentation. As you all know, the consultants, Allman & Partners have been looking at the way we answer the telephone throughout the group and Amy is going to give a short report on their findings. Her presentation will probably finish just before 5.30.

Dinner this evening is at eight o'clock. We'd like everyone to meet in the bar for drinks from about seven o'clock. That way we can enjoy a drink together until the coach leaves for the restaurant at 7.45.

Tomorrow morning we're starting at nine o'clock with a look at ways of marketing the new product. This'll also be a workshop session. Then there'll be a coffee break before we come back together again and share our ideas with a feedback session. And that will bring us to the end of the conference and a farewell lunch. So, that's enough from me. I'd just like to wish you all an enjoyable and successful two days and hand you over to Jodie Cox, who's going to start with a look at Canadian sales.

Tapescript: Listening 2

Colleague So how did the conference go, Jodie?

Jodie Oh it was good. All the sessions were interesting and all the speakers were really good. The organisation was a lot better this year, as well. I think having a smaller number of people there made a big difference. You know, you could actually get things done in the workshops and make decisions a lot more quickly. There were about 30 delegates altogether, which was just perfect.

Colleague And how was the hotel?

Jodie Fine. The conference rooms were a good size and the hotel rooms were clean and very comfortable. I really liked the hotel a lot. I think we should go there again next year.

Colleague And how was dinner on Saturday?

Jodie Ah, that was probably the only thing that people really complained about. The food wasn't very good and the service was slow. If we go back to the same hotel again, we'll have to find another restaurant.

Exam focus: Listening

Objectives:	To familiarise Ss with the content of the Listening Test
	To provide useful tips
	To practise the Listening Test

Materials needed: None

Unit overview

- **The Listening Test**

  T gives an overview of the Listening Test.

- **Before you listen**

  Ss read the listening tips.

  Ss look at some exam questions to practise predicting vocabulary before listening.

- **While listening**

  T takes Ss through information about first and second listenings.

- **After listening**

  Ss read post-listening tips then find mistakes in candidates' answers.

- **Exam practice**

  Part One: Multiple-choice (short texts).

  Part Two: Gap-filling (numbers).

  Part Three: Gap-filling (words or numbers).

  Part Four: Multiple-choice (longer text).

The Listening Test

If T is unfamiliar with the Listening Test, he/she should look at the following:
- *BEC 1: Teachers' Information Pack*
- *UCLES BEC1 Sample Papers*
- *Linguarama Cambridge BEC 1 Practice Tests 1 and 2.*

1 **Warmer (books closed):** T elicits from Ss what the Listening Test consists of.

2 Ss open their books and read the information about the examination. T tells them that they are allowed to write on their examination papers in pencil but must transfer their answers to an Answer Sheet at the end of the test, for which ten minutes is allowed.

3 T takes Ss briefly through the four parts of the test in the unit to ensure Ss understand the requirements of each: in all parts Ss have to listen for specific information rather than for gist and do multiple-choice or gap-fill exercises. T tells Ss that they are going to do each part of the Listening Test during the lesson, focusing in detail on how to do each part successfully.

Before listening

4 **(Books closed),** T asks Ss their experience of doing the listening exercises so far in *Pass Cambridge BEC 1.* T elicits from Ss that they do not need to listen for every word. T also tells Ss that in the exam each text is played twice so Ss always have a chance to check their answers. T then asks Ss to brainstorm a list of good advice for candidates. T divides this into:
Before listening: e.g. read instructions carefully; check what is required - numbers or words; note how many words are needed to fill the gaps; predict probable content from what they read beforehand.
While listening: e.g. don't try to pick up every word and concentrate on the information as a whole, to begin with.
After listening: e.g. check to make sure all the questions are answered; when transferring answers to the Answer Sheet, double-check they have given the required number of answers.

5 **Ex ❶:** Ss then open their books and T takes them through the tips on pre-listening.

6 **Ex ❷:** T reminds Ss of the importance of predicting language from what is already provided in the task. Ss read the two questions and predict vocabulary. (They will not hear the actual recordings in this case but T can encourage them to use the same strategy later in the unit when doing Part One of the test.

Suggested answers:
1 A: *increase/rise slightly, fall/drop sharply*
  B: *increase/rise steadily, steady increase/rise*
  C: *fall/drop sharply, recover strongly, strong recovery, same level*

2 A: *elevator, not working, stuck, stairs*
  B: *food unavailable, sick(ness), out to a restaurant/café, eat sandwiches*
  C: *silence, take a test, candidates*

While listening

7 T takes Ss through the information on first and second listenings.

After listening

8 **Ex ❶:** T takes Ss through the post-listening tips. Ss then work in pairs and find the mistakes in the answers.

The candidate:
- *did not complete all the questions (13 not done)*
- *wrote more than the required word limit (four rather than one or two words in 14)*
- *answered 24 with two answers rather than one.*

T in feedback emphasises the overriding importance of thorough checking and good examination techniques in Cambridge BEC 1. T points out that although the examples on page 82 are presented on the question papers, final answers will, of course, be transferred to the Answer Sheet in the examination. Nevertheless, the point about checking answers very carefully is just as valid.

Exam focus: Listening

The Listening Test

The Cambridge BEC 1 Listening Test has four parts.

Part	Input	Task
1	Short conversations	Multiple-choice
2	Short conversation or monologue	Gap-filling (numbers)
3	Two telephone conversations	Gap-filling (words or numbers)
4	A longer conversation or monologue (3-4 mins)	Multiple-choice

Length: A total of 12 minutes of listening material played twice, plus 10 minutes at the end to transfer answers to the Answer Sheet.

Before listening

1 It is important that you use your time well even **before** you listen. Here are some tips.

- Always read the instructions very carefully before you listen.
- Check the type of answer you need to give. Is it a letter, numbers or words?
- Check the number of words you should write for each answer.
- You will always be given time to read through the questions before you listen. Use this time well. Try to predict words you might hear and what the answer might be.

2 Work in pairs. Look at the Listening Test below. Predict words that you might hear in the recordings.

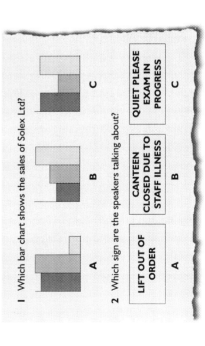

1 Which bar chart shows the sales of Solex Ltd?

2 Which sign are the speakers talking about?

LIFT OUT OF ORDER	CANTEEN CLOSED DUE TO STAFF ILLNESS	QUIET PLEASE EXAM IN PROGRESS
A	B	C

While listening

You will hear every part of the Listening Test twice.

First listening

Try to get an idea of the general context and answer as many of the questions as possible. However, do not worry if you do not understand every word. Also, do not worry if you do not know all the answers yet. The second listening will give you a second chance.

Second listening

Do not stop listening if you think you know the answer with multiple-choice questions the recordings often include words from the incorrect options. Listen for negatives and words such as *but* or *instead of*.

After listening

1 In order to obtain a high mark, you need to check carefully. Here are some tips.

- Make sure that you give only **one** answer for each question.
- Make sure that you answer **every** question.
- Check your answers after transferring them on to the Answer Sheet.

Find the candidates' mistakes on the question papers below.

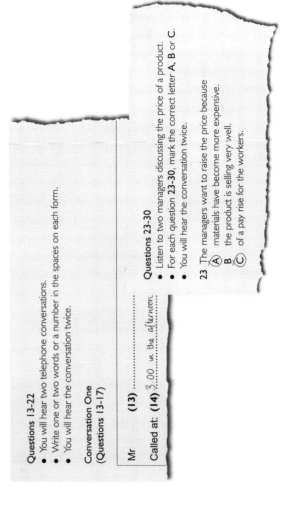

Questions 13-22

- You will hear two telephone conversations.
- Write one or two words or a number in the spaces on each form.
- You will hear the conversation twice.

Conversation One
(Questions 13-17)

Mr **(13)** ....

Called at: **(14)** 3.00 in the afternoon

Questions 23-30

- Listen to two managers discussing the price of a product.
- For each question **23-30**, mark the correct letter A, B or C.
- You will hear the conversation twice.

23 The managers want to raise the price because
   A materials have become more expensive.
   B the product is selling very well.
   C of a pay rise for the workers.

Part One

9   Ss listen to Part One and write their answers.

In feedback T reminds Ss that they should always wait until the end of the dialogue before deciding the answers as distractors may appear in the conversations (e.g. references to Asian food and mention of *spicy* for Question 2 when in fact the answer relates to Italian food). T also reminds Ss that they have the chance to check their answers on the second listening.

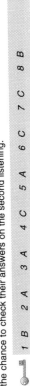

| 1 B | 2 A | 3 A | 4 C | 5 A | 6 C | 7 C | 8 B |

Part Two

10 Ss read through the tips for Part Two. T emphasises that this part of the Listening Test requires candidates to write numbers rather than words. T tells Ss that one or more distractors occur during the listening. They should therefore make their final decision about their answers only after listening to the whole conversation. T repeats the point that Ss will hear the conversation twice so the second listening will enable them to check their answers.

11 Ss listen and complete their answers to Part Two. T goes through the answers with Ss to deal with any queries.

| 9 10 | 10 £10.60 | 11 1,000 | 12 £16.99 |

Part Three

12 Ss read through the tips for Part Three. T emphasises that for this part of the test the candidate is required to find information of a general nature requiring words and numbers. The information could be names, addresses, times, prices, dates or spellings. All names will be repeated and spelt on the cassette unless they are real words (e.g. *Church Street* in question 15). Before listening, T may wish to practise some of the most common S problem areas here by asking Ss to pronounce certain vowels with which they have problems (*i, e, a*) or numbers (*thirty/thirteen*).

13 Ss listen and answer the questions

Conversation 1	13 *Askey*	14 *Riverside Books*	15 *Church Street*
	16 *Managing Tomorrow*	17 *£13.50*	
Conversation 2	18 *8 - 10*	19 *Senator Hotel*	20 *seminar*
	21 *Buffet lunch*	22 *Drinks*	

Part Four

14 T reminds Ss that the listening for this part is a long monologue or conversation and takes them through the tips.

15 Ss should begin by reading the instructions and questions to establish the context and predict the type of language they might hear (as in Part One). Ss report back (job appraisal with probable discussion of negative and positive aspects of the job and improvements/plans to be made).

T elicits good practice for dealing with extended listening texts: do not be distracted by redundant and possibly technical information; focus on listening for the information asked for; listen to all the conversation or monologue rather than stopping listening when you think you have got the answers required. T reminds Ss that there will be distractors within the listening material and that the questions are in the same order as the information appears on the cassette.

16 Ss listen to Part Four and complete the answers.

| 23 B | 24 B | 25 C | 26 B | 27 B | 28 A | 29 C | 30 C |

Part One

Questions 1-8

- For questions **1-8**, you will hear eight short recordings.
- For each question, mark one letter **A**, **B** or **C**.
- You will hear each recording **twice**.

1 What is Maria's job title?
A Sales Executive
B Marketing Manager
C Managing Director

2 Where are they going to take the visitors?

The Italian Experience	The Thai House	The Potato House
A	B	C

3 What was the final decision about the meeting?
A It will take place as arranged.
B It will take place at a later date.
C It will not take place.

4 Which part of the job offer was George unhappy about?
A The amount of pay.
B The number of hours.
C The number of holidays.

5 Which graph is the Head of Department talking about?

A   B   C

6 When are the visitors arriving?
A Ten o'clock.
B Half past ten.
C Eleven o'clock.

7 Which photocopier do they decide to buy?
A The X40.
B The BT100.
C The RX200.

8 Which part of the factory does Alan want to change?
A The packing hall.
B The warehouse.
C The production line.

Part Two

Listening tips

1 Read the instructions carefully.
2 Read the information before you listen.
3 **Do not** write any words as answers.
4 Use the second listening to check your answers.
5 Transfer your answers carefully to the Answer Sheet.

Questions 9-12

- Look at the notes below.
- You will hear two people discussing an order for office equipment.
- Listen to the conversation and write the missing **numbers** in the spaces.
- You will hear the conversation twice.

Order for office equipment

Item	Pack size	Price
Pens - blue	20	£3.40
Highlighters **(9)**	12	£9.40
Markers - fine	12	**(10)** £ ......
Markers - fat	10	£38.30
Envelopes C6 **(11)**		£31.25
Envelopes C4	250	**(12)** £ ......

Part Three

Listening tips

1 Read the instructions carefully.
2 Read the information before you listen.
3 Think about what kind of information the answer might be: a name, address, number etc.
4 Use the second listening to check your answers.
5 Transfer your answers carefully to the Answer Sheet.

Questions 13-22

- You will hear two telephone conversations.
- Write **one or two words or a number** in the spaces on each form.
- You will hear the conversation twice.

Conversation One

Questions 13-17

- You will hear a woman ordering some books.
- Complete the form using the information you hear.

BOOK ORDER FORM

Caller: Michelle **(13)** _____

Date: 12 May

Company: **(14)** _____

Address: *The Riverside Centre*

            (15) _____

            Birmingham B2 5UG

Title: **(16)** _____

Quantity: *50*

Price: **(17)** _____ *per book*

Conversation Two

Questions 18-22

- You will hear a woman confirming some arrangements.
- Complete the form using the information you hear.

Conference details

Company: *Sonic Industries*

Dates: **(18)** _____
            January

Location: *The* **(19)** _____
            Manchester

Delegates: *32*

Rooms: *One conference room*
            Two **(20)** _____
            rooms

Included:
- *Dinner on Friday evening*
- **(21)** _____ *on Saturday*
- *Dinner on Saturday evening*
- *Sunday lunch*
- **(22)** _____ *during dinner*

Part Four

Listening tips

1 Read the instructions and questions carefully.
2 Do not worry if you miss the answer first time.
3 Use the second listening to check your answers.
4 Transfer your answers carefully to the Answer Sheet.

Questions 23-30

- Listen to a Head of Department talking to an employee about her performance.
- For each question **23-30**, mark the correct letter **A**, **B** or **C**.
- You will hear the conversation twice.

23 Sharon started working for the company
A some time last year.
B one year ago.
C over a year ago.

24 Sharon found out about the vacancy from
A a friend.
B a newspaper.
C an internal memo.

25 Sharon does not enjoy
A answering the telephone.
B typing invoices.
C preparing price lists.

26 The biggest problem with the computer is that
A she doesn't know the program very well.
B it regularly stops working.
C the monitor is too small.

27 Sharon would like the company to buy
A new software.
B new computers.
C new monitors.

28 When dealing with complaints, she would like to
A take more responsibility.
B pass the customer on to her boss.
C give the customers money back.

29 Sharon's boss thinks that some customers
A often receive faulty orders.
B often make mistakes.
C are not always honest.

30 Sharon's main aim for next year is to
A get to know the customers a lot better.
B make fewer mistakes.
C learn more about the products.

Production

Objectives:	To enable Ss to talk about production processes and problems at work
	To practise listening for specific information
	To review the passive

Materials needed: Cassette - *Pass Cambridge BEC 1*

Unit overview

● Bread production

Listening 1	Ss order the stages of the baguette making process before listening to the Production Manager to check the order. Ss then listen again and label the machinery in the bakery.
Speaking	Ss say what happens at each of the machines in the production line.
Language focus	Ss review the passive.
Vocabulary	Ss match verbs and nouns taken from the tapescript. Ss think of another noun to go with each verb.
Speaking	Ss describe a process using as many verbs as possible.

● Production problems

Listening 2	Ss work in pairs and decide which type of problems would be most common at the bakery. Ss then listen to the Production Manager and check their answers. Ss listen again and complete sentences halves with *when* and *if*.
Language focus	Ss review the difference between *when* and *if*.
	Ss match sentence halves and complete them with *when/if*.

● Self-study

Language focus	Transformation exercise (passive).
Writing	Describing a process (from a flow chart).
Vocabulary	Word fields (machines/processes).
Exam practice	*Memo writing (Writing Test Part 2).*

Bread production

Although some of the language in this unit looks technical, most of it is very general. T should explain to Ss that bread production is a relatively simple context for the description of a process. The final objective is for Ss to be able to describe a process which is relevant to them.

1 **Warmer (books closed)**: Before Ss open their books, T introduces the subject of making bread and tries to elicit some of the vocabulary by asking Ss whether they have ever made their own bread and what the ingredients are.

2 **Ex ❶**: T asks Ss to read the seven stages of making baguettes and order them. T offers no feedback but plays the cassette when Ss are ready. Ss check their own answers before T offers feedback.

> 1 weigh ingredients (flour, yeast and water)
> 2 mix the dough
> 3 form the baguettes
> 4 bake the baguettes
> 5 cool the baguettes
> 6 wrap the baguettes
> 7 box the baguettes

3 **Ex ❷**: Ss listen again and label the machines on the ground plan of the bakery.

> 2 divider   3 first prover   4 baguette former   5 circuit
> 6 second prover 7 oven   8 cooler

4 **Ex ❸**: Ss say what happens at each of the machines listed in the previous exercise. The task should encourage Ss to use the passive, but at this point it is not essential that they do so as the focus is more on meaning than form. T puts the answers on the board to set up the next exercise.

> 1 mixers   The ingredients are mixed.
> 2 divider   The dough is divided into pieces.
> 3 first prover   The dough proves.
> 4 baguette former The dough is formed into baguettes.
> 5 circuit   The baguettes are taken along the production line.
> 6 second prover   The baguettes prove again.
> 7 oven   The baguettes are baked.
> 8 cooler   Cool air is blown over the baguettes to cool them.

5 **Ex ❹**: The sentences from the previous exercise give examples of active and passive sentences. These can be highlighted by T, who elicits reasons for using the passive (subject unknown, subject unimportant, subject obvious, style, genre). Ss then complete the description of how to form the passive voice.

> **The Passive**
> • The passive is formed with the verb **to be** (in the correct tense) and the **past participle/3rd form** of the verb.

6 **Ex ❺**: Ss complete the table, which includes verbs and nouns taken from the unit. The table offers Ss the chance to refine their understanding of the meaning of the verbs by checking if they can be used with each noun. After completing the table, Ss think of another noun which each verb could be used with. During feedback, Ss give example sentences using the verbs and nouns.

	weigh	mix	bake	cool	wrap	box	despatch
ingredients	✓	✓					
dough	✓	✓	✓				
baguettes			✓	✓	✓	✓	✓
boxes						✓	✓

7 **Ex ❻**: Ss work in pairs and think of the description of a process involving as many of the verbs as possible. (T may wish to make the activity competitive with the winners being the pair who have used the most verbs.) Ss present their answers in the form of a process with each stage listed in order and connected by sequencers, as in the example given. The exercise could also be set as homework.

Production

Bread production

Listening 1 **1** Brian Benfield, Production Manager at Gossens, a UK food group, explains how baguettes are produced. Before you listen, put the following stages of the process into the correct order.

☐ cool the baguettes ☐ box the baguettes ☐ mix the dough
☐ wrap the baguettes ☐ form the baguettes ☐ bake the baguettes
☐ weigh the ingredients (flour, yeast and water)

Now listen and check your answers.

2 Look at the floorplan below. Listen again and write the correct numbers next to the following:

☐ circuit ☐ first prover ☐ baguette former ☐ mixers
☐ divider ☐ second prover ☐ oven ☐ cooler

Floorplan of the bakery

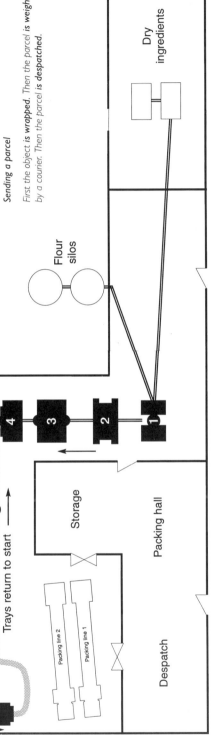

Flour silos

Dry ingredients

Packaging store

Trays return to start

Storage

Packing hall

Packing line 2
Packing line 1

Despatch

Production

Speaking **3** What happens at each of the machines on the production line?

---

4 Complete the information below.

The Passive

The passive is formed with the verb _____ (in the correct tense) and the _____ of the verb.
The *ingredients* **are weighed.**
The *company* **was set up** in 1982.

Vocabulary **5** Which verbs can be used with each noun? Tick (✔) the correct boxes.

	weigh	mix	bake	cool	wrap	box	despatch
ingredients	✔						
dough							
baguettes							
boxes							

Now think of another noun to go with each verb.

weigh .... wrap ....
mix .... box ....
bake .... despatch ....
cool ....

Speaking **6** Work in pairs. Think of three processes. How many of the verbs below can you use to describe each process?

| check | cool | cut | despatch | heat |
| mix | press | weigh | wrap | collect |

Sending a parcel

*First the object **is wrapped**. Then the parcel **is weighed**. It is taken to the post office or **collected** by a courier. Then the parcel **is despatched**.*

Production problems

8 Ss predict which type of problems would be the most common at the bakery and then listen to the Production Manager to check their answers. T replays the cassette to check the answers.

Human problems   Not often. The mixerman can forget to put in yeast and additives.
Electronic problems A lot of problems with sensors, sometimes problems with mixers.
Mechanical   Occasionally an old tray can jam in a prover or oven.

9 **Ex ❷**: Ss listen again and complete the sentences. As Ss have to write a lot down quickly, T tells Ss to make notes the first time, then gives Ss a moment to expand their notes before playing the cassette again. (Although the answers below show exactly the same words as on the cassette, Ss only need to complete the sentences with a logical meaning.)

1 *The computer stops the whole process* **when a sensor stops working properly.**
2 *If the computer gets a mix wrong,* **we have to clean it all out of the mixer.**
3 *If the mixerman forgets the yeast and additives,* **we lose the whole mix.**
4 *When an old tray loses its shape,* **it can jam in an oven or prover.**
5 *We can lose up to an hour and a half of production* **if we have a really bad day.**

10 T then uses the sentences to lead into a focus on the difference in meaning between *when* and *if*. T draws Ss' attention to the **Don't forget!** section. Despite the fact that this unit refers to *if* clauses, it does not focus on conditionals; it simply attempts to clarify the meaning of *when* and *if*. The next unit, 13b, deals with Conditional 1.

11 **Ex ❸**: Ss match the sentence halves using the **Don't forget!** section to help them choose *when* or *if*. T allows the class to correct each other before offering feedback.

2 *The baguettes do not rise if the dough does not prove first.*
3 *The line produces 6,000 baguettes an hour when everything runs properly.*
4 *The baguettes are taken off the trays when they have left the cooler.*
5 *Old trays can damage machines if they get jammed in them.*
6 *The baguettes burn if the oven temperature is too high.*

12 **Ex ❹**: Ss ask each other about typical things that go wrong at work and how they deal with these situations. Feedback could lead to general discussion or the class deciding which problems are the most serious and how they could be dealt with.

Self-study

Ex ❶:
2 *The ingredients are fed into the mixers.*
3 *The baguettes are dropped onto a tray.*
4 *The baguettes are baked for 10 minutes.*
5 *Cool air is blown over the baguettes.*
6 *The baguettes are packed into boxes.*

Ex ❷: *Suggested answer:*

First of all, the production line and sensors are checked before the line is started. If the line does not start, the sensors are re-set and the line is started again. After the line has started, the ingredients are fed into the mixers. If the mix is not correct, the mixer is cleaned out and the ingredients are fed in again. If the mix is correct, the dough is then sent to the divider.

Ex ❸: *Machines:*
cooler, oven, divider, packing machine, former

(The names of many machines are formed by adding -er to the verb.)

Processes:
mix, divide, form, bake, prove, cool, wrap, box, despatch

Ingredients:
water, yeast, additives

Ex ❹: *Suggested answer: (21 words)*

The 8200 packing machines are not set correctly for the new packaging. Please check all settings when using the new packaging.

Essential vocabulary

Process	General
to bake	*circuit*
to box	to damage
to check	*dough*
to collect	electronic
to cool	human
to despatch	production line
to divide	ingredients
to feed	*mechanical*
to form	oven
to mix	*sensor*
to weigh	*shape*
to wrap	*tray*

The words in italics are not on the Cambridge BEC 1 wordlist.

Production problems

Listening 2 **1** Brian Benfield talks about production problems at the bakery. Before you listen, decide which of the following would cause problems most often. Then listen and compare your answers.

- human problems
- electronic problems
- mechanical problems

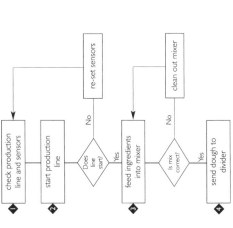
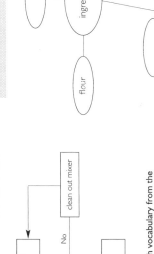

2 Listen again and complete the sentences.

1 The computer stops the whole process ___
2 If the computer gets the mix wrong, ___
3 If a mixerman forgets the yeast and additives, ___
4 When an old tray loses its shape, ___
5 We can lose up to an hour and a half of production ___

When or if?

- **When** is used when we expect something to happen.
  The trays pass through a sensor when they enter the oven.
- **If** is used when we are unsure if something will happen.
  We can lose an hour and a half if we have a really bad day. Unit 46

Grammar **3** Match the following sentence halves and complete the sentences with *when* or *if*.

The trays pass a sensor when they enter or exit any machine.

1 The trays pass a sensor — they get jammed in them.
2 The baguettes do not rise — they enter or exit any machine.
3 The line produces 6,000 baguettes an hour — the oven temperature is too high.
4 The baguettes are taken off the trays — the dough does not prove first.
5 Old trays can damage machines — everything runs properly.
6 The baguettes burn — they have left the cooler.

Speaking **4** Work in pairs. What goes wrong at your partner's place of work? What does he/she do when things go wrong?

Exam practice

- You are the Production Manager at a factory.
- You notice that some packing machines are not set correctly for some new packaging.
- Write a memo to all packing machine operators:
  * explaining the problem
  * saying which machines are having problems
  * asking them to check the machine settings.
- Write about **20 words**.

MEMO

To: All packing machine operators
From: Production Manager

1 Rewrite the following sentences using the passive.

1 We weigh the ingredients.
  The ingredients are weighed.
2 The system feeds the ingredients into the mixers.
3 A machine drops the baguettes onto a tray.
4 Ovens bake the baguettes for ten minutes.
5 A blower blows cool air over the baguettes.
6 Packing machines pack the baguettes in boxes.

2 Look at the flow chart below. Write a short text describing the start-up process for the baguette production line. Add any words which are necessary (articles, sequencers etc.).

1 check production line and sensors
2 start production line
Does line start? → No → re-set sensors / Yes
3 feed ingredients into mixer
Is mix correct? → No → clean out mixer / Yes
4 send dough to divider

3 Complete the diagram with vocabulary from the tapescript for Listening 1 on page 140.

ingredients — flour, weigh
processes
machines — prover

Tapescript: Listening 1

Brian So, this is a diagram of the bakery. Now it all begins with the main ingredients, those are flour and water. They're weighed and fed automatically into mixers. Yeast and additives are then added by hand and everything is mixed together for twelve minutes to make the dough.

Visitor What are the additives for?

Brian They're just to increase the shelf-life of the baguettes. The dough is then divided into pieces. And after the weight is checked, the dough enters the first prover for ten minutes.

Visitor The first what?

Brian Prover.

Visitor What's a prover?

Brian I can tell you haven't baked bread before.

Visitor No, that's very true!

Brian Well, you can't bake the dough straight away. You have to let it stand for a while so the yeast can react before you form it. This is called proving. Well now, the yeast makes the dough rise, and gives the bread shape and volume.

Visitor Oh, right. I see.

Brian So, the dough is then formed into a baguette and dropped onto trays which then continuously go round a circuit. The trays take the baguettes into another prover for 60 minutes. The temperature in the prover is perfect for the yeast to make the bread rise even more.

Visitor 60 minutes, that long?

Brian Well, the prover stage is very important. If the bread doesn't prove properly, you can't bake it. Now the trays then continue around the circuit to the oven, where the bread is baked for ten minutes. And after leaving the oven, the trays enter the cooler. That's where cool air is blown over them for 40 minutes. The baguettes are then taken off the trays and dropped into plastic baskets for packaging. And the trays continue around the circuit and go back to the start again.

Visitor And what happens to the baguettes?

Brian They're taken to the packing hall, where they're wrapped, boxed and despatched.

Visitor And how long does the whole process take?

Brian From flour to boxed products takes about two and a half hours.

Tapescript: Listening 2

Visitor So, Brian, what problems do you have with the production line?

Brian Well, we have a lot of problems with sensors. These are electronic sensors that tell the computer when a tray enters or leaves a prover or oven. The computer monitors the circuit and controls the speed of the trays. The computer stops the whole process when a sensor stops working properly - a complete shutdown.

Visitor Really?

Brian Well, you have to remember that the line produces 6,000 baguettes an hour. The timing has to be perfect or the system stops. The sensors have to be set up exactly right. If they aren't, the computer won't start the system.

Visitor What other problems do you have?

Brian Well, sometimes we have problems with the mixers. If the computer gets the mix wrong, we have to clean out the whole mixer.

Visitor Do you have any problems with your workers?

Brian Not often, no. The system produces a new mix every 12 minutes, so it is possible that a mixerman can forget to put in the yeast and additives. If he forgets the extra ingredients, we lose the whole mix.

Visitor Any other kinds of problems?

Brian Occasionally we have mechanical problems. Like when an old tray loses its shape, it can jam in a prover or oven. That can be a big problem because it can damage a machine and jam the whole system.

Visitor So how much time do you lose a day on average?

Brian That's difficult to say, really. On a good day maybe 6 minutes. We can lose up to an hour and a half of production if we have a really bad day. And that means nearly 10,000 baguettes.

Quality control

<table>
<tr><td>**Objectives:**</td><td>To enable Ss to discuss quality control
To practise listening for specific information
To review Conditional 1 and language for making suggestions</td></tr>
<tr><td>**Materials needed:**</td><td>Cassette - *Pass Cambridge BEC 1*
Cards - 13 cards: *Pass Cambridge BEC 1* Unit 13b/1-13 One set per pair/group</td></tr>
</table>

Unit overview

- ### Monitoring quality

  Warmer   T elicits three verbs related to quality control.

  Speaking   Ss discuss the work of a quality control manager.

  Listening 1   Ss listen to the Head of Quality Control talk about monitoring quality in a factory and complete a table. Ss listen again and answer more detailed comprehension questions.

  Speaking   Ss discuss QC processes at their place of work.

- ### Improving quality

  Listening 2   Ss listen to a discussion of quality problems and answer general questions followed by multiple-choice questions.

  Language focus   Ss look at the tapescript and underline and categorise uses of the present simple. Ss then review Conditional 1. Ss write conditional sentences from prompts.

  Speaking   Factory maze. T (or Ss in turn) read out problems and options. Ss discuss the options and make decisions.

- ### Self-study

  Vocabulary   Matching exercise (word partnerships) followed by a gap-fill exercise with the same words.

                Matching exercise (opposites) followed by a gap-fill exercise with the same words.

  Language focus   Gap-fill exercise (conditional 1).

  Exam practice   *Matching exercise (Reading Test Part 2).*

Monitoring quality

1 **Warmer (books closed):** Before Ss open their books, T writes QC on the board and elicits that it stands for *quality control*. T asks Ss to think of three verbs connected with quality control. Ss open their books and compare with the verbs in **Ex ❶**. T may need to point out that although the noun *control* is used with the idea of checking (*quality control*, *passport control* etc.), the verb is not. In English the verb *control* has the idea of being in charge or in power; it does not mean *check*.

2 **Ex ❶:** T explains the meaning of the verbs in the box. Ss talk about their understanding of the job of a quality control manager using the verbs.

Check: He/she *checks* the quality of the raw materials, *checks* quality during the production process and *checks* the finished products.
Monitor: He/she *monitors* the production process.
Inspect: He/she *inspects* the raw materials, *inspects* the product at various stages of production and *inspects* the finished goods.
Sample: He/she *samples* the product during production and at the finished goods stage.
Reject: He/she *rejects* any products where the quality is too low/unacceptable.

3 **Ex ❷:** T introduces Coopers and elicits from Ss quality problems there might be with snacks (crispness, flavour/taste, freshness, hygiene, size) to feed in essential vocabulary. Ss then listen and complete the table.

Quality control - Inspection points

1 Suppliers	2 Goods in	3 *Production*	4 *Finished goods*
• QC processes	• quantities	• *cooking oil*	• *packet weight*
• *factory hygiene*	• quality	• *flavouring*	• *packet seal*
	• *transport*	• *size*	• *taste*
	packaging	• *crispness*	

4 **Ex ❸:** Ss listen again and answer more detailed questions.

1 *Because if Coopers are not happy with their hygiene, they'll cancel the supply contract.*
2 *Because if the packaging is damaged, the warehouse shelf-life can be reduced.*
3 *If the snacks are too oily, they go soft.*
4 *By eating them. Also by doing chemical analysis to check things like fat levels.*

5 **Ex ❹:** Ss discuss QC processes. This does not have to be in production. It may, for example, be a system to ensure customer satisfaction in a hotel or a system to ensure accuracy and timeliness in an accounts department.

For pre-experience Ss, T could put the names of famous companies on the board (e.g. Volkswagen, Benetton, Pepsi) and ask Ss to describe what they think their QC processes are.

Improving quality

6 Before beginning this section, T may wish to elicit the process of making such snacks in order to base the listening in a firmer context. T does not need to do this, but should T want further information, the process is as follows:

1 *Ingredients are mixed (maize, water, additives).*
2 *The mix is formed into shapes.*
3 *The snacks are cooked in oil.*
4 *They are then put into a flavour drum, where flavouring is added.*
5 *The snacks are put into bags, and boxed.*

7 **Ex ❶:** Ss answer the four questions which check their general understanding of the situation.

1 *Reject levels are high. (They have increased by 5% over the last three weeks.) The suggestion is that because of high demand, they are running at full capacity.*

2 *The oil temperature in the cookers keeps rising and falling so the samples don't always pick up high fat levels. (T might wish to explain that if the fat doesn't reach the correct temperature, the snacks don't cook properly. This leaves them soft and greasy. The higher the volume which is processed, the dirtier the oil becomes, potentially causing problems.)*

3 *Keith: Increase the sampling rate*

   Pauline: Change the cooker temperature sensors
   *   Change the cooking oil more often*

4 *Jack decides to try all three things for two weeks on a trial basis: change the oil more often and monitor the sensors; he also wants to increase the sampling rate by just 10%.*

8 **Ex ❷:** Ss listen for more detail and answer the multiple-choice questions.

1 B   2 B   3 C   4 A   5 A

Quality control

Monitoring quality

Speaking **1** What does the job of a quality control (QC) manager at a snacks factory involve? Use the verbs below.

check   monitor   inspect   sample   reject

Listening 1 **2** Pauline Carr is Head of Quality Control at Coopers, a UK snack producer. She talks about monitoring quality. Listen and complete the table below.

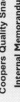

Quality Control at Coopers

Inspection points

1 Suppliers	2 Goods in	3 _____	4 Finished goods
• QC processes	• quantities	• cooking oil	• _____
• _____	• _____	• flavouring	• packet seal
• _____	• _____	• crispness	• _____

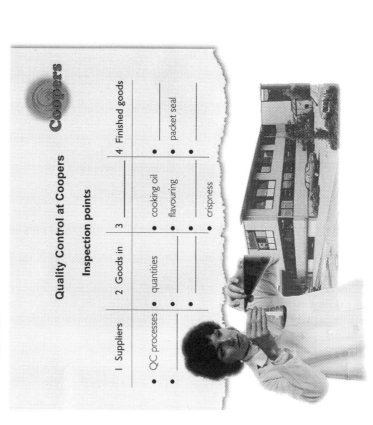

3 Listen again and answer the questions.

1 Why is hygiene very important for the supplier?
2 Why is it important to check transport packaging?
3 What happens if the snacks are too oily?
4 How do they check the taste of the snacks?

Speaking **4** Work in pairs. What QC processes are there at your partner's place of work?

Improving quality

Listening 2 **1** Pauline is in a meeting with Jack Simmons, the Production Director, and Keith Taylor, the Operations Manager. Read the memo below. Then listen to their discussion and answer the questions.

1 What is the problem?
2 What causes it?
3 Which proposals do Keith and Pauline each support?
4 What action does Jack decide to take?

Coopers Quality Snacks
Internal Memorandum

To: Pauline Carr
cc: Keith Taylor
From: Jack Simmons
Date: 8 March 1999

Re: QC Meeting   9 March 1999

Our reject levels have risen by over 5% in three weeks. Chemical analysis shows that fat levels are above the acceptable maximum. Please be prepared to discuss them at the meeting.

Here are some ideas for dealing with the problem.

   1 Increase the sampling rate
   2 Change the cooker temperature sensors
   3 Change the cooking oil more often

2 Listen again and choose the best option to complete the sentences.

1 The samples do not pick up the high fat levels because
  A the cooker does not work properly.
  B the oil temperature changes too quickly.
  C the factory is running at full capacity.

2 Pauline does not want to increase the sampling rate because she
  A thinks the rate is already good enough.
  B has not got enough staff in her department.
  C does not think it will make a difference.

3 Keith does not want to change the sensors because
  A the sensors are very expensive.
  B it would mean losing production.
  C he has already changed them.

4 The temperature sensors do not work properly
  A when the cooker oil gets dirty.
  B if samples are not taken regularly.
  C because the cookers are old.

5 Keith does not want to change the oil more often because
  A it will be expensive and cut production.
  B he thinks changing sensors is a better idea.
  C he does not think it will make a difference.

Self-study

Ex 1:
2 inspection points
3 shelf-life
4 finished goods
5 goods in
6 chemical analysis

1 finished goods
2 inspection points
3 quality control
4 shelf-life
5 goods in
6 chemical analysis

Ex 2:
2 goods in   finished goods
3 rise   fall
4 reject   accept
5 reduce   increase

1 demand
2 goods in/finished goods
3 finished goods/goods in
4 increase
5 suppliers
6 fall
7 rise
8 reject
9 reducing
10 accept

Ex 3:
2 change
3 doesn't make
4 increases
5 'll happen / 's going to happen
6 'll have to/'re going to have to
7 don't arrive
8 won't be/aren't/isn't going to be

won't make/isn't going to make
'll talk
'll have to/'re going to have to
keep
want
'll look/'re going to look
increase

Ex 4: 1 H   2 A   3 E   4 B   5 C

Essential vocabulary

Quality control	Factory	General
to analyse	capacity	demand
analysis	finished goods	flavouring
to inspect	goods in	hygiene
to reject	packaging	quality
to sample	shelf-life	quantity
	supplier	soft
	warehouse	taste
		workforce

The words in italics are not on the Cambridge BEC 1 wordlist.

---

9 **Ex 3:** The objective of this exercise is to lead Ss into an awareness of Conditional 1 forms. (A deliberate decision has been taken not to refer to Conditionals 1 and 2 in the student material as this suggests that conditionals consist of only a small number of discrete forms; however, for the sake of convenience, Conditional 1 and 2 are used in the Teacher's Guide.) T asks Ss to underline all examples of the present simple but not to describe the use of every example. T elicits the five categories below with suitable examples.

Suggested answers: Uses of the present simple

Stative verb,
e.g. we all **know** there's a problem

General facts,
e.g. that's why the samples **don't** always pick up high fat levels

Routines or regular activities,
e.g. It **keeps** falling or rising suddenly.

To refer to future time in time clauses,
e.g. before we **look** at ways of dealing with it

Conditionals (in the if clause - when referring to real possibilities in the future),
e.g. If we **take** samples more often, we'll pick up the rejects sooner.
We're going to lose capacity if we **stop** the line more often.

10 T draws Ss' attention to the comments in the **Don't forget!** section. It is over-simplistic to suggest that this is formed only by if + present simple, + will ...; going to is often used interchangeably with will. Moreover, might (or indeed may and could) are used when the speaker is not sure of the result.

11 **Ex 4:** This exercise is simply to practise the form of conditional sentences to refer to real possibilities. (T should draw Ss' attention to the fact that the comments are in note form only and therefore articles are omitted.)

Suggested answers:
2 If we spend more money on training, we might improve quality.
3 If we work more overtime, we'll have/we're going to have problems with the workforce.
4 If we increase the workforce, we'll have to spend too much time training new people.
5 If we increase our QC activities, we might reduce reject levels.
6 If we only offer a 2% pay rise, the workers will never/are never going to accept it.

12 **Ex 5:** This is basically a fluency maze activity. Before starting, T draws Ss' attention to the language of suggestions in the box. There are three ways in which T might choose the do this activity.

Option 1: T writes the card numbers on the back of the cards (they are only on the front). T starts off the maze by taking Card 1 and reading out the options. Ss discuss and choose an option. One S picks up the relevant numbered card and reads out the problem and the options. Ss continue to take turns to read out the next card. This way every body in the class is involved.

Option 2: T keeps all of the cards, reading out all the problems and options. Ss discuss the options and tell T what they have decided.

Option 3: T delegates his/her role to one member of the group, who reads out what is on the the cards.

Grammar

3 Look at the tapescript on page 141. Underline examples of the present simple. What are the different uses of the present simple in the conversation?

Conditional (real possibility)

• We can use the following conditional forms to talk about the possible results of an action:

> If + present simple, will
> going to + infinitive
> might

• We can use **will/going to** when we are sure of the result.
• We can use **might** when we are not sure of the result.

Unit 15

4 You are discussing changes to the place where you work. Here are some of your colleagues' suggestions. Your thoughts are in brackets. Write responses using conditional sentences.

1 "I think we should buy new machinery." (Very expensive!)
If we buy new machinery, it'll be expensive.

2 "We need to spend more on training." (Possibly improve quality)
_____

3 "We have to work more overtime." (Problems with the workforce!)
_____

4 "Why don't we increase the workforce?" (Spend too much time training new people)
_____

5 "Let's increase our QC activities." (Possibly reduce reject levels)
_____

6 "We can only offer workers a 2% pay rise." (Never accept it!)
_____

Speaking

5 You are the directors of a small soft drinks producer. You are going to hear descriptions of different problems at your company and possible solutions. Discuss the problems and decide what action to take. Use some of the words below.

Let's ...   Why don't we ...?   We should ...

---

1 Match the words. Then use them to complete the sentences below.

1 quality — life
2 inspection — control
3 shelf — analysis
4 finished — in
5 goods — goods
6 chemical — points

1 All _____ are stored in a warehouse ready for despatch.

2 There are five main _____ in our quality control programme.

3 The _____ department is next to the production hall.

4 The _____ of our ingredients is about two weeks. After that we throw them away.

5 We check all _____ when they arrive at our warehouse.

6 The _____ is carried out in a laboratory in the QC department.

2 Match the words with their opposites. Then complete the text with the correct form of the words. Do not use any word more than once.

1 demand — fall
2 goods in — increase
3 rise — accept
4 reject — supply
5 reduce — finished goods

The problems started about 6 months ago. We were already at full capacity when (1) _____ suddenly went up by 30%. We only had one warehouse so both (2) _____ and _____ were in the same place. There (3) _____ was no way we could (4) _____ our storage space so we worked very closely with our (5) _____, who delivered the ingredients just when we needed them and not before. On the production side, both workers and machinery had to work overtime and our quality levels began to (6) _____. We soon noticed a (7) _____ in our (8) _____ levels and we had to throw away more and more finished goods. But we couldn't really do anything about it without (9) _____ capacity so we just had to (10) _____ the situation.

3 Complete the following sentences with the correct form of the verb in brackets.

1 We (need) *'ll need* to increase capacity if we (get) *get* any more orders.

2 Even if we (change) _____ the sensors, it (not/make) _____ any difference.

3 If it (not/make) _____ any difference, we (talk) _____ about it again next week.

4 If demand (increase) _____, we (have to) _____ increase overtime.

5 What (happen) _____ if we (keep) _____ the oil in the cooker longer?

6 We (have to) _____ spend more on training if we (want) _____ to improve quality.

7 If the goods (not/arrive) _____ soon, we (look) _____ for a new supplier.

8 The QC department (not/be) _____ happy if we (increase) _____ the sampling rate.

Exam practice

4
• Look at the notice below. It shows the different divisions of a manufacturing company.
• For questions 1-5, decide where each activity takes place.
• For each question, mark the correct letter **A-H.**
• Do not use any letter more than once.

> **A** Production line
> **B** Warehouse
> **C** Despatch
> **D** Research & development
> **E** Quality control
> **F** Packing line
> **G** Canteen
> **H** Washrooms

1 Workers get changed here before and after their shift.

2 This is where the goods are actually manufactured.

3 Samples are taken there for inspection.

4 Goods in arrive here for storage.

5 The division handles the distribution of finished goods.

Tapescript: Listening 1

Visitor	Could you tell me a bit about quality control at the factory?
Pauline	Well, there are four main quality control inspection points. We begin by visiting our suppliers to make sure we are happy with their quality control. Next, we inspect all goods in on arrival at our factory and the third inspection point is during production. And the final stage is chemical analysis of our finished goods.
Visitor	And what do you look for at each of the four inspection points?
Pauline	Well each stage is different. With our suppliers, for instance, we inspect their QC processes and, even more importantly, their factory hygiene. If we're not happy with their hygiene, we'll cancel the supply contract. At the goods in stage we make sure that order quantities are correct and the quality is OK. We also check the transport packaging. If the packaging is damaged, the warehouse shelf-life can be reduced.
Visitor	And what quality checks do you run during production?
Pauline	We take samples to check there isn't too much cooking oil on the snack and that each snack has the minimum amount of flavouring. We also check the size of the snacks and their crispness. If the snacks are too oily, they go soft.
Visitor	So that leaves the finished goods. What do you check for at the final QC stage?
Pauline	We check individual bags to make sure that the packet weight is above the acceptable minimum and that the packet is sealed properly. We also check the taste.
Visitor	And how do you do that?
Pauline	Well, we eat them. How else? We also do chemical analysis to check things like fat levels and other information that we have to put on the packets.

Tapescript: Listening 2

Jack	OK, so we all know there's a problem with reject levels, but before we look at ways of dealing with it, what I'd like to know is why don't we find the rejects sooner. How can they get all the way to the finished goods chemical analysis before we find them? Keith?
Keith	Well, Jack. The problem is the oil temperature in the cookers. It keeps falling or rising suddenly. And that's why the samples don't always pick up high fat levels. The problem is worse when demand is high and we're running at full capacity, well, like we are at the moment.
Jack	So what can we do about it?
Keith	Well I think the first idea on your memo is the best one. We should increase the sampling rate. You see, if we take samples more often, we'll pick up the rejects sooner.
Pauline	That's true, but if we do that, we'll need extra human resources in the QC department. I prefer the second idea. I'd rather just change the temperature sensors in the cookers.
Keith	We've already tried that, but it didn't make any difference. The problem is the oil in the cookers. When it gets dirty the temperature sensors don't work properly.
Pauline	So why don't we change the oil more often?
Keith	Well it would help, but we have to stop production to change the oil. We're going to lose production capacity if we stop the line more often. And the extra oil will increase our costs, of course.
Jack	Hmm. That's a point.
Pauline	Yes, but if it reduces the reject levels, a bit of lost production won't be a problem.
Keith	It might not be a problem if we can reduce reject levels to zero, but I don't think that's possible.
Jack	OK let's try it anyway. Keith, I'd like you to change the oil more often and monitor the sensors. Pauline, I'd like you to increase the sampling rate by just 10 per cent. That means you won't need extra staff. Let's do that for the next two weeks and see what happens. OK?
Pauline	Right.

Direct service providers

Objectives:	To enable Ss to talk about insurance and changes in working practices
	To practise listening for specific information
	To review language of future possibility/probability
Materials needed:	Cassette - *Pass Cambridge BEC 1*

Unit overview

- **The call centre**

Warmer	Ss discuss the advantages and popularity of call centres.
Listening 1	Ss listen to a manager talk about why his company uses call centres and complete notes about the company. Ss then listen again and answer multiple-choice questions.
Vocabulary	Ss match insurance words with definitions.
Language focus	Ss review the language of future possibility and probability.
Speaking	Ss discuss four statements about the future.

- **Working in a call centre**

Listening 2	Ss decide if statements about a call centre are true or false then listen to the manager and check their answers.
Reading	Ss look at descriptions of people and say who might be interested in working in a call centre.
Speaking	Ss discuss what changes direct services and the Internet might bring.

- **Self-study**

Vocabulary	Keyword exercise (*insurance*).
	Odd one out exercise.
	Gap-filling exercise (*insurance*).
Exam practice	*Multiple choice gap-fill test (Reading Test Part 6).*

The call centre

1   **Ex ①**: T introduces the subject of call centres and asks Ss what they might be, how they work and whether they are popular in their country or not. The following details might help Ts give Ss some background information about call centres. Ss listen to George Watt, the National Sales Manager at Direct Line, and compare their answers with his information.

> Call centres are one of the fastest growing sectors in the UK. As more and more financial service companies such as insurance companies and banks change to telephone-based business practices, they are setting up centralised telephone centres which handle all national calls. The call centres are usually set up in business parks and out-of-town locations, often in areas with relatively cheap land such as Scotland or the north-east. Open much longer than high street shops, the customer service centres offer an instant response at almost any time of day. Powerful databases and new telephone technology allow the companies to handle large volumes of calls efficiently, monitor the quality of their service easily and reduce costs dramatically. The UK has more call centres than any other European country and at present about one in every 100 employees works in one. This figure is expected to rise to one in fifty in the foreseeable future.

2   **Ex ②**: Before playing the cassette, T tells Ss to read the gapped notes and points out that the gaps can be filled with up to three words or a number (as in the exam). T plays the cassette and Ss complete the notes about Direct Line. T then elicits answers, replaying passages of the cassette where necessary.

1 6	*2 3,000*	*3 costs*	*4 prices*
5 response	*6 house*	*7 loans*	*8 pensions*
9 find good staff	*10 work from home*		

3   **Ex ③**: Ss read through the multiple-choice questions before listening to the cassette again.

1 B	*2 C*	*3 C*	*4 B*

If requested to, T explains the difference between *operator* and *operative* (*operator* being a general term for people who answer telephone enquiries full-time while *operative* is used by George Watt as a technical term referring to Direct Line staff).

4   **Ex ④**: Ss match the insurance/financial services words and their definitions. T reminds Ss that they can use the tapescript on page 142 to help them. During feedback Ss quote from the tapescript in support of their answers.

2 premium	*money you pay for insurance*
3 claim	*request for money to be paid by an insurer*
4 policy	*insurance contract*
5 mortgage	*loan to buy a house*
6 commission	*money paid to a salesperson for every sale he/she makes*

5   T elicits from Ss ways of expressing future possibility and probability. T then draws Ss' attention to the **Don't forget!** section. T reminds Ss that *will* is normally reduced to *'ll* in speech.

6   **Ex ⑤**: The statements give opinions about how basic business practices will develop in the future. Ss offer their own views.

Direct service providers

The call centre

Speaking **1** Call centres are a rapidly growing business sector in the UK. Why do you think companies are investing so much money in them?

Listening 1 **2** George Watt, the National Sales Manager at Direct Line, talks about call centres. Listen and complete the journalist's notes.

Notes: *Direct Line* _____

No. of call centres: (1) _____
Total staff: (2) _____

Advantages
Lower (3) _____ for the company
and lower (4) _____ for the clients.
When customers call, they get an immediate
(5) _____

Products
• Insurance lines: motor. (6) _____
travel and life.
• Financial services: mortgages. personal
(7) _____ savings and
(8) _____
• Vehicle breakdown service.

Future
Will become harder to (9) _____
Staff might (10) _____

3 Listen again and choose the correct option to complete the sentence or answer the question.

I Direct Line's costs are lower because the company does not have to
  A pay as many claims as competitors.
  B rent shops or pay commission.
  C pay for advertising.

2 Operatives can deal with a call quickly because
  A they are good at making decisions.
  B the company employs a lot of staff.
  C of the technology.

3 Call centre technology means that operatives
  A need a lot of special training.
  B have a lot of responsibility.
  C can deal with almost every call.

4 In future, direct service providers will have to
  A reduce the size of their call centres.
  B make job offers more attractive.
  C cut wages to keep prices down.

Vocabulary **4** Match the words with the meanings.

I broker   money you pay for insurance
2 premium   person who buys and sells things, e.g. insurance, for other people
3 claim   money paid to a salesperson for every sale he/she makes
4 policy   loan to buy a house
5 mortgage   request for money to be paid by an insurer
6 commission   insurance contract

Future possibility and probability

• We can express possibility in different ways.
  Call centre staff **will possibly** *work from home.*
  Companies **could/might** *find it hard to compete in the future.*

• We can also talk about probability in different ways.
  Companies **will probably** *have difficulty finding staff.*
  Prices **are likely to** *fall in the next few years.*

Unit 61

Speaking **5** Work in pairs. Are the following situations possible in your country?

I Companies will provide more of their services by telephone.
2 The price of insurance will fall because of cheap competition.
3 Fewer insurance companies will use agents in the future.
4 Call centres will use video-phones for face-to-face contact.

40,000

Direct Line's motor telesales operators handle around 40,000 incoming calls a day.

Direct service providers

Working in a call centre

7 **Ex 1**: Ss read the statements and discuss them in pairs before deciding which are true and which are false. T elicits feedback before playing the cassette for Ss to check their answers.

1 true   2 true   3 false   4 false   5 false   6 true   7 true

8 **Ex 2**: Ss read the descriptions and discuss them before deciding who would be interested in working in a call centre. Ss quote from the profiles in support of their answers. T asks other Ss for their comments before giving feedback.

Suggested answers:

Zoe Connolly	Possibly	*Needs some money, might like a temporary job.*
Steven Gregory	Possibly	*Although not suited to call centre (likes travelling and meeting people), he is unemployed and has experience of sales.*
Helen Taylor	Possibly	*Would suit evening work, secretarial experience.*

9 **Ex 3**: In pairs Ss discuss how direct services and the Internet might change our daily lives. As both of these are made possible by cheap telephone technology, the discussion could broaden out to other telephone-based innovations such as video-conferencing and video-phones. The technology will undoubtedly find its way into the home so even Ss with no experience of direct services or the Internet should eventually be affected in some way by these changes.

Self-study

Ex 1: *house, life, travel* - **insurance**
insurance - *policy, line, company*

Ex 2: 1 *memorandum* (the others are all types of agreement)
2 *claim* (the others are all something the customer pays)
3 *location* (the others are all something you pay)
4 *exciting* (the others are all to do with speed)
5 *loan* (the others are all lines of insurance)
6 *quality* (the others are all quantity)
7 *provider* (the others are all financial services)

Ex 3: 1 *premium*   2 *loan*   3 *broker*
4 *commission*   5 *enquiry*   6 *monitor*
7 *claim*   8 *policy*   9 *supervisor*

Ex 4: 1 C   2 B   3 B   4 C   5 A
6 A   7 C   8 B   9 C   10 A

Essential vocabulary

Insurance
broker
claim
commission
policy
premium

General
call centre
competitor
competition
direct provider
loan
mortgage
operative
response
supervisor

The words in italics are not on the Cambridge BEC 1 wordlist.

Working in a call centre

1 Work in pairs. George Watt talks about working conditions in a call centre. Before you listen, decide whether the following statements are true or false. Then listen and check your answers.

1 The computer system monitors the workers every minute of their shift.
2 Call centre operatives can earn productivity bonuses for selling a lot of policies.
3 Operatives normally work a lot more hours than office workers.
4 Operatives work the same hours every month.
5 The call centre is open from 9am until 5pm on weekdays.
6 Call centres employ a lot of young people and women.
7 The company tries to make working in the call centre more interesting.

2 Which of the following people would be interested in working in a call centre? Why?

Zoe Connolly, 22

I've just finished university and I'm looking for a job. I've got a degree in business studies but I'm not really sure what I want to do. I'd like to take some time off and travel around the world but I don't have any money.

Steven Gregory, 32

I'm unemployed at the moment. I've worked in sales a lot and I'd like to continue in that area. I really enjoy working with people and visiting customers. Sales is always interesting because you know you can always sell more, so you never relax.

Helen Taylor, 26

I worked as a secretary after leaving school but I stopped work last year to start a family. My daughter is now nearly six months old and I would like to go back to work. My husband works in an office from 9 to 5.

3 Work in pairs. More and more organisations are offering their services and products directly over the telephone and on the Internet. What changes could this make to our daily lives?

- Read the newspaper article below about call centres.
- Choose the correct word from **A**, **B** or **C** below.
- For each question, mark the correct letter **A**, **B** or **C**.

New call centre creates 2000 jobs in north-east

Barclays Bank is to set up a new call centre in Sunderland because of the rapid growth of its telephone banking service. The decision is good news for the north-east, **(1)** _____ companies considered less attractive **(2)** _____ other regions such as London, Scotland and the north-west in **(3)** _____ list of the most attractive locations for setting up a call centre. The centre will open early next year and **(4)** _____ expected to employ 2,000 people over the next three years. Barclaycall, the bank's specialised telephone banking service, **(5)** _____ set up in 1994 and now has **(6)** _____ than 600,000 customers. The service employs 650 at a call centre in Coventry and another 200 at a centre opened in Manchester last year. The service is **(7)** _____ 25,000 new customers every month and the bank expects to add another one million customers **(8)** _____ the next two years. Gary Hoffman, a Barclays director said: "Our decision to open another call centre shows **(9)** _____ popular our telephone banking service is **(10)** _____ our customers. It is essential that our resources grow in order to meet their needs."

1 A where   B what   C which
2 A that   B than   C as
3 A there   B their   C its
4 A are   B be   C is
5 A was   B were   C have
6 A more   B many   C much
7 A attractive   B attracted   C attracting
8 A at   B over   C on
9 A why   B very   C how
10 A with   B between   C through

---

1 Look back through the unit (including the tapescripts). How many words connected with *insurance* can you find? Now write words which go **before** the word *insurance* and words which go **after**.

_____ _____ _____ broker.
_____
_____   **insurance**
_____

2 Which is the odd one out?

1	contract	policy	agreement	memorandum
2	cost	claim	premium	price
3	premium	location	price	commission
4	instant	immediate	exciting	fast
5	life	loan	motor	house
6	volume	total	quality	number
7	loan	mortgage	provider	pension

3 Complete the sentences with the words below.

supervisor	loan	premium
policy	monitor	broker
claim	commission	enquiry

1 I changed my car insurance because the _____ was lower.
2 I bought the car with a _____ from the bank.
3 We know a _____ who advises us on insurance.
4 As an insurance salesman he earns _____ on everything he sells.
5 A new customer phoned me to make an _____
6 The system lets us _____ what the operatives are doing at any time.
7 My car has just been stolen so I need to make a _____
8 Her house insurance _____ ran out last month.
9 A _____ makes decisions if operatives have to deal with large or unusual risks.

Tapescript: Listening 1

Journalist Direct Line was the first direct provider of insurance in the UK when it started 13 years ago. How many call centres does the company now operate?

George We have 6 regional centres which employ between 300 and 700 people each. In total we have about 3,000 staff in our centres.

Journalist Why did the company decide to offer its products directly by phone and Internet rather than the usual way through insurance brokers or high street shops?

George Well, the major reason was probably cost. You see with a call centre you don't have to pay high rents for good high street locations or pay commission to brokers and agents. You can then pass on these cost savings to your customers through competitive pricing of your products.

Journalist Right and how does a call centre affect the quality of service a customer gets?

George When a customer calls they get an instant response. The computer database shows all the customer's details, which saves a lot of time. This means we can offer our customers good products, quick service and lower premiums.

Journalist And what products does Direct Line offer?

George Our insurance policies include motor - we're the UK's biggest direct motor insurer - house, travel and life. We also offer financial services such as mortgages, personal loans, savings and pensions. We've also recently started to offer a vehicle breakdown service.

Journalist Gosh, so many. Are your operatives able to deal with all these different products?

George Some operatives only deal with one product, whilst multi-skilled staff can deal with 2 or 3 products. But the system is programmed to guide operatives in dealing with 80 - 90% of enquiries and claims, so they don't have to make any decisions themselves. Unusual or large risks are assessed by supervisors. The important thing is to get as much information at your operative's fingertips as possible. The more information they have in front of them, the less training they need.

Journalist How do you see the future for call centres?

George They're definitely here to stay. But as more and more new call centres are set up, it'll probably become harder to find good staff, so companies'll have to offer better conditions. In the future staff might even work from home on closed computer networks.

Tapescript: Listening 2

Journalist George, we sometimes read negative stories about working conditions in call centres. Is it true, for example, that you know exactly where workers are for every minute of their shift?

George Yes, the computer system does monitor whether operatives are at their desks, but we make sure that they get an hour for lunch and plenty of other breaks.

Journalist Does the monitoring affect their pay?

George Yes, but in a positive way. Operatives receive bonuses based on the number of calls they take, the products they sell and the mistakes they make. This way we reward good work.

Journalist So what kind of hours do the operatives work?

George They work flexible shifts of 35 hours a week. Plus overtime if they want it.

Journalist What do you mean by flexible shifts?

George Well, the computer system works out a shift plan based on the calls it expects and plans exactly the right number of operatives for each time of day. So shift times are flexible.

Journalist So, do the operatives also work evenings?

George We're open from 8 till 8 Monday to Friday and from 9 till 5 on Saturdays. A lot of our operatives are young mothers or students, so they're happy to work evening shifts.

Journalist And what about job satisfaction?

George Some people believe that working in a call centre isn't the most exciting job in the world - so it's very important to remember that your operatives are human. So we organise them into teams. The team that sells the most policies, for example, wins a prize. We also organise fun competitions during big sporting events like the World Cup or the Olympics.

The banking sector

Objectives:	To enable Ss to talk about banking services and changes within an industry
	To practise reading for gist and specific information
	To practise listening for specific information
	To raise awareness of -ing

Materials needed: Cassette – *Pass Cambridge BEC 1*

Unit overview

● The banking revolution

Reading	Ss look at a headline and predict the content of an article. They then read the article and match headings with paragraphs. Ss take notes from the article then answer multiple-choice comprehension questions.
Language focus	Ss categorise different uses of -ing and focus on the fact that prepositions are often followed by -ing.
Vocabulary	Ss complete a word-building table.
Speaking	Ss discuss the changes affecting their sector/industry.

● Home banking

Listening 1	Ss listen to an enquiry about home banking and take notes.
Listening 2	Ss listen and complete an application form.
Speaking	Ss discuss the services offered by their own banks.

● Self-study

Vocabulary	Crossword (banking words).
	Matching exercise (verb + noun).
	Matching exercise (noun + preposition + noun).
Exam practice	*Note-taking (Writing Test Part 1).*

The banking revolution

1 Warmer (books closed): T writes the headline from the article on the board. Ss work in pairs to predict the possible contents of the article. The possible issues can be elicited and put on the board. Ss then open their books and quickly scan through the text to search for the issues listed on the board.

2 Ex ❶: Ss read the four paragraph headings in the box and read the article again more carefully in order to match the headings with the paragraphs. During feedback Ss quote from the text in support of their answers.

1 Warnings of redundancies
2 Reasons for reducing costs
3 New banking products
4 The future of banking

3 Ex ❷: Ss read the text again and complete the table by taking notes under the three headings.

The banks' plans	Reasons for cutting costs	Banking services
Cut jobs	Competition from supermarkets	Telephone banking
Close domestic branches	and direct providers	Smart cards
Develop electronic	Investment in IT	PC banking
banking	Millennium bug	
	European monetary union	

4 Ex ❸: Ss carefully read the questions before reading through the text again. During feedback Ss quote from the text in support of their answers.

1 B   2 A   3 C   4 A

5 Ex ❹: Ss scan the texts to underline examples of -ing forms in the article. The underlined items are then grouped according to the columns in the table. T brings the highlighted **Don't forget!** note to the Ss' attention. (T points out that not all words with -ing necessarily fall into these three categories.) The point could be quickly practised by giving Ss incomplete sentences finishing with a preposition and asking them to provide an -ing form and a noun to finish each sentence.

-ing as a noun	-ing after prepositions	-ing in the present continuous
banking sector	of dealing	are warning
electronic banking	with ... planning	is becoming
telephone banking	of cutting/using	is hoping
PC banking		are testing
day-to-day banking		

The banking sector

The banking revolution

Reading ❶ Read the article and match the headings with the paragraphs.

New banking products   Warnings of redundancies
The future of banking   Reasons for reducing costs

Stormy times for Europe's banks

In spite of all the recent mergers and cost-cutting in the European banking sector, experts are warning that thousands of jobs are still at risk. UK banks could cut up to 20,000 jobs over the next two years as they try to compete with supermarkets and direct providers. Switzerland and Germany, with their over-crowded retail banking markets, could see even greater job losses.

The need to reduce non-IT costs is becoming increasingly important as Europe's banks invest heavily in electronic banking and meet the costs of dealing with the millennium bug and European economic and monetary union (Emu) all at the same time. The domestic branch networks will suffer most, with several European banks planning to close up to 15 per cent of their smaller branches.

The staff reductions are made possible by the development of electronic banking services such as telephone banking, smart cards and PC banking. Alan Higgins,

Manager of Direct Financial Services at Carlisle NSB, a UK bank, is hoping that home banking technology will put the company ahead of its competitors. "We are testing a product called HomeBank with 2,000 of our customers who have a 24-hour direct modem connection."

The banks have to find a way of cutting staff and using technology without affecting the quality of service. "We have to take the bank to the customer" says Alan Higgins. "I do a lot of my day-to-day banking on a Sunday."
However, in spite of the warnings about jobs, recent figures suggest that banks will continue to make record profits.

	France	Germany	Italy	Netherlands	Spain	Sweden	Switzerland	UK
Number of banks	627	3,730	1,004	128	315	107	395	591
Bank branches per million inhabitants	445	600	397	317	893	460	1,066	339
Average pre-tax return on capital 1996	9.6%	13.7%	8.8%	14.5%	17.1%	31.8%	5.0%	28.1%

26 | Finance

Writing ❷ Take notes from the text under the following headings.

The banks' plans	Reasons for cutting costs	Banking services
Cut jobs		

❸ Choose the correct option to complete the sentences or answer the questions.

1 Over 20,000 jobs could be cut by
   A supermarkets and direct providers.
   B banks in the United Kingdom.
   C Swiss and German banks.

2 The banks have to cut staff costs
   A so they can finance IT investment.
   B in order to expand the branch network.
   C because they are losing money.

3 How does HomeBank work?
   A Customers telephone the bank during office hours.
   B The bank answers telephone calls 24 hours-a-day.
   C Customers do their banking on a home computer.

4 How are the banks performing?
   A They are making more money than ever before.
   B Increased competition means they are making less money.
   C The cost of IT investment has reduced profits.

Grammar ❹ Find words ending in -ing in the article. Write them in the groups below.

-ing as a noun	-ing after prepositions	-ing in the present continuous
cost-cutting		

Preposition + -ing
- Prepositions are usually followed by -ing or a noun.
  Banks have to meet the costs of dealing with the euro.
  Banks are investing in new technology.

Unit 19
Unit 37

Unit 14b

The banking sector

6 **Ex 5**: Ss complete the table by providing the correct noun or verb form. If necessary, Ss can return to the text a final time to find the missing forms. Alternatively, they can find the answers in a dictionary.

Verb	Noun	Verb	Noun
merge	merger	compete	**competition**
increase	increase	invest	**investment**
reduce	**reduction**	**close**	closure
cut	cut	**develop**	development

7 **Ex 6**: In pairs Ss discuss changes taking place in their own industry/sector. This could include the impact of new technology, market trends, economic trends or the development of new business practices.

Home banking

8 T elicits what home banking is and how it works. Ss can briefly discuss whether they use it, its advantages etc. as a class.

9 **Ex 1**: T sets the scene and Ss read through the handwritten notes before listening to the cassette. Ss may have difficulties with *PIN number* (Personal Identification Number) - especially as *number* is actually repeated in the phrase. After the listening, T points out that the services available also appear on the visual.

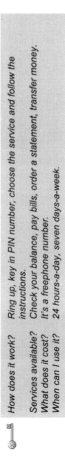

How does it work? Ring up, key in PIN number, choose the service and follow the instructions.
Services available? Check your balance, pay bills, order a statement, transfer money.
What does it cost? It's a freephone number.
When can I use it? 24 hours-a-day, seven days-a-week.

10 **Ex 2**: The second listening continues on from the first with the customer now actually applying for the telephone banking service. Ss read the blank form and then listen to the conversation and complete the form.

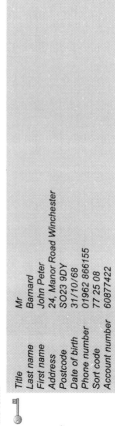

Title	Mr
Last name	Barnard
First name	John Peter
Address	24, Manor Road Winchester
Postcode	SO23 9DY
Date of birth	31/10/68
Phone number	01962 866155
Sort code	77 25 08
Account number	60877422

11 **Ex 3**: In pairs Ss discuss their own banks' services: which they use and which they wish they could have. This could lead to an open class discussion about banks in the country.

Ex 1:

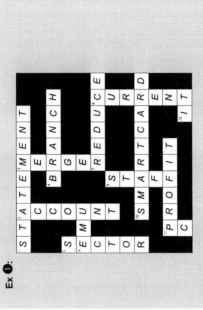

Ex 2: 2 transfer money
3 pay bills
4 order a statement
5 sign a form
6 follow instructions
7 key in a PIN number

Ex 1: 1 Accounts
2 Andy Smith/The bank
3 386SX or higher
4 4MB
5 Windows 3.0 or higher

Ex 3: 2 deal with problems
3 invest in new technology
4 pay for a service
5 fill in a form
6 note down some details

Essential vocabulary

Banking
balance
bank account
bank statement
branch
current account
PIN number
sort code
to transfer money

General
to compete (with)
date of birth
Emu (European monetary union)
to fill in (a form)
to follow (instructions)
to finance
IT (information technology)
merger
Millennium bug
PC (personal computer)
postcode
redundancy
sector
to warn

The words in italics are not on the Cambridge BEC 1 wordlist.

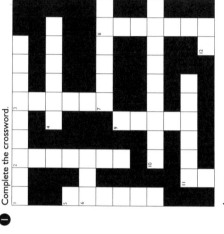

Vocabulary

5 Complete the table with the correct verb or noun.

Verb	Noun	Verb	Noun
merge	merger	compete	....
....	increase	invest	....
reduce	cut	....	closure
....	....	....	development

Speaking

6 Work in pairs. What changes are taking place in your partner's sector?

Home banking

Listening 1

1 John Barnard enquires about telephone banking. He has noted down some questions. Listen and take notes to answer his questions.

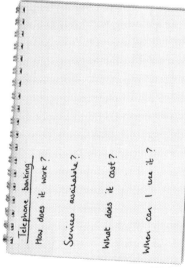

Check transactions on accounts
1 (ABC) 2 (DEF) 3
Check your balance
(GHI) 4 (JKL) 5 (MNO) 6
Order a statement
(PRS) 7 8 (WXY) 9
Transfer money
(OPER) 0 #
Pay bills

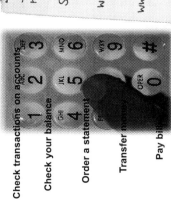

Telephone banking
How does it work?
Service available?
What does it cost?
When can I use it?

Listening 2

2 John applies for the telephone banking service. Listen and complete the form.

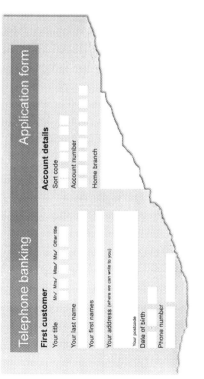

Telephone banking   Application form

First customer
Your title   Mr/ Mrs/ Miss/ Other title
Your last name
Your first names
Your address (where we can write to you)
Your postcode
Date of birth
Phone number

Account details
Sort code
Account number
Home branch

Speaking

3 Work in pairs. What home banking services does your partner's bank offer? Does your partner use any of them? What other services would he/she like?

---

1 Complete the crossword.

[crossword grid]

Across
1 A print-out with information about your account.
4 A local office of a bank.
6 Abbreviation for European Monetary Union.
7 To make something smaller.
10 A plastic card with a computer chip on it.
11 The banks are still making a lot of it.
12 Abbreviation for information technology.

Down
2 Where you keep your money at the bank.
3 A joining together of two companies.
5 An area of economic activity.
8 A type of bank account.
9 The people who work for an organisation.
11 You need one for computer banking.

2 Match the verbs and nouns.

1 check	bills
2 transfer	a balance
3 pay	a form
4 order	a PIN number
5 sign	a statement
6 follow	money
7 key in	instructions

3 Match the words below to make phrases from the unit.

1 compete	in	a service
2 deal	with	a form
3 invest	down	another company
4 pay	in	some details
5 fill	for	problems
6 note	with	new technology

4

Exam practice

- Read the fax and note below.
- Complete the note to Jane Little.
- Write a word, phrase or number in spaces 1-5.

To: Lisa Jones
        Island Clothing Co.
From: Andy Smith
        HomeBank Customer Services
        Carlisle NSB
Date: 22 February 1999
Pages: 1

Hello Lisa

Here's the information you needed about using your computer for PC banking. Using your PC shouldn't be a problem as you can even use the software on old computers.

Anyway, what you need is an IBM compatible PC with a 386SX processor or higher. We recommend you use a computer with at least 4MB of RAM. You'll also need Windows software, version 3.0 or higher.

Finally, you'll need a fast modem. I hope that answers all your questions. If you need any more help, give me a call.

All the best

Andy

Peter
Jane in Accounts wants to know whether her computer is OK for PC banking. Here's a fax I received from the bank. Could you send her a note with the information she needs?

Thanks

Lisa

To: Jane Little
From: Peter Hargreaves   Dept.

(1) _____ contacted us with the information you wanted about PC banking.
Here are the requirements:

Processor (3) _____
RAM (4) _____
Software (5) _____

Tapescript: Listening 1

Clerk   Hello. Can I help you?
Customer   Yes, I'd like some information on your telephone banking service.
Clerk   Certainly. Do you have an account with us?
Customer   Yes, I do. This is my home branch.
Clerk   Well, with our telephone banking service you can do all your day-to-day banking over the telephone at any time of day or night.
Customer   How does it work?
Clerk   All you do is ring up, key in your PIN number, choose the service you want and then just follow the instructions. It's as easy as that.
Customer   And what can I actually do over the phone?
Clerk   You can check your balance, pay bills, order a statement or transfer money. All your normal day-to-day banking.
Customer   Does it cost anything?
Clerk   No. The number is a freephone number, so you don't pay for your calls and the service is part of your normal bank account.
Customer   Oh right and can I phone at any time of the day?
Clerk   Yes, you can. There's an automated answering machine and staff are available 24 hours-a-day, seven days a week.
Customer   Could I fill in a form now?
Clerk   Certainly. One moment, I'll just get an application form …

Tapescript: Listening 2

Clerk   Right, could I have your full name, please?
Customer   Yes, it's John Peter Barnard.
Clerk   And your address, Mr Barnard?
Customer   24, Manor Road, Winchester.
Clerk   And the postcode?
Customer   SO23 9DY.
Clerk   Could I have your date of birth, please?
Customer   Yes It's 31 October 1968.
Clerk   Thank you. And your daytime phone number?
Customer   01962 866155.
Clerk   And all I need now are your account details. Would you like the telephone banking just for your current account or for more than one account?
Customer   Just for my current account, please.
Clerk   OK. So, the sort code is 77 25 08 and could I have your account number, please?
Customer   60877422.
Clerk   60877422.
Customer   That's right.
Clerk   If you could sign the form here, Mr Barnard, and then that's it. I'll register you and then we'll send you your information pack and membership number.

Exam focus: Speaking

Objectives: To familiarise Ss with the content of the Speaking Test
To provide useful tips
To practise the Speaking Test

Materials needed: Cards - 11 cards: *Pass Cambridge BEC 1 Unit 15/1-11* One set per pair/group

Unit overview

- ### The Speaking Test

  T gives an overview of the Speaking Test.

- ### How to succeed

  Ss brainstorm tips for success based on four assessment criteria then compare their ideas with the tips in the book.

- ### Personal information

  Ss practise answering questions about general topics in preparation for Part One. First they write questions to ask their partner, then mingle asking people about topics on cards.

  Ss listen to a bad version of Part One of a Speaking Test and compare it with a good version.

- ### Information exchange

  T elicits question forms for a Part Two information exchange. Ss read exam tips then improve their questions.

  Ss listen to a bad then a good version of Part Two of a Speaking Test.

  Ss do an information exchange activity, taking into account the tips from the lesson.

- ### Exam practice

  Part One: Form-filling.

  Part Two: Note.

  Part Three: Long memo.

The Speaking Test

If T is unfamiliar with the Speaking Test, he/she should look at the following:

- *BEC 1: Teacher's Information Pack*
- *UCLES BEC 1 Sample Papers*
- *Linguarama Cambridge BEC 1 Practice Tests 1 and 2.*

Assessment criteria

The assessment criteria used by UCLES for the Speaking Test are **Interactive communication, Grammar and vocabulary, Pronunciation** and **Discourse management**. These categories have been used in this unit with the exception of **Discourse management**, which refers to a candidate's ability to use English beyond the sentence level. It was decided to simplify this category to make the criteria more tangible for Ss. Ss will obtain good marks for **Discourse management** if they follow the advice given under **Interactive communication** and **Organisation of ideas**. For a complete description of the marking criteria for the Speaking Test refer to *BEC 1: Teacher's Information Pack*.

1 **Warmer (books closed):** T elicits what the Ss know about the Speaking Test (length, parts, number of candidates/examiners etc.).

2 Ss open their books and read the overview of the exam format. T reassures Ss that the examiners will be sympathetic and friendly.

How to succeed

3 Ss close their books. T writes the four headings: *Interactive communication, Organisation of ideas, Grammar and vocabulary* and *Pronunciation* on the board and Ss brainstorm tips for succeeding in the Speaking Test.

4 Ss open their books and read through the tips to compare their answers. T may want to add some of the following extra information:

• Interactive communication
The examiners will pay attention to how well the Ss work together. Ss need to ask polite, if possible indirect, questions and frame interactions with common courtesies.

• Organisation of ideas
Ss have few opportunities to produce extended turns or use connectors. However, Part One of the test allows the Ss the chance to express opinions and justify them. Ss can use connectors such as *because, but, also, as well*. Ss should also try to frame their answers with fluency phrases such as *I think that, The best thing about X is ..., What I really like about X is ...*.

• Grammar and vocabulary
Although marks are given for range, accuracy and appropriateness are more important. Therefore, Ss should restrict themselves to grammar that they feel comfortable with. Before Part Two, the examiner will give Ss time to digest the input information. Ss should use this time to quickly think of how to form all the questions before they ask them.

• Pronunciation
The examiners will listen for the pronunciation of individual sounds, intonation and sentence stress. Many Ss are nervous and launch into answers only to hesitate and have to rethink in mid-sentence. A slightly slower, but natural, rhythm is better than a fast but disjointed delivery.

Personal information

5 **Ex ❶:** T now focuses on the general topics that might arise in Part One of the Speaking Test in which Ss will have to answer but not ask questions. T writes *family* on the board and elicits questions to do with the topic. Ss then write three questions for each of the remaining words in Ex ❶. Ss ask each other their questions. T reminds them of the need to offer further information if possible.

Suggested answers:
Transport: Have you got a car? How do you get to work? Do you like travelling by train?
Free time: What do you do in your free time? Do you play any sports? Do you have any hobbies?
Places to live: Where do you live? Do you live in a house? What is it like?

6 **Ex ❷:** T gives Ss cards with conversation topics on them. Ss do the task as a mingling activity and try to find out as much as possible about their partner and the topic on the card. T can limit the time to make Ss work more spontaneously.

7 T points out the visual showing the layout of the Speaking Test room with the second examiner sitting silently apart.

8 **Ex ❸:** T explains that the cassette contains bad and good versions of simulated BEC 1 Speaking Tests (stressing that the focus is entirely on exam technique, not language). The simulation has been recorded as a whole; T therefore needs to stop the cassette at appropriate places.

Suggested answers:
Juana
- *Often only gives one word answers (**Where are you from? Madrid. Do you like living there? Yes**).*
- *Often neglects to use connectors (**It's a big city, too many people there**).*

Jean-Pierre
- *Speaks very fast, launching into answers, at times impeding clarity. (The examiner has to ask him to repeat the spelling of his name.)*
- *Does not listen carefully to questions (i.e. spells his Christian name, not surname).*
- *Often digresses (talks about Paris, not Lille, when asked where he lives; talks about France when asked about England etc.).*
- *Does not think before he speaks, pauses in mid sentence (when describing why he likes living in Lille).*

9 **Ex ❹:** T plays the second version of the same part of the test, in which the candidates demonstrate improved exam technique.

Suggested answers:
Juana
- *Gives fuller answers (although she still lists information without connectors).*
- *Uses fluency phrases (**I think, you know, the palace and everything**).*

Jean-Pierre
- *Answers questions correctly and gives full, relevant answers.*
- *Speaks with a better rhythm, fewer hesitations, more relaxed.*
- *Uses connectors in longer turns (**because I just arrived in September and since September I've got really a lot of work so I really didn't have to occasion to visit...**).*

Information exchange

10 **Ex ❶:** In the information exchange in Part Two of the Speaking Test question forming is essential. Ss look at the exam style input and T elicits possible question forms, either as direct or indirect questions.

Exam focus: Speaking

The Speaking Test

The Cambridge BEC 1 Speaking Test always takes place with two or three candidates and two examiners.

Part	Format	Input	Task
1	Examiner talks to both candidates.	Examiner asks questions.	Giving personal information. Expressing preferences.
2	Candidate talks to candidate.	Written input. Instructions from examiner.	Asking for and giving information.

Length: A total of 10 minutes. Each part lasts between 3-4 minutes. Interviews with 3 candidates will be slightly longer.

How to succeed

During the Speaking Test one examiner will ask questions and give instructions. The second examiner in the Speaking Test does not speak to the candidates but is also there to assess your English. Here are some simple tips to remember in the test.

Interactive communication

- Listen carefully to all instructions and respond appropriately. Perfect grammar is useless if you do not answer the question you are asked.
- Ask the examiner to repeat any instructions you are not sure about.
- Give full answers, not just one or two words.
- Keep to and complete the task. Do not talk about other things.
- Good communication means helping the other candidate by asking questions, checking understanding and giving very clear information.
- Work **together** with the other candidate to complete the task in Part Two. Remember to speak to the other candidate and not the examiner.

Organisation of ideas

Show that you can organise your ideas. They can be organised in many ways, such as:

- sequence *(first of all, then, after that etc.)*
- importance *(I think the most important thing is …)*
- contrast *(but, although etc.).*

Grammar and vocabulary

- Do not try to use complicated words and structures. It is better to use simple words well than difficult ones badly.

Pronunciation

- Speak clearly and at a natural speed.
- Relax and think before you speak. It is better to pause before a sentence than in the middle of it.

Personal information

1 After introducing him/herself, the examiner will check that the information on your entry form is correct. He/she will then ask both candidates a few general questions. Write three questions for each of the topics below.

family	transport
free time	places to live

Now work in pairs. Ask and answer questions about the topics.

2 Work in pairs. Your teacher will give you some cards with possible Cambridge BEC 1 conversation topics on them. Take a card and ask your partner about the topic on it. Then take another card and find a different partner.

Listening

3 Listen to Juana and Jean-Pierre doing Part One of a Speaking Test. Read the exam tips again and listen to the test. What do they do wrong?

Interview 1, Part One

Juana

_____

Jean-Pierre

_____

4 Now listen to the same candidates doing Part One of the test again. Is it better this time? In what way?

Interview 2, Part One

Juana

_____

Jean-Pierre

_____

Information exchange

Speaking

1 Part Two is a test of your ability to exchange information with the other candidates. Look at the task below. Decide what questions you need to ask.

> You need to ask Candidate B for this information about a business hotel.
>
> Name ....
> Address ....
> Distance from airport ....
> Business facilities ....
> Room price per night ....

Exam focus: Speaking

Exam practice: Writing

The Exam Practice for this unit focuses on the Writing Test. All three parts are included.

Questions 1-5
1   CLOSE & SONS
2   TIM NICHOLLS
3   10 DEC 1998
4   TEK 200
5   £3495

Question 6
Suggested answer: *(23 words)*

Louise
If Mr Jablonski calls, please tell him I'm in a meeting with a supplier until 1pm. I'll call him back then.

Anne

Question 7
Suggested answer: *(60 words excluding header)*

(To: Jim)
(From: Paul)
(Date: 13 January 1999)

I have seen a hotel in Barcelona. The rooms have communication facilities and it has a business centre. Moreover, it is in the city centre, only 35 minutes from the airport and 25 minutes from the exhibition centre.

Therefore, it seems suitable for us for the trade fair. I think I should book rooms soon. Could you confirm the dates?

---

11 **Ex ②**: T reads through the tips about the information exchange in Part Two. T stresses that simple things can make a positive impression on the examiner, e.g. asking the other candidate if he/she is ready and thanking him/her at the end.

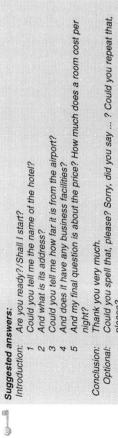

Suggested answers:
Introduction: Are you ready?/Shall I start?
1   Could you tell me the name of the hotel?
2   And what is its address?
3   Could you tell me how far it is from the airport?
4   And does it have any business facilities?
5   And my final question is about the price? How much does a room cost per night?

Conclusion: Thank you very much.
Optional: Could you spell that, please? Sorry, did you say ... ? Could you repeat that, please?

12 T refers to the visual showing the layout of Part Two of the Speaking Test with the candidates talking to each other.

13 **Ex ③**: Before Ss listen to bad and good versions of Part Two of the Speaking Test, T asks Ss to look at the **Conference Speakers Activity sheets** on page 130. T talks them through the materials. Once again Ss listen for what Juana and Jean-Pierre do wrong.*

Suggested answers:
Juana
● *Gives minimal answers.*
● *Does not ask complete questions (**What the name of the speaker? What place?**).*
● *Speaks to the examiner and not Jean-Pierre.*
Jean-Pierre
● *Does not wait for Juana to read through her information.*
● *Speaks very quickly, which impedes clarity at times.*
● *Is rude and aggressive. Does not listen carefully to Juana's answers (**He's from Hamburg, Germany. From Bonn?**).*
● *Does not form complete or polite questions.*
● *Points to the answers on Juana's sheets. Ss should not try to read each other's information.*
● *Asks the examiner for confirmation (**I think it's finding the right supplier, isn't it?**).*

* Jean-Pierre does not say *Mr* or *Mrs* when giving Josianne Boscariol's name, which leads Juana to refer to the speaker as *he*. It is important to use titles when giving names in the exam.

14 **Ex ④**: Ss listen to the improved version of the same.

Suggested answers:
Juana
● *Gives full, helpful answers.*
● *Asks if Jean-Pierre is ready to start and thanks Jean-Pierre at the end of the test.*
Jean-Pierre
● *Politely asks Juana if she is ready to start.*
● *Attempts to form polite indirect questions. Although in terms of interactive communication this is good, he is attempting to use a structure that is too sophisticated for him (**Could you tell me what's the name of the speaker?**). Direct questions would be sufficiently polite if delivered with the appropriate intonation.*

15 **Ex ⑤**: Finally Ss refer to Activity sheets on pages 127 and 133 and run through a mock Part Two activity, taking into account all the tips on communication and language that they have had. The activity could be recorded and used for feedback.

Questions 1-5
- Read the memo and the information about office laser printers.
- Complete the form below.
- Write each word, phrase or number in **CAPITAL LETTERS**.

Close & Sons
Memo

To: Tim Nicholls
From: Rachel West
Date: 10 December 1998

New Colour Laser Printer

We'll have to order the new printer today or it won't be delivered before Christmas. Could you look at these 3 printers and choose one? We need a printer that is fast but not the most expensive. Could you place the order for me this morning and leave me a copy of the order form?

Thanks

	560Pro	Tek200	Pro-jet
Width	50cm	40cm	62cm
Depth	53cm	50cm	49cm
Height	40cm	33cm	37cm
Pages per min.	3	6	4-5
Memory	12MB	24MB	20MB
Price	£2995	£3495	£3900

ORDER FORM

Company name: (1) ....
Contact person: (2) ....
Date of order: (3) ....
Product: (4) ....
Price: (5) ....

Question 6
- You have been waiting all morning for Mr Jablonski, an important client, to return a phone call. Now you have a meeting with a supplier.
- Leave a note for your colleague Louise White:
  * saying where you are
  * saying when you will be back
  * telling her what to say if Mr Jablonski calls.
- Write **about 20 words**.
- **Do not write in capital letters.**

Question 7
- You are visiting a trade fair in Barcelona with your boss. You have seen this hotel in a brochure.

Hotel Gaudí
Rambla de Catalunya 38, Barcelona

The Gaudí is situated in the heart of Barcelona city centre with its exciting nightlife. The hotel has 120 rooms including 42 business rooms specifically designed for the business traveller and fully-equipped with communication facilities.

The hotel enjoys direct bus and train connections to the airport (35 mins) and exhibition centre (25 mins). Other facilities include express check-in and check-out, 24-hour room service, two bars, restaurant, fitness room and full business centre.

- Write a memo to your boss:
  * mentioning the hotel in the brochure
  * describing some of the facilities listed
  * saying why you think you both should stay there
  * asking him which dates you should book.
- Write **50-60 words**.
- **Do not write in capital letters.**

---

2 Look at the tips for Part Two of the Speaking Test below.
- Check that the other candidate is ready to start.
- Use polite questions.
- Ask the other candidate to repeat anything that is not clear.
- Use connectors such as *and, also, as well*.
- Thank the other candidate when the task is complete.

Work in pairs. Now improve and expand your questions from the previous exercise.
Also write a short introduction and a conclusion. Refer to all the tips above.

Introduction: *Are you ready?*

1   *Could you tell me ...*
2
3
4
5

Conclusion:

Listening **3** Look at the Activity sheet on page 130. Juana and Jean-Pierre do Part Two of the Speaking Test. What do they do wrong?

Interview 1, Part Two

Juana

Jean-Pierre

Candidate 1 ←→ Candidate 2
Examiner 1
Examiner 2

4 Now listen to the same candidates do Part Two again. What are the differences between the way they do the two tests?

Interview 2, Part Two

Juana

Jean-Pierre

Speaking **5** Work in pairs. Student A: Look at the Activity sheet on page 127. Student B: Look at the Activity sheet on page 133. Use the information to practise Part Two of the Cambridge BEC 1 Speaking Test.

As Unit 15 contains extended extracts from a simulated Speaking Test, no tapescript is provided.

Delivery services

Objectives: To enable Ss to discuss delivery services
To practise reading for specific information
To review prepositions of time

Materials needed: Cassette - *Pass Cambridge BEC 1*
Cards - 16 cards: *Pass Cambridge BEC 1 Unit 16a/1-16* One set per pair/group

---

Unit overview

• Parcel carriers

Reading   Ss decide on figures about UPS before reading a brochure extract to check their answers. Ss complete sentences with the correct UPS service features.

Vocabulary   Ss identify repetition and language used to make a favourable impression on the reader.

Language focus   Ss review prepositions of time and match sentence halves with time prepositions.

Speaking   Ss decide on the most important features of a parcel delivery service.

• Sending a parcel

Reading   Ss read information in order to calculate the cost of sending three different packages by UPS.

Speaking   Ss work in pairs and exchange information about the delivery services used by their companies.

Speaking   Ss work in pairs and brainstorm alternative ways of sending items abroad and discuss their advantages and disadvantages.

                 Ss work in pairs with two sets of cards (items and destinations). Ss select cards to decide the best way to send the items to the destinations.

• Self-study

Vocabulary   Gap-fill exercise (prepositions).

                 Gap-fill exercise (delivery vocabulary).

Exam Practice   *Multiple-choice reading comprehension exercise (Reading Test Part 1).*

Parcel carriers

1 **Warmer (books closed):** T writes *UPS* on the board and asks Ss what the letters stand for and what UPS is. T elicits names of other parcel carriers (e.g. *DHL*) and asks Ss which, if any, their own companies use. T also introduces relevant vocabulary by asking Ss which carrier service has the best reputation and why (*reliability, guaranteed delivery time, reasonable prices, fast service* etc.).

2 **Ex ❶:** Ss work in pairs and guess which figures complete which statement about UPS.

This activity is to prepare Ss for the reading activity (a 'reason for reading'). Before Ss read the text, T may wish to collect Ss' suggested answers across the class in order to create even more motivation for reading to find the answers.

3 **Ex ❷:** Ss read the first part of the brochure and check their answers.

1 22 billion	2 3.04 billion	3 157,000	4 500	5 12 million	6 326,000

4 **Ex ❸:** Ss read the text for detail in order to match the correct feature with the correct phrase.

1 D	2 E	3 G	4 B

5 **Ex ❹:** T asks Ss if they can remember, without looking, any facts and figures which UPS used in the brochure to impress the reader. These figures are basically those used in the quiz. T then asks Ss to look at language which is repeated. Ss then search for other language which is designed to impress.

Repeated words and phrases
quality, guarantee, reliability, on time, every time, rely on us

Other language written to impress
more than over …, full (tracking), hundreds of, fastest, largest, commitment to quality, (customers) trust us, rely on us, ideal

6 T focuses on *in time* and *on time* to ensure Ss understand the difference. T also checks Ss understand the use of *by* vs *until*. Ss then read the **Don't forget!** section to round off the activity.

7 **Ex ❺:** Ss complete sentences with times or time phrases.

2 *An Express parcel will get there within 24 hours.*
3 *In order to arrive tomorrow, the package needs to leave by 3.30.*
4 *I'll stay here until UPS collects the parcel.*
5 *It arrived at 8.30, which was exactly on time.*
6 *We sent the document by UPS Express, so it should arrive in time.*

8 **Ex ❻:** After Ss have discussed and prioritised the parcel delivery service features, they compare their list with other Ss' as a whole class activity.

Delivery services

Parcel carriers

Speaking **1** Work in pairs. Complete the information about UPS (United Parcel Service) with the figures below.

326,000	22 billion	3.04 billion
157,000	500	12 million

1 Its turnover is more than _____ dollars a year.
2 Each year UPS delivers _____ parcels and documents.
3 The company owns _____ vehicles (cars, vans, trailers etc.).
4 UPS also owns over _____ aircraft.
5 UPS delivers _____ parcels and documents daily.
6 The company employs about _____ people worldwide.

Reading **2** Now read the first part of the UPS brochure and check your answers.

Welcome to UPS

UPS is the world's largest package distribution company with an annual revenue of $22.5bn. Our customers understand our commitment to quality service and trust us to deliver over 12 million of their parcels and documents to over 200 countries every day. This means our 157,000 vehicles and over 500 aircraft deliver more than three billion parcels annually. The UPS Worldwide Guarantee ensures documents and packages arrive on time, every time. Because you can rely on us, your business partners can rely on you. Whichever UPS service you choose, our 326,000 employees guarantee its quality and reliability will be the same.

UPS Express Plus
This is UPS's fastest service for your your most urgent documents and packages. It guarantees delivery by 8.30 am next day to hundreds of cities across Europe and the USA. The service also includes automatic confirmation of delivery by phone as soon as your shipment is delivered.

UPS Express
This is the ideal service for most of your urgent deliveries. It guarantees delivery by 10.30 am the next business day to over 200 countries. Full electronic tracking means confirmation of delivery is available within minutes in many cases.

UPS Expedited
UPS Expedited offers quality, reliability and scheduled delivery for your less urgent shipments. The service guarantees door-to-door deliveries within 48 hours. Full electronic tracking means confirmation of delivery is available within minutes in many cases.

UPS Standard
The UPS Standard service offers the benefits of UPS's quality,

Reading **3** Match the phrases below with one of the features of the UPS services.

1 Only UPS Express Plus guarantees …
2 All three services provide …
3 With UPS Expedited you can arrange …
4 Both UPS Express Plus and Express guarantee …

A same day delivery
B next day delivery
C delivery to only EU countries
D next day delivery by 8.30am
E confirmation of delivery
F worldwide next day delivery by 10.30am
G delivery on a particular day

Vocabulary **4** Read through the brochure again and find examples of the following.

- words and phrases that are repeated several times
- words and phrases written to impress the reader

Prepositions of time

- **By/until** **By** refers to a point in time. **Until** refers to a period of time.
  *I can do it **by** 10 o'clock. (I can finish it sometime before 10 o'clock.)*
  *We'll wait **until** 10 o'clock. (We'll wait for the period between now and and 10 o'clock.)*

- **Within** refers to a period of time. It can always be replaced by **in**.
  *We can deliver the package **within** two days.*

- **In/on time.** You arrange to meet a colleague at 1 o'clock.
  *Don't worry, she'll arrive **in time**. (She'll arrive before 1 o'clock.)*
  *Don't worry, she'll arrive **on time**. (She'll arrive at exactly 1 o'clock.)*

Speaking **5** Match the following sentence halves.

1 Don't worry, an Expedited parcel will arrive in — 3.30.
2 An Express parcel will get there within two days.
3 To arrive tomorrow, the package needs to leave by on time.
4 I'll stay here until in time.
5 It arrived at 8.30, which was exactly 24 hours.
6 We sent it by UPS Express, so it should arrive UPS collects the parcel.

Speaking **6** Work in pairs. Which three of the following features do you think are the most important for a parcel delivery service?

next day delivery reliability global network
confirmation of delivery low prices high quality of service

Sending a parcel

9 **Ex 1**: T introduces the exercise by telling Ss the three texts come from the same UPS brochure as in the first section. T introduces the notion of shipping charges and asks Ss to suggest what such charges are based on (*speed of service, destination and weight*). Ss then complete the task. They will also need to look at the descriptions of UPS services on the first page of the unit.

Helsinki	Express	Zone 4	3kg	= **£42.30**
Warsaw	Expedited	Zone 5	1.2kg	= **£43.40**
USA	Expedited (scheduled delivery)	Zone 3	2.4kg	= **£43.25**
	To arrive on Thursday			

In feedback T may need to review how sterling amounts are expressed/pronounced.

10 **Ex 2**: Ss ask one another about their company's delivery service. If Ss work for the same company, T may wish to expand the task to include a question as to how much each S's own department sends documents and parcels, where to and why.

11 **Ex 3**: Ss brainstorm other ways of delivering documents and parcels abroad (e.g. *personal courier, state postal system, lorry*). Possible disadvantages could include *length of time taken, expense, unreliability, poor security, lack of expertise in dealing with customs paperwork* etc. Advantages could include *security (e.g. courier carrying diamonds), lower cost, greater control of the process.*

12 **Ex 4**: T gives each pair of Ss two sets of cards face down. Ss proceed to pick up one pair of the cards, one from each set, and work out the best way of sending the various items. T may wish to give the task an outcome so that Ss are motivated to do the exercise well by indicating that there will be a feedback session for Ss to compare their suggestions. Alternatively, T could use smaller items and a UPS brochure and ask Ss to calculate the cost of sending the items to the locations on the cards.

Self-study

Ex 1: 2 *in/within*
3 *on*
4 *in/within*
5 *until*
6 *on*
7 *by*
8 *until*

Ex 2: 1 *documents*
2 *charge/rate*
3 *vehicles*
4 *urgent*
5 *rate/charge*
6 *destinations*
7 *packages*
8 *weight*

Ex 3: 1 B
2 A
3 C
4 C
5 A

Essential vocabulary

Delivery service
aircraft
carrier
charge
delivery
document
electronic tracking
express
network
package
parcel
shipment
vehicle

General
commitment
to rely on
urgent
worldwide

The words in italics are not on the Cambridge BEC 1 wordlist.

Sending a parcel

Reading **1** Your company wants to send three packages to different countries. How much will each item cost?

Weight: 3000g
To: Helsinki
To arrive by tomorrow morning

Weight: 1200g
To: Warsaw
To arrive within 48 hours

Weight: 2400g
To: United States
Zip code: 30341
To arrive Thursday

How to use the guide

All shipping charges are based on three considerations: the service selected, the weight of the shipment and the zone number for the destination. To find the correct rate for your shipment, follow these three steps:

1 Select your service
UPS offers a choice of Express, Expedited or Standard. Refer to the zone chart to see which services are available.

2 Select the zone
Locate the destination country and find its zone number.

3 Find the rate
Turn to the rate chart and match the shipment rate with the correct zone number.

zone chart

Destination	Express	Expedited
Finland EU	4	
Poland	5	2
United States *For areas below*	6	
New Jersey: 07000 - 07999 08500 - 08999		
New York: 10000 - 11999	7	3
Other destinations		

...kage shipments

■ Express Packages

Weight	zone 4 £	zone 5 £	zone 6 £	zone 7 £	zone 8 £
0.5 kg	27.70	33.50	28.50	34.00	37.50
1.0 kg	31.90	36.80	31.00	37.00	42.00
1.5 kg	34.50	39.40	33.00	40.00	46.50
2.0 kg	37.10	42.00	35.00	43.00	49.10
2.5 kg	39.70	44.60	37.00	46.00	51.70
3.0 kg	42.30	47.20	38.80	48.30	54.30

■ Expedited Packages

Weight	zone 1 £	zone 2 £	zone 3 £	zone 4 £	zone 5 £
1.0 kg	35.80	27.40	34.25	37.80	37.80
2.0 kg	40.80	31.20	38.75	43.40	43.40
3.0 kg	45.80	34.60	43.25	48.90	48.90
4.0 kg	50.00	38.00	47.75	54.30	54.30
5.0 kg	54.20	41.40	52.25	59.70	59.70
6.0 kg	57.20	43.00	55.05	63.70	64.10

Speaking **2** Work in pairs. What kind of parcel delivery service does your partner's company use? Why?

3 What other ways are there to send documents and parcels abroad? What are the advantages and disadvantages of each method?

 4 Work in pairs. Your teacher will give you two sets of cards showing items and destinations. Take one from each set and decide the best way to send the item to that destination.

Delivery services

---

1 Complete the sentences with the prepositions.

in   on   by   until   within

1 We sent it by Express Plus so it should arrive ___by___ 8.30 tomorrow morning.

2 We chose UPS Expedited in order to guarantee delivery _____ 24 hours.

3 She's very punctual. She always arrives exactly _____ time.

4 If you e-mail it, it'll get there _____ minutes.

5 We can't send it _____ we've weighed it.

6 If you want delivery _____ a particular day, you can send it Expedited for scheduled delivery.

7 It needs to arrive _____ tomorrow so we'll have to send it Express.

8 Please wait _____ I inform you that I have received the package.

2 Complete the sentences with the words below.

destinations   urgent
charge   weight
documents   packages
vehicles   rate

1 UPS will deliver both your _____ and parcels.

2 If you have the zone and the weight, you can work out the delivery _____.

3 Most UPS delivery _____ are vans.

4 You can send really _____ parcels to arrive before 8.30am the following day.

5 There is a standard postal _____ for EU countries.

6 They deliver to _____ in almost every country.

7 It is more expensive to send heavy _____ by post than by parcel delivery services.

8 The cost of the service depends on the _____ of the package and the speed of the service.

---

③

Exam practice

- Look at questions 1-5.
- In each question, which phrase or sentence is correct?
- For each question, mark the correct letter **A**, **B** or **C**.

1

> For additional charges, please refer to page 10.

You should turn to page 10

A to see about possible discounts.
B to find out about extra costs.
C for information about the product.

2

> Guaranteed delivery within 48 hours.

The parcel will arrive

A in less than two days from now.
B in exactly two days' time.
C in at least two days' time.

3

> Export documentation may be required for non-EU destinations.

Packages sent outside the EU

A must be documents only.
B will need special documents.
C might need special documents.

4

> Payment to be made by cash on delivery.

The invoice has to be paid

A after the shipment arrives.
B before the shipment arrives.
C when the shipment arrives.

5

> Transport papers must include an approximate value of the shipment.

The transport documents have to show

A how much the shipment is worth.
B the delivery charges for the shipment.
C a list of what is in the shipment.

Delivery services

Trading

Objectives:
To enable Ss to talk about trading
To practise listening and reading for specific information
To practise letter writing
To review tenses

Materials needed: Cassette - *Pass Cambridge BEC 1*
Cards - **9 cards:** *Pass Cambridge BEC 1*, Unit 16b/1-9 One set per pair/group

Unit overview

● An import agent

Warmer	T writes *agent* on the board. Ss discuss what the job involves.
Listening	Ss listen to the Managing Director of an import agency talking about his company and complete a factfile. Ss listen again and answer multiple-choice questions.
Speaking	Ss work in pairs, ordering cards which show the sequence of events surrounding a customer order. Ss decide which of the faxes etc. referred to on the cards match certain descriptions.
Language focus	Ss underline examples of tenses in the tapescript and categorise their uses.
Speaking	Ss interview each other in pairs in order to get information for a company factfile.

● Ordering parts

Reading	Ss read a quotation for some spare parts and answer multiple-choice questions.
Speaking	Ss work in pairs discussing things their companies order and the means by which they order them.
Writing	Ss write (collaboratively) a letter in reply to the earlier quotation.

● Self-study

Vocabulary	Matching exercise (verbs and nouns).
Language focus	Matching sentence halves.
	Jumbled sentences (letter phrases).
Exam practice	*Matching exercise (Reading Test Part 2).*

An import agent

1 **Warmer (books closed):** T writes *agent* on the board and asks Ss what they think an agent does. (Ss might suggest that the agent deals with enquiries from customers, deals with the supplier abroad and deals with paperwork.) T asks Ss what they think the advantages of using an agent are.

2 **Ex 1:** Before Ss listen to Wolfgang Rauch, the Managing Director of Raupack, talking about his company, T asks them to look at the gapped Factfile. T asks Ss what they know about the company even before they listen; it is helpful if T reinforces the idea that it is useful to base listening on knowledge and predictions rather than listen in a void. Ss then complete the Factfile to get an overview of the company's activities. (Mr Rauch is German but has worked in the UK for a long time.)

Company Raupack Ltd
Activities Agent for German packing machine manufacturers.
Services • Provide UK sales network.
 • (1) *translate* documents, specifications and (2) *parts* lists.
 • Deal with customer enquiries and (3) *correspondence*.
 • Arrange (4) *customers' visits* to Germany.
Founded In (5) *1982*.
Customers Major companies include SmithKline Beecham, Boots and (6) *Glaxo*.

3 **Ex 2:** Ss listen again and answer the multiple-choice questions.

1 B   2 A   3 B   4 C

4 **Ex 3:** Ss work in pairs and order the cards. It is probably easiest for Ss if T tells them to imagine three columns, with the British customer on the left, Raupack in the middle and the German supplier on the right. They then arrange the cards according to whether they are correspondence to or from the customer or the supplier.

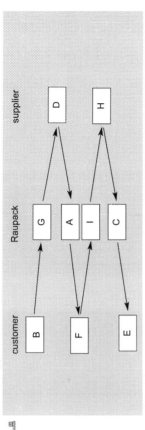

customer   Raupack   supplier

T asks Ss to leave the cards on the desk while doing the second part of Ex 3.

1 Enquiry: the fax in B
 Quotation: the fax in D and A
 Confirmation: the fax in F and I
 Invoice: the supplier bills Raupack in H also Raupack invoices the client in C

2 Written in English: the faxes in B, A and F. Important documents accompanying the shipment to the client and the invoice to the client in C.

 Written in German: the faxes in G and D. The confirmation from Raupack to the supplier in I. The documentation accompanying the goods in H.

5 **Ex 4:** Ss underline examples of the present simple, past simple, present perfect and present continuous in the tapescript. This is to lead into a review of these tenses which have already been referred to in earlier units. T then elicits uses of the tenses and reviews further if he/she feels it is necessary.

Suggested answers:
Present simple (already given)

Past simple - definite time (e.g. *in 1982 I left and set up my own company*) finished actions (e.g. *before I started Raupack, I worked in sales for eight years, ... these machines helped us to expand, ... our sales people were very good at ... so Raupack got a name for delivering excellent products*)

Present perfect - an action that started in the past and is still continuing (e.g. *how has the company developed since then?*)

Present continuous - an activity happening now (e.g. *at the moment we're looking for new staff* - there is only one example of the present continuous in the tapescript)

6 **Ex 5:** T elicits questions which Ss may wish to ask and ensures that Ss are confident about question formation. Ss then work in pairs, asking and answering similar questions to those asked by the interviewer. The factfile which Ss are going to write should cover similar categories to those in the Raupack factfile. Ss will have to use a variety of tenses in their questions and answers.

T may ask Ss to write the factfile in the lesson (perhaps with Ss from the same company working together). Alternatively, the task can be given for homework.

For pre-experience Ss, T can ask them to write a factfile about a company which has appeared earlier in the book, e.g. Direct Line or UPS.

Trading

An import agent

Listening **1** Raupack Ltd is a small company based near London. Listen to Wolfgang Rauch, the Managing Director, and complete the factfile.

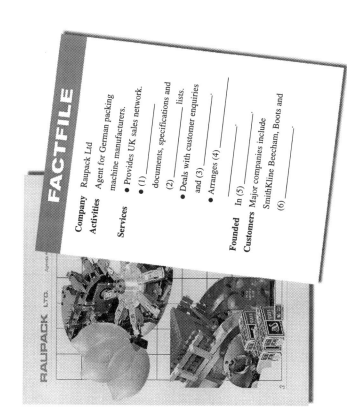

FACTFILE

Company Raupack Ltd

Activities Agent for German packing machine manufacturers.

Services
- Provides UK sales network.
- (1) _____ documents, specifications and (2) _____ lists.
- Deals with customer enquiries and (3) _____.
- Arranges (4) _____.

Founded In (5) _____.

Customers Major companies include SmithKline Beecham, Boots and (6) _____.

2 Listen again and choose the best phrase to complete the sentence.

1 Wolfgang Rauch left his job in 1982 because
   A he did not like the company.
   B he saw a good business opportunity.
   C the company had financial problems.

2 Raupack expanded because
   A its suppliers built very good machines.
   B the whole market grew very quickly.
   C its prices were very low.

3 Raupack became known for the
   A fair prices of its products.
   B quality of its products and service.
   C skill of its sales people.

4 Raupack's suppliers will have to develop
   A their machines and customer support services.
   B reliable and low priced machines.
   C technically advanced and reliable machines.

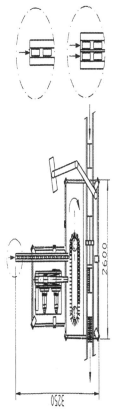

Product Collator

2600

3250

Speaking **3** Work in pairs. Your teacher will give you some cards describing how a customer orders parts through Raupack. Read the cards and put the process into the correct order.

1 Now decide which of the faxes or letters is
   - an enquiry
   - a quotation
   - confirmation
   - an invoice

2 Which of the faxes or letters would be
   - in English?
   - in German?

Grammar **4** Look at the tapescript on page 143. Underline examples of the following tenses. How does Mr Rauch use them?

1 Present simple   company activities (e.g. we translate their documents)

                          opinions (e.g. I think)

2 Past simple

3 Present perfect

4 Present continuous

Speaking **5** Work in pairs. Ask your partner questions and write a factfile for his/her company.

Ordering parts

7   Ex ❶: Ss read the quotation and answer the multiple-choice questions.

    1 A   2 B   3 C   4 A

8   Ex ❷: Ss work in pairs and discuss how orders are made in their companies. T encourages them to expand about the problems involved with the different types of communication.

9   Ex ❸: Ss read the Post-it note and work in pairs to plan the reply to Raupack. T encourages them to think of some typical letter phrases which could be useful. Ss then write the letter alone. Before T reads the letters, T may wish to encourage peer feedback and correction. The word limit in Part Three of the Writing Test must be respected. Therefore, if Ss have exceeded the 50-60 word limit, they could work in pairs, trying to make the letters more concise.

Alternatively, T may wish to ask Ss to write the letter for homework.

Self-study

Ex ❶: 1 *deal with **enquiries, correspondence***
        2 *translate **documents, specifications, a parts lists***
        3 *provide **a sales network, a service, support***

Ex ❷: 2 C   3 H   4 B   5 A   6 E   7 F   8 D

Ex ❸: 1 *Thank you for your enquiry.*
        2 *We are pleased to quote as follows.*
        3 *Our standard terms and conditions apply.*
        4 *The price is quoted in euros.*
        5 *The price does not include VAT.*
        6 *We look forward to hearing from you.*

Ex ❹: 1 C   2 G   3 A   4 E   5 F

Essential vocabulary

Import agent	General
ex works	availability
invoice	fair
packing	receipt
to quote	skill
parts list	*technically advanced*
spare parts	to translate
specifications	

The words in italics are not on the Cambridge BEC 1 wordlist.

Ordering parts

Reading **1** A customer has received a quotation from Raupack. Read the letter and Jenny's note and choose the best phrase to complete the sentences.

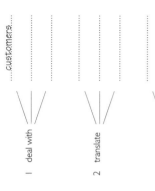

RAUPACK LTD

11 CASTLE STREET
GUILDFORD
SURREY
GU1 6KG

Tel: (01483) 564700
Fax: (01483) 564710
e-mail: sales@raupack.com

Fax no: 32725

Date: 08.04.99
To: Eversham Dairy Products
FAO: Jennifer Tanner

Dear Ms Tanner

Re: Parts Quotation for SM300/Machine type 3000.002.93

Thank you for your enquiry. We are pleased to quote as follows:

Qty	Description	Parts No	Unit Price
100	Tension spring	RZ-0531 9907.15	
10	Starting disc	3000.010.19	
4	Grooved bearing	6007-2RS1 9908	
1	Level switch	WF02	

The above prices are quoted in euros and are ex works in Germany. These prices do not include packing, transport, insurance and VAT. Our standard terms and conditions apply.

The parts would be ready for despatch from Germany approximately six weeks after receipt of the order.

Kind regards

Gisela Mason
RAUPACK LTD

[Jenny's note:] Could you write back to Raupack and order these spares? Could you also ask how much the extra costs will be and how long they'll take to get here. Thanks Jenny

1 The customer would like to
  A buy some spare parts for a machine.
  B buy a new packing machine.
  C enquire about a new machine.

2 The letter is in reply to a
  A confirmation of an order.
  B request for information.
  C letter of complaint.

3 The customer has to pay
  A no extra costs.
  B only import tax.
  C all extra costs.

4 The order could
  A leave the factory in about six weeks.
  B be delivered in about six weeks.
  C leave the factory immediately.

Speaking **2** Work in pairs. Find five things your partner's company orders. Does it order them by telephone, fax, e-mail or letter? Which type of communication is best? Why?

Writing **3** Work in pairs. Read the note again and write a reply to Raupack. Write about 50-60 words. Plan your letter carefully with your partner before you write it.

---

3 Re-arrange the words to make phrases from a written quotation.

1 you / enquiry / thank / your / for

2 pleased / to / follows / we / quote / are / as

3 apply / our / conditions / terms / standard / and

4 in / is / price / quoted / euros / the

5 does / price / include / the / not / VAT

6 hearing / forward / from / look / we / to / you

1 Look at the tapescript on page 143. Find the nouns that go with the verbs below.

1 deal with ....customers........

2 translate

3 provide

2 Match the sentence halves about the history of Raupack.

1 Mr Rauch began by ... G
2 The company's smaller suppliers wanted ...
3 So Mr Rauch set up ...
4 His suppliers were very good at ...
5 Moreover, his company developed a name for ...
6 Raupack is now looking for new staff ...
7 In the future, suppliers will have to develop the machines technically without ...
8 And Raupack will have to continue ...

A the quality of its products and service.
B developing technically advanced machines.
C someone to sell only their machines.
D to provide the best possible service.
E to help the company grow.
F losing any of their reliability.
G working in sales for an international company.
H his own company.

Exam practice

4
- Look at the checklist below. It shows the documents **A-H** which are needed to export machinery.
- For questions 1-5, decide which documents **A-H** the people are talking about.
- For each question, mark the correct letter **A-H**.
- Do not use any letter more than once.

> A Shipping papers
> B Drawings
> C Invoice
> D Specifications
> E Handbook
> F Parts list
> G Registration form
> H Guarantee

1 2% discount if payment is within ten days.
2 The customer fills it in and returns it in order to go on our customer mailing list.
3 If they aren't correct, the machine won't get through customs.
4 It's translated so the engineers know how to operate the machine properly.
5 We normally mark on it the spares that we think the customer should always keep in stock.

Tapescript: Listening

Journalist Could you tell me about Raupack and its activities?

Mr Rauch We're an agent for German manufacturers of packing machinery. We provide them with a British sales network and translate their documents, specifications and parts lists into English. We also deal with the British customers and all their enquiries and correspondence. And we arrange customers' visits to Germany.

Journalist Mm, that's very interesting. How did this company begin?

Mr Rauch Before I started Raupack, I worked in sales for eight years for an international company here in the UK. We had to use some small suppliers of packing machinery to complete our product range, but working with both large and small suppliers caused problems. The smaller companies wanted someone to sell only their products, so in 1982 I left and set up my own company, Raupack Ltd.

Journalist That was a big step. And how has this company developed since then?

Mr Rauch Well, I began selling to the drinks industry. Our suppliers began developing excellent new machines that were technically more advanced than our competitors'. These machines helped us to expand into the food and pharmaceutical industries. And our sales people were very good at understanding and selling these new machines so Raupack got a name for delivering excellent products and providing a service that was fair to both customers and suppliers. Since then turnover has grown to nearly £10m a year and our customers now include companies such as SmithKline Beecham, Boots and Glaxo. We moved into these new offices last year and at the moment we're looking for new staff to help the company grow further.

Journalist Very good. And the future? How do you see the future?

Mr Rauch I think technical development is the key to the industry. Companies have to produce and pack more and more specialised goods to satisfy their customers. So, in future, our suppliers'll have to develop their machines technically but without losing any reliability. Our job, of course, is going to be to sell these new machines and continue to provide the best possible support for both our customers and our suppliers.

Recruiting staff

Objectives:	To enable Ss to talk about recruitment
	To practise reading and listening for gist and for specific information
	To focus on Conditional 2 for hypothetical situations

Materials needed: Cassette - *Pass Cambridge BEC 1*

Unit overview

● Recruitment methods

Reading	Ss read an article about recruitment and complete a diagram, then look for the advantages and disadvantages of each method.
Speaking	Ss discuss extracts from the article.
Language focus	Ss review *would* and *could/might* for expected and possible results of hypothetical situations.
Speaking	Ss work in pairs and discuss how they would recruit people for a range of occupations.

● Advertising a vacancy

Reading	Ss read two advertisements for the same job and answer questions.
Listening	Ss then listen to a conversation related to the job vacancy, decide which advert will be placed first and listen again for the disadvantages of each of the two types of advertisement.
Language focus	Ss identify the uses of the past simple verbs in the tapescript then focus on Conditional 2.
Speaking	Ss exchange ideas on how they would recruit people for their own jobs.

● Self-study

Vocabulary	Sentence completion exercise (personal vocabulary).
	Matching exercise (noun and verb collocates).
Language focus	Sentence completion (Conditional 2).
Exam practice	*Matching statements with graphs (Reading Test Part 3).*

Recruitment methods

1 **Warmer (books closed):** T writes the title of the unit *Recruiting staff* on the blackboard and asks Ss what they think it means. T uses this to introduce the topic and elicit/teach important vocabulary for the unit: *to apply for, application, applicant, candidate, vacancy, to recruit, recruitment*. T checks that Ss can pronounce *recruit* and *recruitment*.

2 **Ex ❶:** T elicits from Ss how they were recruited to their present job. Ss then work in pairs brainstorming ways to recruit staff (*external* or *internal advertising, agency* etc.).

3 **Ex ❷:** Ss read the article and complete the diagram. Ss check their answers with a partner before general feedback.

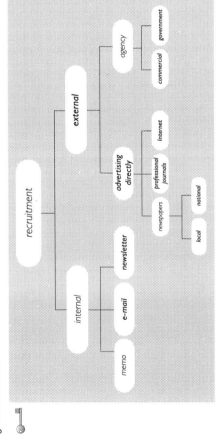

4 **Ex ❸:** Ss read the article to identify the advantages and disadvantages of each recruitment method.

Method	Advantages	Disadvantages
Internal recruitment	Easy to recruit applicants Easy to assess Applicants know the company well	Rarely bring fresh ideas to a position If rejected, people could become unhappy and leave the company
External recruitment Local newspapers	Good for blue-collar or clerical jobs	
National newspapers or professional journals	Good for senior management positions	
The Internet	One of the best ways of advertising IT vacancies or recruiting abroad	Risk of receiving unsuitable applications from all over the world
Government employment centre	Good for blue-collar workers	
Commercial employment agency	Good for white-collar staff	Expensive. Applicants less likely to stay with the company

5 **Ex ❹:** The objective of this exercise is to stimulate discussion. There are no right or wrong answers.

6 T draws Ss' attention to the use of *could/might* in the article in **Ex ❹** to refer to the possible results of a hypothetical situation: *which could cause personnel problems for the whole department/a rejected internal candidate might become unhappy and leave the company*. T broadens out the idea of consequences of a hypothetical situation to cover *would* for expected results. T then refers Ss to the **Don't forget!** section.

7 **Ex ❺:** Ss discuss ways of advertising specific jobs. T encourages Ss to think of the advantages and disadvantages of any methods chosen.

Recruiting staff

Recruiting staff

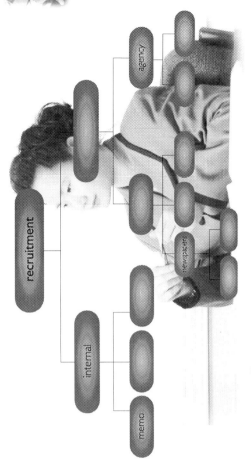

Recruitment methods

Speaking ❶ Work in pairs. How many different ways can a company recruit applicants to fill a job vacancy?

Reading ❷ Read the magazine article about recruiting staff and complete the diagram on the opposite page.

profile

The right person for the right job

Finding the right job applicant to fill a vacancy is never easy. Julie Bain looks at the pros and cons of different recruitment methods.

Recruiting the right candidate to fill a vacancy can be a difficult and costly task. Appointing the wrong person could be an expensive mistake which could cause personnel problems for the whole department. And, as every HR Manager knows, it is much more difficult to get rid of someone than it is to employ them.

The HR Manager's first decision is whether to recruit internal applicants or advertise the vacancy outside the company. Internal applicants are easy to recruit by memo, e-mail or newsletter. Furthermore, they are easy to assess and know the company well. However, they rarely bring fresh ideas to a position. Moreover, a rejected internal candidate might become unhappy and leave the company.

Recruiting outside the company means either advertising the vacancy directly or using an employment agency. If the company decides to advertise the vacancy directly, it has to decide

where to place the advertisement. Traditionally this has meant newspapers and professional journals but now the Internet is also very popular. The decision normally depends on the vacancy. Companies advertise blue-collar or clerical jobs in local newspapers and senior management positions in national papers or professional journals, while the Internet is one of the best ways of advertising IT vacancies or recruiting abroad. However, with the Internet there is a risk of receiving unsuitable applications from all over the world.

An agency can be either a commercial business or a government employment centre. A company often uses a government agency to recruit blue-collar workers but normally prefers a commercial agency for its white-collar staff. However, a commercial agency could be very expensive and the applicants are less likely to stay with the company for a long time.

❸ What are the advantages and disadvantages of each recruitment method?

❹ Look at the following extracts from the article and answer the questions.

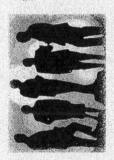

Appointing the wrong person could be an expensive mistake which could cause personnel problems for the whole department. And, as every HR Manager knows, it's much more difficult to get rid of

assess and know the company well. However, they rarely bring fresh ideas to a position. Moreover, a rejected internal candidate could

fresh ideas to a position. Moreover, a rejected internal candidate might become unhappy and leave the company.

for the whole department. And, as every HR Manager knows, it's much more difficult to get rid of someone than it is to employ them.

1 How could the wrong candidate cause problems for the whole department?
2 Why is it difficult to get rid of someone?
3 Why don't internal applicants have fresh ideas?
4 Why might an unsuccessful candidate leave the company?

Don't forget! Hypothetical situations

- We can use **would** to talk about the expected results of a hypothetical situation.
  A large company would advertise in a national newspaper.
- We can use **could/might** to talk about the possible results of a hypothetical situation.
  Appointing the wrong person could/might be an expensive mistake.

Units 21–23

Speaking ❺ Work in pairs. How would you advertise the following vacancies?

finance director · graphic designer · marketing manager
bilingual secretary · truck driver · computer programmer

Self-study

Ex 1:
1 applicants
2 an application form
3 appointed
4 vacancy
5 recruit
6 candidates

Ex 2:
1 **to fill**
  to advertise   a vacancy
  to apply for
2 **internal**
  external   applicants
  to recruit
3 recruit   **a candidate**
                           internal applicants
                           workers
4 advertise   **a vacancy**
                           jobs
                           a position

Ex 3:
2 you would have to advertise.
3 I'd look for a different kind of work.
4 I'd miss my family.
5 the job was/were offered to you?

Ex 4: 1 D   2 F   3 C   4 H   5 B

Essential vocabulary

Recruitment
application (form)
to apply (for)
to appoint
blue-collar worker
white-collar staff
clerical job
curriculum vitae (CV)
employment agency
external
internal
to fill (a vacancy)
to place (an advertisement)
position
to promote
to recruit
recruitment
to get rid of
to take on
vacancy

The words in italics are not on the Cambridge BEC 1 wordlist.

Advertising a vacancy

8 **Ex 1:** Ss read the two advertisements and answer the questions. They compare their answers with a partner before feedback.

1 The advertisement on the left would appear on an office notice board or as a memo circulated to staff.
   The advertisement on the right would appear in a national newspaper.
2 The advertisement on the left is organised as a memo and is brief and to the point. It has a memo-style heading and has three paragraphs: the fact that the vacancy exists, the requirements of the job, how to apply.
   The advertisement on the right is laid out more clearly as an advertisement: centred information with bolding to make the company name, the company and the job and how to apply stand out. There are four main paragraphs: the job and the company, the requirements of the job, a reference to rewards and how to apply.
3 The newspaper advertisement contains more information about the company itself (package holiday company etc.). It also contains (somewhat non-specific) reference to salary, benefits etc. The full address of the company is given.
4 The newspaper advertisement. The company is described in terms suggesting size, quality and success (**largest, quality products, partners worldwide**). The rewards mention career development and that there will probably be performance-related pay.

9 **Ex 2:** Ss predict which of the two advertisements they would place first before listening to compare their answers with what the managers decide.

   They will advertise internally first because it is company policy: the company policy is to promote its own people and help them develop a career in the company.

10 **Ex 3:** Ss may well be able to answer this question from their first listening. T therefore first elicits possible answers from Ss before playing the cassette again. Ss then listen to check their answer.

   The disadvantages are not enough applicants and a lot of internal political problems. If one internal applicant is given the job, the others aren't happy.

11 **Ex 4:** Ss work in pairs and find the verbs in the past simple form in the tapescript

   decided, advertised, did, didn't advertise, promoted, took, had (to do), didn't get.

   Had (to do) and didn't get refer to the past.

   T elicits the various hypothetical situations from Ss plus their possible consequences:

   If we decided to to take someone on, where would we advertise the vacancy? (Internally)
   If we advertised the job internally, we'd have the same old problems.
   If we did (ie., advertise the job outside), a lot of people wouldn't be very happy …
   It'd look a bit funny if we didn't advertise it internally first.
   If we promoted one of our own people, the other internal applicants wouldn't be very happy …
   If we took someone on from outside the company, we'd bring some new ideas …

12 Ss complete the **Don't forget!** section.

   If + **past simple** tense, **would/could/might** + infinitive

13 **Ex 5:** Ss work in pairs to exchange ideas on how they would recruit people. To round off the activity, T asks for Ss' ideas in a general feedback session.

Advertising a vacancy

Reading **1** Read the two advertisements below and answer the questions.

1 Where would the advertisements appear?

2 How is the information organised in the two advertisements?

3 What extra information does the newspaper advertisement include?

4 Which advertisement tries to "sell" the position more? How?

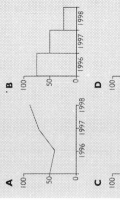

06-MAR-1999 12:28 FROM: GOLDSMITHS HOLIDAYS TO: ALL OFFICES P.01/01

Goldsmiths
H O L I D A Y S

To: All offices
From: Rick Hayward
Date: 6 March 1999

Re: Vacancy for Senior Marketing Assistant

Senior Marketing Assistant - London

Goldsmiths Holidays has a vacancy at its main London offices for an assistant to the Marketing Director.

The successful candidate will be a graduate with at least 3 years' marketing experience and preferably a second European language. Key responsibilities will include helping to plan and manage our range of package holidays and building relationships with partners.

If you wish to apply for the vacancy, please speak with your office manager and contact Rick Hayward at Heath Villas by 13 March.

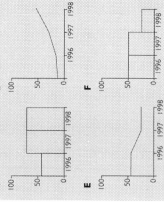
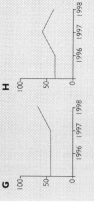

Goldsmiths
H O L I D A Y S

requires a

Senior Marketing Assistant

Goldsmiths, one of Europe's largest package holiday companies, requires a **Senior Marketing Assistant** at our main London offices. Working closely with the Marketing Director, you will help plan and manage our range of quality products and maintain relationships with our partners worldwide.

A confident and skilled communicator, you will be a graduate with a minimum of 3 years' marketing experience within the travel industry. A second European language would also be an advantage.

The rewards in terms of salary, benefits and career development will fully reflect your contribution to the success of Goldsmiths Holidays Ltd

If you think that you have the ability and the confidence, please apply in writing enclosing your CV to: Goldsmiths Holidays, 24 Heath Villas, The Vale of Heath, London NW3 1AW. Fax: 0171 444 3879. e-mail: refima@goldsmiths.com

Closing date: Friday 26 June 1999

Goldsmiths Holidays is an Equal Opportunities Employer

PRESS OFFERED

Listening **2** Two HR managers discuss the vacancy at Goldsmiths. Listen to the conversation. Which advertisement do they decide to place first? Why?

3 Listen again. What are the disadvantages of each type of advertisement?

Grammar **4** Look at the tapescript on page 143. Underline all the verbs in the past simple. How many of them refer to the past? What do the others refer to? Now complete the information below.

Hypothetical conditionals

• We can use the following conditional forms to talk about the results of an action which we do not expect to happen.

If + _____ tense, _____ would _____ + infinitive

Unit 6

Speaking **5** Work in pairs. How would your partner recruit people for his/her own job?

Recruiting staff

4
• Look at the graphs A-H below. They show how a company has recruited its staff over a three-year period.
• Which method does each sentence 1-5 describe?
• For each question, mark the correct letter A, B or C.
• Do not use any letter more than once.

A

B

C

D

E

F

G

H

[graphs A–H showing recruitment figures for 1996, 1997, 1998, with vertical axes marked 0, 50, 100]

1 The number of employees recruited on the Internet rose steadily throughout the period.

2 Recruitment through national newspapers remained steady in 1996 and 1997 but fell in 1998.

3 After a sharp rise in 1997, internal recruitment levelled off.

4 The number of employees recruited directly from universities peaked at the end of 1997.

5 Over the three-year period there was a continuous decline in recruitment through local newspapers.

Recruiting staff

116

---

1 Choose the best word to complete the sentences.

1 We had over 30 *applicants/assistants* for the vacancy we advertised in the local paper.

2 I had to fill in a *CV/an application form* and return it to the Personnel Department.

3 We *appointed/filled* someone to the position over two weeks ago.

4 We advertised the *employment/vacancy* on the Internet.

5 We need to *apply/recruit* ten more people before the summer.

6 I am going to interview the *candidates/appointments* tomorrow.

2 Look back through the unit and tapescript. Find three words to go with each of the following.

1 _____ _____ a vacancy

2 _____ _____ applicants

3 recruit _____ _____

4 advertise _____ _____

3 Complete the sentences below. Use your own words.

1 If I decided to change my job, *I'd look for a different type of work.*

2 If you wanted to recruit more people to work in your department, _____

3 If I lost my job, _____

4 If I worked abroad, _____

5 Would you accept it if _____

Recruiting staff

Tapescript: Listening

Rick   So Patricia, have you given any more thought to taking on an assistant in marketing?

Patricia   Yes and I'm still not sure about it. If we decided to take someone on, where would we advertise the vacancy?

Rick   Well, I guess we'd advertise the position internally as we always do.

Patricia   But if we advertised the job internally, we'd have the same old problems - not enough applicants and lots of internal political problems. Couldn't we advertise the job outside the company for once?

Rick   Well I suppose we could. But if we did, a lot of people wouldn't be very happy about it.

Patricia   So? Would that be a problem?

Rick   Well, yes. I mean, the company always talks about how we like to promote our own people and how you can develop a career with us. So it'd look a bit funny if we didn't advertise it internally first.

Patricia   But even if we promoted one of our own people, the other internal applicants wouldn't be happy anyway. So what's the difference? Why couldn't we just advertise it in the national papers?

Rick   But it's company policy. You know that. We always advertise internally first.

Patricia   Yes, I know. But why can't we try something different for a change? If we took someone on from outside the company, we'd bring some new ideas into the department. It's what we need, Rick.

Rick   Look, why don't we just advertise it internally as we always do, right? That'll keep everyone happy and then, after a couple of weeks, we can put an advert in the paper as well. What do you say?

Patricia   Oh all right. But I'm not going to do the interviews. You can. I had to do the interviews last time and the people who didn't get the job didn't speak to me for weeks afterwards.

Applying for a job

Objectives: To enable Ss to talk about job applications and interviews
To practise reading and listening for specific information
To practise writing a letter of application
To review indirect questions

Materials needed: Cassette - *Pass Cambridge BEC 1*

Unit overview

● Application letters

Reading	Ss read an advertisement for a secretarial job and answer questions. Ss then order an applicant's notes about the advertisement.
Language focus	Ss match typical application letter language with the notes.
Writing	Ss work in pairs and write the applicant's letter of application.

● Attending an interview

Listening	Ss transform the interviewer's notes into polite questions. They then listen to the interview and compare the questions used. Ss listen again and write down the applicant's answers to the questions.
Language focus	Ss review the form and use of indirect questions.
Speaking	Ss ask and answer polite questions in pairs in order to fill in their partner's application form. Ss then discuss how to answer four awkward interview questions and compare their ideas with those in Exercise 4 of **Self-study**.

● Self-study

Language focus	Transformation exercise (indirect questions).
Vocabulary	Word-field (qualities and skills).
Language focus	Jumbled sentences (letter-writing).
Exam practice	*'Right, Wrong, Doesn't say' questions (Reading Test Part 4).*

Attending an interview

6 **Ex ❶**: Ss work in pairs to make polite questions from the handwritten notes. They listen to the cassette and compare their own questions with those in the interview.

1 Could you tell me which countries you have dealt with?
2 Could you tell me how good your French is?
3 Could you tell me how many words a minute you can type?
4 Could you tell me why you left?
5 Could you tell me a bit about which programs you use?
6 Did you design the presentations yourself?

T focuses on the functions of polite questions. (T focuses on their form in **Ex ❸**.) T leads discussion of why indirect questions are used. T should elicit that they enable the speaker to be polite and relatively distant, as in a formal interview with strangers. Also indirect questions can be used for potentially embarrassing or difficult information-gathering. T makes the point that polite indirect questions are particularly useful when a new topic is being introduced but they are unlikely to be useful for follow-up questions. For example, here the first question about computer software is indirect but it is followed up by a direct question (Did you design the presentations yourself?). As long as the intonation is all right, direct questions can also be polite.

7 **Ex ❷**: Ss listen again and note down Almudena's answers to the questions. They compare answers in pairs before general feedback.

1 America, Britain and Italy.
2 Basic (not as good as her English and Italian).
3 About 50 wpm.
4 She never used her languages and had always been interested in publishing.
5 Microsoft Word and Powerpoint.
6 The Training Director planned them, but Almudena did the actual computer work and made sure the computer worked during the presentation.

Application letters

1 **Warmer (books closed)**: T elicits what Ss normally expect to find in a job advertisement. Ss then open their books and scan the GlobalTV advertisement to see if this information is included.

2 **Ex ❶**: Ss read the advertisement and answer the questions.

16K = £16,000 salary   O/T = overtime
60 wpm = 60 words per minute   langs = languages

1 Temporary (until 2000)
2 Support the television production team
3 Shorthand and word-processing skills (60 wpm); European languages an advantage but not required
4
5 Flexible, motivated, enthusiastic with good communication skills

3 **Ex ❷**: Ss then look at the applicant's notes and discuss the correct order.

Suggested answers:
1 how I heard about the job
2 qualifications
3 experience
4 why I want the job
5 CV and photo

There should probably be four paragraphs: 1) reference to the advertisement, 2) educational and work background, 3) why she wants the job, 4) enclosures.

In feedback T asks Ss what they normally include in letters of application. This can be a discussion before the letter writing activity.

4 **Ex ❸**: After Ss have matched the phrases, T checks Ss are sure of their meaning as a full group activity.

1 how I heard about the job   2 qualifications   3 experience
4 why I want the job   5 CV and photo

5 **Ex ❹**: Ss use the information provided to plan and write a letter of application.

Suggested answer:
PRODUCTION SECRETARY
I am writing with reference to your advertisement for a Production Secretary in the Guardian of 23 July 1998.

I graduated from Madrid University in 1994 with a degree in Modern European languages. My first full-time job was as a support secretary for the Training Director of a company which ran courses for software designers and IT managers. Since 1996 I have been working as a bilingual secretary for a large international publishing company.

I am very interested in the position because I would like to use my languages. I am enthusiastic about working for a TV company and feel that I have the flexibility, motivation and communication skills you require.

Please find enclosed my curriculum vitae and a photo.

I look forward to hearing from you.

In feedback T asks Ss to exchange and compare versions of the letter. T points out the different pronunciations of a graduate/to graduate.

Applying for a job

Application letters

Reading **1** Almudena Ribera is a secretary in Madrid. She is looking for work in Britain and replies to the advertisement below. Read the advertisement and answer the questions.

1 What do the following abbreviations mean?
   £16K   O/T   60wpm   langs
2 Is the position permanent or temporary?
3 What are the duties?
4 What skills are required for the job?
5 What personal qualities are looked for?

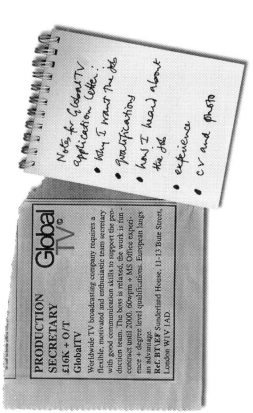

PRODUCTION SECRETARY
£16K + O/T
GlobalTV

Worldwide TV broadcasting company requires a flexible, motivated and enthusiastic team secretary with good communication skills to support the production team. The boss is relaxed, the work is fun - contract until 2000. 60wpm + MS Office experience + degree level qualifications. European langs an advantage.
Ref: BTUEF Sunderland House, 11-13 Bute Street, London W1V 1AD.

Notes for GlobalTV application letter:
- Why I want the job
- qualifications
- how I heard about the job
- experience
- CV and photo

2 Almudena begins to plan her application letter. Put her notes above into the correct order for the letter. How many paragraphs should there be?

3 Match the phrases below with Almudena's notes.

1 I am writing with reference to your advertisement in the ...
2 I graduated from Madrid University with a degree in ...
3 Since 1996 I have been working as ...
4 I am very interested in the position because ...
5 Please find enclosed ...

Writing **4** Work in pairs. Write Almudena's letter of application to GlobalTV. Decide what information you should include. Use the phrases above and the information in the curriculum vitae (CV) on the opposite page.

Attending an interview

Listening **1** Almudena attends an interview at GlobalTV. Before you listen, read the HR Manager's notes about Almudena's CV. Change his notes on the CV into polite questions. Then listen and compare your questions with his.

CURRICULUM VITAE
ALMUDENA Ribera

Duncan — Thanks for agreeing to do the interview for me on Tuesday. Here's the candidate's CV - I've marked a few things you should ask her about. And don't forget to take notes! Thanks

Personal details

Name:	Almudena Ribera
Address:	c/ Lozano n°24 1°B 28019 MA
Telephone:	00 34 91 6342918
Date of birth:	10.02.1973
Marital status:	Single
Nationality:	Spanish

Key skills

- Ability to work to deadlines.
- Experience of dealing with clients in different countries. — *Which countries?*
- Good written and spoken knowledge of English and Italian. — *What about French?*
- Good keyboard skills and knowledge of current software packages. — *Wpm?*

Work experience

1996 - present
Ediciones Gómez S.A., Madrid
Currently working as a bilingual secretary for Ediciones Gómez, a Madrid-based publisher. Duties include dealing with international partners both on the phone and in writing, sending invoices, making arrangements for visitors and general office duties.

1994 - 1996 — *Why did she leave?*
Informática S.A., Madrid — *Which software?*
Support Secretary for the Training Director. Used various software packages. Assisted the Director in the organisation of training courses for software designers and presentations to IT managers. Responsibilities also included dealing with correspondence and general office duties. — *What kind? With computers?*

Summer work 1992 -1994
Instituto Calderón de la Barca, Madrid
Teaching Spanish as a foreign language. Duties included planning and teaching Spanish lessons to adults. I also organised cultural trips to museums and exhibitions.

Qualifications

1991 - 1994
Complutense University, Madrid
Graduated with an honours degree in Modern European Languages, specialising in English and Italian. The degree also included French language studies, English commercial correspondence and IT skills.

- 1 -

2 Now listen again and write down Almudena's answers to the questions.

8 **Ex ❸**: Ss answer the questions about the form of indirect questions. T focuses on the form of indirect questions and elicits from Ss how the word order in direct question changes for indirect questions (the subject and verb stay in their normal position). T also points out that auxiliaries are not used with indirect questions.

Direct questions	Indirect questions
Wh-questions:	
verb subject Which programmes **do you use**?	*subject verb* Can you tell me which programmes **you use**?
Yes/no questions:	
verb subject **Did you** design the presentations yourself?	*subject verb* Could you tell me if **you designed the** presentations yourself?

T may then wish to drill Ss, giving them various direct questions to make indirect in order to check that they understand the rule. T might want to point out that *whether* can be used instead of *if* in yes/no questions.

9 **Ex ❹**: T does the first question with the whole class as a model before Ss work in pairs to complete their partner's form. To round off this activity, T may wish to go through the exercise, eliciting Ss' questions at random. T should ensure that Ss do not only use indirect questions. If they do, it will be extremely unnatural. T checks that Ss used block capitals as instructed on the form.

If there is no time to do this activity in class, it may still be useful to ask Ss to fill in the form. (Ss have a much simpler form to complete in Part One of the Writing Test.) Ss could either fill the form in for themselves or transfer the information from Almudena's CV. T may wish to make extra photocopies of the form so that Ss can do both the oral exercise and fill in the form for themselves/Almudena.

10 **Ex ❺**: T reminds Ss that indirect questions help people to ask for potentially difficult or sensitive information. Ss look at the four questions and make them indirect. T may need to check Ss' understanding of *professional objectives*.

T asks Ss to consider how they would answer such questions (i.e. not just the answers but their general attitude when faced with such questions). Ss discuss in pairs before general feedback.

Ss read the text from **Ex ❹** of **Self-study** and compare their own answers with the advice in the text.

Self-study

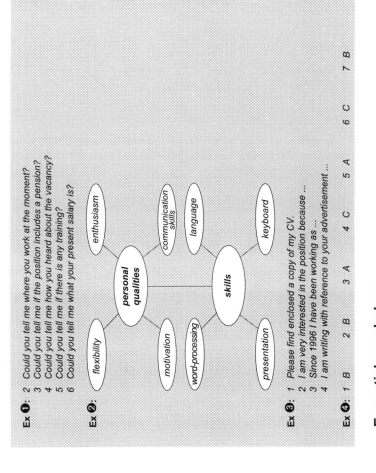

Ex ❶: 2 Could you tell me where you work at the moment?
3 Could you tell me if the position includes a pension?
4 Could you tell me how you heard about the vacancy?
5 Could you tell me if there is any training?
6 Could you tell me what your present salary is?

Ex ❷:

personal qualities — enthusiasm, communication skills, language, flexibility, motivation, word-processing

skills — keyboard, presentation

Ex ❸: 1 Please find enclosed a copy of my CV.
2 I am very interested in the position because …
3 Since 1996 I have been working as …
4 I am writing with reference to your advertisement …

Ex ❹: 1 B   2 B   3 A   4 C   5 A   6 C   7 B

Essential vocabulary

Applying for a job
degree
experience
graduate
to graduate
higher education
marital status
nationality
permanent
temporary
qualifications

Skills and qualities
bilingual
communication skills
enthusiastic
keyboard skills
motivated

General
honest
to lie
software package
weakness
words per minute (wpm)

The words in italics are not on the Cambridge BEC 1 wordlist.

Grammar

3 Look at the direct and indirect forms of the question below. What are the grammatical differences?

- Which programs do you use?
- Could you tell me which programs you use?

- Can you leave your present job immediately?
- Could you tell me if you can leave your present job immediately?

Speaking

4 Work in pairs. Imagine your partner is applying for a job at GlobalTV. Complete the application form with your partner's details.

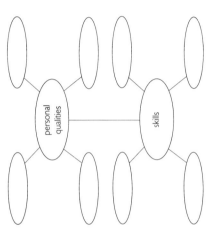

Please write clearly in BLOCK CAPITALS.

Position applied for:

Title:

Full name:

Nationality:

Marital status:

Date of birth:

Address:

Phone number:

e-mail:

Current employment:

Higher education:

Professional qualifications:

Computer skills:

Language skills:

Interests:

Signature: Date:

5 Work in pairs. Look at the interview questions below. How would you answer them?

What don't you like about your current position?

Where does your employer think you are today?

What are your professional objectives?

What are your weaknesses?

Now look at the text **Attending interviews** on the opposite page. It contains a recruitment consultant's advice on how to answer these questions. Do you agree?

Rewrite the following as indirect questions.

1 Where is the interview room?
   Could you tell me where the interview room is?

2 Where do you work at the moment?

3 Does the position include a pension?

4 How did you hear about the vacancy?

5 Is there any training?

6 What is your present salary?

2 Complete the diagram with vocabulary from the unit.

```
        ( )           ( )

              personal
              qualities

        ( )           ( )


        ( )           ( )

               skills

        ( )           ( )
```

3 Re-arrange the following words to make phrases from a letter of application.

1 Please / copy / my / CV / a / find / enclosed / of

2 I / because / position / am / in / the / interested / very

3 Since / as / been / have / 1996 / I / working

4 I / reference / am / advertisement / writing / with / to / your

---

Exam practice

- Read the text below which advises candidates how to answer difficult interview questions.
- Are the sentences below 'Right' or 'Wrong'?
- If there is not enough information to answer 'Right' or 'Wrong', choose 'Doesn't say'.
- For each question, mark the correct letter **A, B** or **C.**

Attending interviews

Good interviewers prepare their questions carefully in advance according to the candidate's application and CV. So candidates need to prepare just as carefully. Here are some useful tips on answering interview questions.

1 What don't you like about your current position?
No job is perfect; there's always something we don't like. Be honest but don't give a list of complaints. The important thing is to talk positively about how you deal with problems at work.

2 Where does your employer think you are today?
Be honest. If you lie to your current employer, you'll lie to your next employer. Don't phone in sick on the day of the interview. Take a day's holiday but don't say why.

3 What are your professional objectives?
Think about these before the interview. Your objectives should be relevant to the job you have applied for and achievable. If the new job can't offer you everything you want, the interviewer will think that you probably won't stay with the company very long.

4 What are your weaknesses?
Be honest: no-one is perfect. Think about this before the interview and choose your answer carefully. Talk about how you deal with a weakness; this is far more important than the weakness itself.

1 Interviewers ask every candidate the same questions.
   A Right   **B** Wrong   **C** Doesn't say

2 You shouldn't mention problems with your current job.
   A Right   **B** Wrong   **C** Doesn't say

3 You should arrange to have a day off for the interview.
   A Right   **B** Wrong   **C** Doesn't say

4 You should give your personal objectives.
   A Right   **B** Wrong   **C** Doesn't say

5 Your objectives should suit the position you apply for.
   A Right   **B** Wrong   **C** Doesn't say

6 You should practise your answers at home.
   A Right   **B** Wrong   **C** Doesn't say

7 You shouldn't discuss things you aren't good at.
   A Right   **B** Wrong   **C** Doesn't say

Tapescript : Listening

Duncan	So, Ms Ribera, I'd like to ask you a few questions about your professional experience and qualifications, if I may?
Almudena	Sure.
Duncan	Now your CV says that you've experience of dealing with clients from different countries. Could you tell me which countries you've dealt with?
Almudena	My department publishes translations of foreign books. Most of them are English language books so I deal with America a lot and Britain. And sometimes Italy, too.
Duncan	So, America, Britain and Italy. So your English is obviously very good and you speak Italian too. Could you tell me how good your French is?
Almudena	It's OK. I did French as part of my degree but it isn't as good as my English or Italian.
Duncan	So, that's reasonable French. Now, on your CV you say you have good keyboard skills. Could you tell me how many words a minute you can type?
Almudena	About 50. I learned to type as part of my studies but I need to practise a bit more.
Duncan	You're not the only one. I still use two fingers! And what about computers? Could you tell me a bit about which programs you use?
Almudena	At the moment I use Microsoft Word as I only need the computer for correspondence. In my last job I also used Powerpoint for our presentations.
Duncan	You used Powerpoint? Did you design the presentations yourself?
Almudena	The Training Director planned them, but I had to do the actual computer work and make sure it worked properly during the presentations.
Duncan	So that was at Informática. But it says here in your CV that you left in 1996. Could you tell me why you left?
Almudena	I think the main reason was languages. I liked my job at Informática but all our clients were Spanish so I never got to use my languages. Then one day I saw the advertisement for the job at Ediciones Gómez and I'd always been interested in publishing, so I applied.
Duncan	So why do you want to change jobs now?
Almudena	Well, I still feel that I don't get enough practice with my languages ...

Exam practice

Objectives: To enable Ss to practise for the Reading, Writing and Listening Tests
To give an indication of time pressure and introduce Ss to UCLES Answer Sheets

Materials needed: Cassette - *Pass Cambridge BEC 1 Exam focus*
Sample UCLES Answer Sheets (One per S for each test)

Unit overview

● **Reading Test**

Questions 1-5 *(Part One)*   Multiple-choice.

Questions 6-10 *(Part Three)*   Matching (graphs and charts).

Questions 11-20 *(Part Six)*   Multiple-choice gap-filling.

● **Writing Test**

Questions 21-25 *(Part One)*   Form-filling.

Question 26 *(Part Two)*   Memo.

Question 27 *(Part Three)*   Letter.

● **Listening Test**

Questions 28-35 *(Part One)*   Multiple-choice (short texts).

Questions 36-43 *(Part Four)*   Multiple-choice (longer text).

Questions 6-10
6 D   7 E   8 F   9 B   10 C

Questions 11-20
11 B   12 C   13 B   14 A   15 A
16 C   17 A   18 B   19 A   20 C

Reading and Writing Test

This Exam Practice Test is not a complete exam because of constraints of space and time. Ts are advised to use this test:
- for exam practice
- to give Ss an indication of time pressure
- to introduce Ss to the fact that in the exam itself they have to transfer their answers to an official Answer Sheet.

However, Ts are advised also to give their Ss a complete mock exam at another time (which will need to be planned in advance as it will require more time than a standard lesson). T can choose from the following for the mock exam:
- *UCLES BEC 1 Sample Papers*
- *Linguarama Cambridge BEC 1 Practice Tests 1 and 2.*

If Ts have any questions about the exam, they should refer to the *BEC 1: Teacher's Information Pack.* Sample *UCLES Answer Sheets* can be found in the pack.

Reading

1   T explains the purpose of the Exam Practice Test and emphasises that one aim is to practise transferring their answers to the Answer Sheet so that they are not distracted by the procedure on the day of the exam itself. T distributes photocopied blank Answer Sheets for the Reading and Writing Tests and explains how Ss have to use them.

2   T explains the timing of the Reading and Writing Test. In the exam Ss have 1 hour 10 minutes including the time necessary for transferring their answers to their Answer Sheet. Ss need to leave 25 minutes for the Writing component. As this unit contains half a Reading Test (Parts Two, Four and Five are omitted) and a complete Writing Test, T gives Ss 45 minutes to do Questions 1-27. T emphasises that within this 45 minutes, Ss must give themselves 25 minutes for the Writing and allow time for transferring answers.

3   T quickly goes over the answers to the Reading Test and Questions 21-25 of the Writing Test and collects in the rest of the Writing tests for marking later.

Reading Questions 1-5
1 A   2 C   3 C   4 A   5 B

Exam practice

Reading and Writing Test

Reading

Questions 1-5
- Look at questions 1-5.
- In each question, which phrase or sentence is correct?
- For each question, mark the correct letter **A**, **B** or **C**.

1

The Supplies Department will provide overalls.

The company provides
A special clothing.
B a uniform.
C a suit.

2

Mrs Rothe called – she's unavailable for the meeting tomorrow.

Mrs Rothe will
A be late for the meeting tomorrow.
B take part in the meeting tomorrow.
C not be at the meeting tomorrow.

3

| 8.7.98
Mike called yesterday to say he's flying to Turkey tomorrow. |
| --- |

Mike is flying to Turkey on
A 7 July.
B 8 July.
C 9 July.

4

European sales have recovered this year.

Compared to last year, European sales have
A improved.
B remained steady.
C decreased.

5

Thank you for your enquiry of 18 February.

The company received a letter asking for
A a delivery date.
B information.
C an order.

Questions 6-10
- Look at the graphs and charts below. They show the passenger volumes for eight different airlines.
- Which airline does each sentence 6-10 describe?
- For each sentence, mark the correct letter **A-H**.
- Do not use any letter more than once.

A   1996 1997 1998

B   1996 1997 1998

C   1996 1997 1998

D   1996 1997 1998

E   1996 1997 1998

F   1996 1997 1998

G   1996 1997 1998

H   1996 1997 1998

6 After a sharp fall in 1997, business recovered slightly the following year.

7 Passenger volumes showed strong growth in 1997 but levelled off in 1998.

8 The number of passengers decreased steadily throughout the three year period.

9 Passenger volumes peaked in 1997 and then fell steadily afterwards.

10 The number of passengers remained steady between 1996 and 1998.

Questions 11-20
- Read the newspaper article below about a new alliance in the packaging industry.
- Choose the correct word from **A**, **B** or **C** below.

Packaging alliance

DD Holdings, the UK packaging group, has announced an alliance with three other European packaging companies. The company hopes the alliance will help (11) ...... members to win more orders from multinational pharmaceutical groups.

There is a (12) ...... trend in the pharmaceutical industry for large multinationals to use pan-European suppliers. (13) ...... has presented problems particularly for small and medium-sized companies (14) ...... produce in just one country.

DD Holdings, based in Yorkshire, is teaming up (15) ...... partners in France, Germany and Spain to form an alliance called Pharmapak. (16) ...... the partners will continue to work as separate companies, they will share (17) ...... of their sales and marketing resources. The deal (18) ...... customers with the opportunity to negotiate Europe-wide contracts.

DD is the (19) ...... of the four companies, with 15 production facilities throughout Europe and (20) ...... annual turnover of about £120m.

11 **A** our	**B** its	**C** their
12 **A** grown	**B** growth	**C** growing
13 **A** These	**B** This	**C** That
14 **A** which	**B** what	**C** who
15 **A** with	**B** to	**C** in
16 **A** However	**B** Despite	**C** Although
17 **A** some	**B** any	**C** lot
18 **A** provided	**B** provides	**C** provide
19 **A** largest	**B** larger	**C** large
20 **A** some	**B** a	**C** an

Exam practice

Writing

4   T should check that the answers are in capital letters for Questions 21-25.

Five minutes before the end of this part of the test, T should warn Ss that they have five minutes left. If they are transferring answers to the Answer Sheet, they need to do that now.

21	BUDDY HOLLY
22	PALACE THEATRE
23	3 JULY
24	20.00
25	6

5   T takes in the rest of the Writing Tests for marking later. A table of descriptors for marking Parts Two and Three of the Writing Test can be found in the Answer key of the *Linguarama BEC 1 Practice Tests*.

Question 26
Suggested answer: (23 words)

The company is closed Friday 25 December - Monday 4 January. Please confirm your holiday dates. Holiday forms must be returned by 15 October.

Question 27
Suggested answer: (55 words excluding salutation and closing phrase)

(Dear Christine)

I am sorry I had to cancel the meeting. I am afraid I am travelling in China at the beginning of April and cannot get a flight back before the 12th.

I suggest we meet on Tuesday 19 April at 10.30. Could you confirm the new date and time if it is convenient for you?

(Best regards)

Listening Test

6   T distributes Answer Sheets and prepares Ss for the Listening Test. T reminds Ss that there would normally be four parts to the Listening Test but that only two parts are included here (Parts One and Four). The Listening Test in the exam is 40 minutes long including 10 minutes' transfer time. As this is a half test, T allows five minutes' transfer time after listening and ensures Ss' answers are correctly entered.

7   T checks Ss' answers and discusses any issues arising.

Questions 28-35

| 28 A | 29 B | 30 C | 31 A | 32 C | 33 B | 34 C | 35 B |

Questions 36-43

| 36 C | 37 B | 38 A | 39 A | 40 A | 41 B | 42 C | 43 B |

Writing

Questions 21-25

- Read the memo and the information about office laser printers.
- Complete the form below.
- Write each word, phrase or number in **CAPITAL LETTERS.**

Memo

To: Jane Little
From: Howard Morgan
Date: Thursday 2 July

Epcom visit on Friday

Could you book some theatre tickets for tomorrow for the five Epcom visitors and me? We'll be in a meeting all day until about 4.30 and then we'll have an early dinner together at the hotel. Could you phone the ticket agency and find a play or something that starts after half past seven? Use the company VISA card to pay for the tickets.

What's on: Theatre

Hamlet at the Barbican.
Performances start at 19.15. Tickets
£8.50 - £44

West Side Story at the Playhouse. Show
starts at 19.00. Tickets £7 - £55

Buddy Holly at the Palace Theatre.
Performances at 15.30 and 20.00. Tickets
£8 - £60

```
                  BOOKING

Name of show:   (21) ...............

Venue:          (22) ...............

Date:           (23) ...............

Time:           (24) ...............

No. of tickets: (25) ...............
```

Question 26

- It is the beginning of December and you have been asked to find out how many days' holiday staff in your department intend to take over Christmas.
- Write a memo to all staff in the department:
  * saying on which days the company is closed
  * asking them to confirm their holidays
  * giving a deadline for filling in holiday forms.
- Write **about 20 words.**
- **Do not write in capital letters.**

Question 27

- You had arranged to meet Christine Hendrikson but had to cancel the meeting at short notice. You receive the fax below from her.

```
To:     Fiona Andrews
From:   Christine Hendrikson
Date:   6 April 1999
Pages:  1

Dear Fiona

I received a message this morning saying
that our meeting on Tuesday 12 April
had been cancelled. Unfortunately, the
message didn't give any more details or
any alternative dates.

Could you just confirm that the meeting
has indeed been cancelled and possibly
suggest another date?

Best regards

Christine
```

- Write a fax to Christine:
  * apologising for cancelling the meeting
  * giving a reason for the cancellation
  * offering a new date and time
  * asking her to confirm the new date and time.
- Write **50-60 words.**
- **Do not write in capital letters.**

Listening Test

Questions 28-35

- For questions **28-35**, you will hear eight short recordings.
- For each question, mark one letter **A, B** or **C.**
- You will hear each recording twice.

28 What does Alison order?

  A Fish
  B Steak
  C Chicken

29 Which is the flight to Sydney?

  LH4521   LH4152   LH4125
    A   B   C

30 Which hotel does Graham's colleague recommend?

  A The Orion
  B The Grand Hotel
  C The Plaza

31 Which machine are the people talking about?

  A A fax machine
  B A printer
  C A photocopier

32 What happens to the phone call?

  A The receptionist puts the caller through.
  B The receptionist takes a message.
  C The caller offers to ring back later.

33 How much does the retailer pay for each game?

  A $7 a unit
  B $8 a unit
  C $9 a unit

34 How long will the order take to arrive?

  A 3 days
  B 4 days
  C 5 days

35 What is wrong with the printer?

  A It has run out of paper.
  B The paper has jammed.
  C It needs a new ink cartridge.

Questions 36-43

- Listen to the Manager talking to staff about the way they answer the telephone.
- For questions 36-43, mark the correct letter **A, B** or **C** for the correct answer.
- You will hear the conversation twice.

36 The information was

  A recorded by the company.
  B given by the company's customers.
  C collected by a consultancy.

37 The company's staff answer the phone

  A very quickly.
  B reasonably quickly.
  C far too slowly.

38 The groups average friendliness score was

  A six out of ten.
  B seven point five out of ten.
  C eight out of ten.

39 When dealing with enquiries, staff usually

  A know who to pass the caller on to.
  B can't answer the caller's questions.
  C have to take a message.

40 When putting a call through, staff should always

  A ask for the caller's name.
  B play the hold music.
  C ask the caller to wait.

41 Employees should answer the phone after

  A two rings.
  B three rings.
  C four rings.

42 The company is most worried about how

  A quickly staff answer the phone.
  B efficiently staff deal with enquiries.
  C friendly staff sound on the phone.

43 The handout has a list of

  A pieces of good hold music.
  B useful telephone phrases.
  C extension numbers.

Activity sheets

Draw the graph that your partner describes.

Sales (£)

10,000

8,000

6,000

4,000

1994   1995   1996   1997   1998

Ask your partner for the information to complete the conference programme below.

Amtech Marketing Conference 1999 Programme

Hotel
The Plaza
Drobárova 8
130 00 Praha 3
Czech Republic

Tel + 420 (2) 768 897   Fax + 420 (2) 717 544 88
E-mail: Plaza_Pra@compuserve.com

Friday 25 September
_____ Drinks reception (hotel bar)
19.30   Dinner at _____

Saturday 26 September
9.00   Opening session (Dvořák room)
11.00   Coffee
11.30   Plenary session
13.00   Buffet lunch
14.00   Workshops (Dvořák room and
         Smetana room)
_____   Coffee
16.30   Plenary session
18.00   End of session
_____   Dinner at a local restaurant

Sunday 27 September
9.30   _____ (Dvořák room and
         Smetana room)
11.00   Coffee
11.30   Plenary session
13.00   End of conference
13.15   _____
14.45   Departure from hotel

1 You have an appointment with Andrew Jones of Collingwood Pharmaceuticals on 14 May at half past two. Telephone him to:
- confirm the date
- change the time to 3 o'clock
- give the name of the colleague who is attending the meeting with you.

2 You are a receptionist at Isis, a company based in Los Angeles. Someone calls to speak to Rosemary Burton. She is not in the office today. Offer to to take a message.

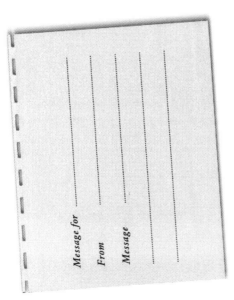

Message for _____

From _____

Message _____
_____

Describe the graph below to your partner.

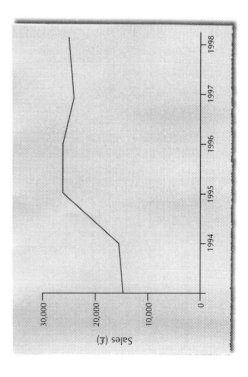

Sales (£)

30,000

20,000

10,000

0

1994   1995   1996   1997   1998

Student A

Your questions

You need to ask Student B for this information about a storage cupboard.

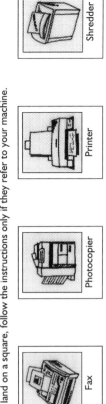

Name of cupboard: ....

Height of cupboard: ....

Number of doors: ....

Colour: ....

Price: ....

Your information

This is the information about the filing cabinet which Student B is interested in.
Try to answer Student B's questions.

New from Accent Office Supplies:

Stor-a-lot™

The safest and biggest storage system available.
This 72cm (h) x 60cm (w) steel filing cabinet has four steel drawers, each with a strong lock for security.

Colour: coffee
Price: £160.00
The *Stor-a-lot*™ cabinet can be delivered in 14 days.

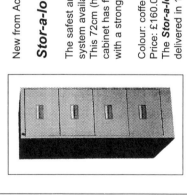

The Business Equipment Game

Play the game in a group of 2–4. Each player has a counter to represent one of these machines. When you land on a square, follow the instructions only if they refer to your machine.

Fax   Photocopier   Printer   Shredder

Toss two coins.

= 1 space
= 2 spaces
= 3 spaces

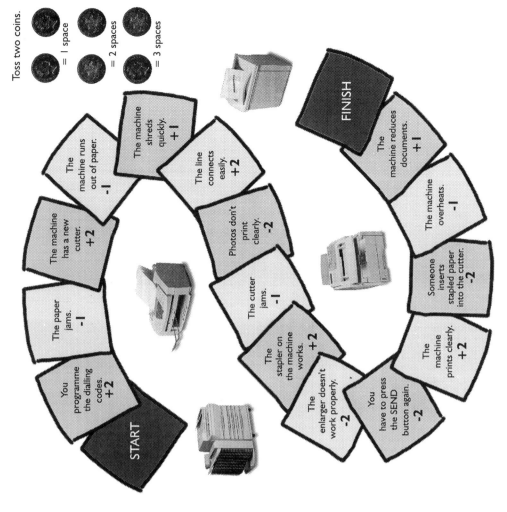

START

You programme the dialling codes. +2

The paper jams. −1

The machine has a new cutter. +2

The machine runs out of paper. −1

The machine shreds quickly. +1

The line connects easily. +2

Photos don't print clearly. −2

The cutter jams. −1

The stapler on the machine works. +2

The enlarger doesn't work properly. −2

You have to press the SEND button again. −2

The machine prints clearly. +2

Someone inserts stapled paper into the cutter. −2

The machine overheats. −1

The machine reduces documents. +1

FINISH

Conference speakers

Student A - Your questions

You need to ask Student B for this information about a conference speaker.

Name of speaker ....

Subject of speech ....

Place ....

Date ....

Time ....

Student B - Your information

This is the information about the conference speaker. Try to answer Student A's questions.

Mrs Josianne Boscariol
Purchasing Manager, Galerie Lafarge, Paris
will give a presentation about "Finding the Right Supplier"
The Grand Hotel, Paris
(Victor Hugo Room)
at 15.30 on 8 August
RSVP by 20 July

Student B - Your questions

You need to ask Student A for this information about a conference speaker.

Name of speaker ....

Company ....

Nationality ....

Location ....

Date ....

Student A - Your information

This is the information about the conference speaker. Try to answer Student B's questions.

As part of his visit to Britain
Mr Gerhardt Braun
HR Manager, Euro Finance GmbH
from Hamburg, Germany
will give an after dinner talk about *Building Multinational Teams*
at the Queen Elizabeth Trade Centre, Manchester on 22 March
Dinner will be served at 22.00

The Commuter Game

You have to get to work for a very important meeting at 9.00. When you land on a red or green traffic light, another player will pick up a card and tell you what to do or ask you a question. If you decide to break the law, toss a coin to see whether the police catch you. Heads: the police catch you and you return to the start. Tails: they don't and you continue as normal. If you land on amber, do nothing. The first person to arrive at work is the winner.

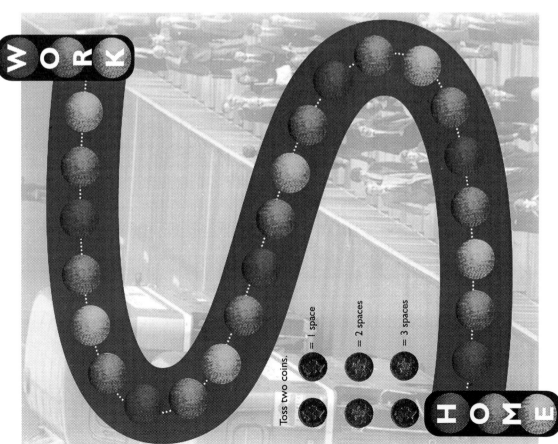

Toss two coins:

● = 1 space

●● = 2 spaces

●●● = 3 spaces

Describe the graph below to your partner.

Sales (£)

10,000

8,000

6,000

4,000

1994 1995 1996 1997 1998

Ask your partner for the information to complete the conference programme below.

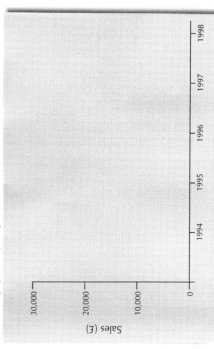

**Amtech Marketing
Conference 1999
Programme**

Hotel
*The Plaza
Drobárova 8
130 00 Praha 3
Czech Republic*

*Tel + 420 (2) 768 897   Fax + 420 (2) 717 544 88
E-mail: Plaza_Pra@compuserve.com*

Friday 25 September
18.30   Drinks reception (hotel bar)
19.30   Dinner at hotel

Saturday 26 September
9.00   (Dvořák room)
11.00   Coffee
11.30   Plenary session
13.00   Workshops (Dvořák room and
                        room)
_____
16.00   Coffee
16.30   Plenary session
18.00   End of session
19.30   Dinner at a local restaurant

Sunday 27 September
9.30   Workshops (Dvořák room and
                        room)
_____
11.30   Coffee
         Plenary session
         End of conference
13.15   Lunch
14.45   Departure from hotel

---

1 You are a receptionist at Collingwood Pharmaceuticals. Someone calls to speak to Andrew Jones. He is in a meeting. Take a message.

Message for ....

From ....

Message ....

....

....

2 You are flying to Los Angeles to visit Rosemary Burton at a company called Isis. Telephone her to:

• say that your flight on Thursday 22 April lands at 10:00 not 14:30
• confirm the flight number: BA 348
• ask who will meet you at the airport.

Draw the graph that your partner describes.

Sales (£)

30,000

20,000

10,000

0

1994 1995 1996 1997 1998

Map of London

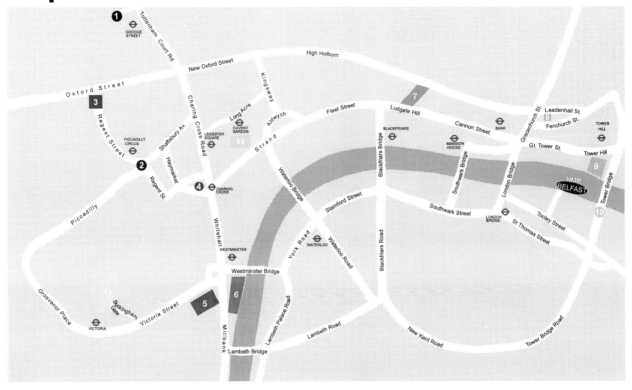

1 Telecom Tower	**4** Nelson's Column	**7** St. Paul's Cathedral	**10** Tower Bridge
2 Piccadilly Circus	**5** Westminster Abbey	**8** Lloyd's Building	**11** Covent Garden
3 Regent Street	**6** The Houses of Parliament	**9** Tower of London	**12** Buckingham Palace

Unit 15

Student B

Your information

This is the information about the storage cupboard which Student A is interested in. Try to answer Student A's questions.

The perfect solution to all your office storage problems!

The MaxiStore 200

This two-door cupboard has maximum storage space for all your office documents. This strong steel cupboard also offers maximum security for all your important records.

Dimensions: 220cm (h) x 100cm (w) x 30cm (d)
Colour: grey
Price: £312.00

Your questions

You need to ask Student A for this information about a filing cabinet.

Height of cabinet: ....
Made of: ....
Number of drawers: ....
Price: ....
Delivery time: ....

Card list

Unit number	Number of cards
Unit 2a	8
Unit 7b Set A	9
Unit 7b Set B	6
Unit 10a	12
Unit 10b	12
Unit 11a	7
Unit 11b	10
Unit 13b	13
Unit 15	11
Unit 16a	16
Unit 16b	9

Supplies of pre-printed cards are available from Alton.

The company tests the new drugs on animals.
Pass Cambridge BEC 1 — Unit 7b Set A 3/9

The company finishes tests on humans.
Pass Cambridge BEC 1 — Unit 7b Set A 2/9

The company keeps a record of test results for the authorities.
Pass Cambridge BEC 1 — Unit 7b Set A 1/9

The company can launch the drug.
Pass Cambridge BEC 1 — Unit 7b Set A 6/9

The authorities approve the drug.
Pass Cambridge BEC 1 — Unit 7b Set A 5/9

The company tests the drug on a larger number of patients.
Pass Cambridge BEC 1 — Unit 7b Set A 4/9

The company tests the new drug on a small number of patients to see how well it works.
Pass Cambridge BEC 1 — Unit 7b Set A 9/9

The company applies to the authorities for approval.
Pass Cambridge BEC 1 — Unit 7b Set A 8/9

The company tests the new drug on healthy people to check safety.
Pass Cambridge BEC 1 — Unit 7b Set A 7/9

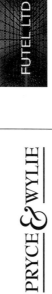

plans for the next six months
Pass Cambridge BEC 1 — Unit 7b Set B 3/6

personal plans for the weekend
Pass Cambridge BEC 1 — Unit 7b Set B 2/6

work schedule for next week
Pass Cambridge BEC 1 — Unit 7b Set B 1/6

holiday
Pass Cambridge BEC 1 — Unit 7b Set B 6/6

business trip
Pass Cambridge BEC 1 — Unit 7b Set B 5/6

work schedule for the next six months
Pass Cambridge BEC 1 — Unit 7b Set B 4/6

EUROPLANT MACHINERY
This medium-sized machine manufacturer is a wholly-owned subsidiary of Delstar.
Pass Cambridge BEC 1 — Unit 2a 2/8
Linguarama

DELSTAR
This is the largest company in the engineering division. The company has a major subsidiary, which has a controlling stake in a subsidiary of its own.
Pass Cambridge BEC 1 — Unit 2a 1/8
Linguarama

FUTEL LTD
The telecommunications division is the smallest in the group and is active in high-growth overseas markets.
Pass Cambridge BEC 1 — Unit 2a 4/8
Linguarama

PRYCE & WYLIE
Invest 1 has a 40% share of this London-based investment management firm.
Pass Cambridge BEC 1 — Unit 2a 3/8
Linguarama

telefonica brasil
This Brazilian joint-venture is 50% owned by Futel and 50% owned by the Brazilian government.
Pass Cambridge BEC 1 — Unit 2a 6/8
Linguarama

HOWELL ENGINEERING
This small company became part of the group when its parent company was taken over by Delstar five years ago.
Pass Cambridge BEC 1 — Unit 2a 5/8
Linguarama

invest
Invest 1 is the only company in the financial services division. It also has a minority stake in an investment management firm.
Pass Cambridge BEC 1 — Unit 2a 8/8
Linguarama

MNE
The holding company controls the three divisions of the whole group.
Pass Cambridge BEC 1 — Unit 2a 7/8
Linguarama

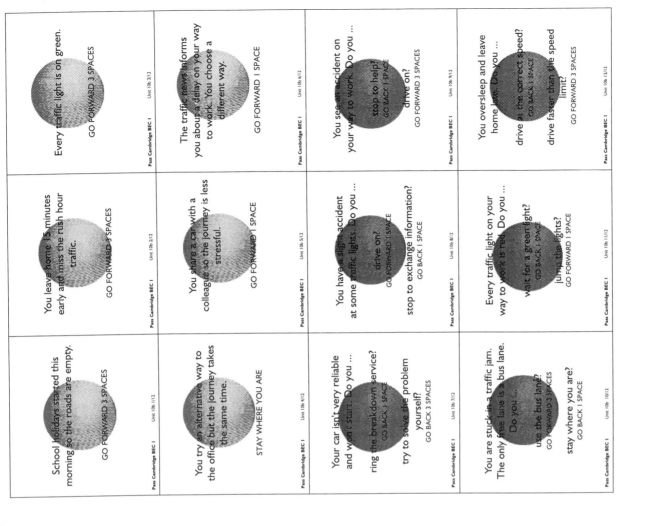

Every traffic light is on green.
GO FORWARD 3 SPACES
Pass Cambridge BEC 1   Unit 10b 3/12

The traffic news informs you about a delay on your way to work. You choose a different way.
GO FORWARD 1 SPACE
Pass Cambridge BEC 1   Unit 10b 6/12

You see an accident on your way to work. Do you …
stop to help?
GO BACK 1 SPACE
drive on?
GO FORWARD 3 SPACES
Pass Cambridge BEC 1   Unit 10b 9/12

You oversleep and leave home late. Do you …
drive at the correct speed?
GO BACK 1 SPACE
drive faster than the speed limit?
GO FORWARD 3 SPACES
Pass Cambridge BEC 1   Unit 10b 12/12

You leave home 15 minutes early and miss the rush hour traffic.
GO FORWARD 3 SPACES
Pass Cambridge BEC 1   Unit 10b 2/12

You share a car with a colleague so the journey is less stressful.
GO FORWARD 1 SPACE
Pass Cambridge BEC 1   Unit 10b 5/12

You have a slight accident at some traffic lights. Do you …
drive on?
GO FORWARD 1 SPACE
stop to exchange information?
GO BACK 1 SPACE
Pass Cambridge BEC 1   Unit 10b 8/12

Every traffic light on your way to work is red. Do you …
wait for a green light?
GO BACK 1 SPACE
jump the lights?
GO FORWARD 1 SPACE
Pass Cambridge BEC 1   Unit 10b 11/12

School holidays started this morning so the roads are empty.
GO FORWARD 3 SPACES
Pass Cambridge BEC 1   Unit 10b 1/12

You try an alternative way to the office but the journey takes the same time.
STAY WHERE YOU ARE
Pass Cambridge BEC 1   Unit 10b 4/12

Your car isn't very reliable and won't start. Do you …
ring the breakdown service?
GO BACK 1 SPACE
try to solve the problem yourself?
GO BACK 3 SPACES
Pass Cambridge BEC 1   Unit 10b 7/12

You are stuck in a traffic jam. The only free lane is a bus lane. Do you …
use the bus lane?
GO FORWARD 3 SPACES
stay where you are?
GO BACK 1 SPACE
Pass Cambridge BEC 1   Unit 10b 10/12

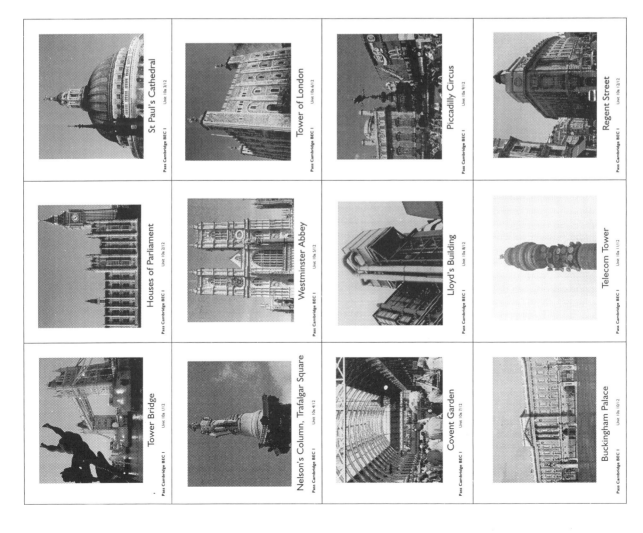

Tower Bridge
Pass Cambridge BEC 1   Unit 10a 1/12

Houses of Parliament
Pass Cambridge BEC 1   Unit 10a 2/12

St Paul's Cathedral
Pass Cambridge BEC 1   Unit 10a 3/12

Nelson's Column, Trafalgar Square
Pass Cambridge BEC 1   Unit 10a 4/12

Westminster Abbey
Pass Cambridge BEC 1   Unit 10a 5/12

Tower of London
Pass Cambridge BEC 1   Unit 10a 6/12

Covent Garden
Pass Cambridge BEC 1   Unit 10a 7/12

Lloyd's Building
Pass Cambridge BEC 1   Unit 10a 8/12

Piccadilly Circus
Pass Cambridge BEC 1   Unit 10a 9/12

Buckingham Palace
Pass Cambridge BEC 1   Unit 10a 10/12

Telecom Tower
Pass Cambridge BEC 1   Unit 10a 11/12

Regent Street
Pass Cambridge BEC 1   Unit 10a 12/12

Welcome speech — Pass Cambridge BEC 1 — Unit 11b 1/10

National sales reports — Pass Cambridge BEC 1 — Unit 11b 2/10

Lunch — Pass Cambridge BEC 1 — Unit 11b 3/10

Targets for next year — Pass Cambridge BEC 1 — Unit 11b 4/10

Coffee — Pass Cambridge BEC 1 — Unit 11b 5/10

Guest speaker: Amy Carter (Allman & Partners) — Pass Cambridge BEC 1 — Unit 11b 6/10

Drinks in the bar — Pass Cambridge BEC 1 — Unit 11b 7/10

Dinner at a restaurant — Pass Cambridge BEC 1 — Unit 11b 8/10

Workshop: Marketing the new product — Pass Cambridge BEC 1 — Unit 11b 9/10

Farewell lunch — Pass Cambridge BEC 1 — Unit 11b 10/10

Decide on the duration — Pass Cambridge BEC 1 — Unit 11a 1/7 — Linguarama

Invite the delegates — Pass Cambridge BEC 1 — Unit 11a 2/7 — Linguarama

Organise the equipment required (overhead projector etc.) — Pass Cambridge BEC 1 — Unit 11a 3/7 — Linguarama

Choose a location — Pass Cambridge BEC 1 — Unit 11a 4/7 — Linguarama

Finalise the programme details — Pass Cambridge BEC 1 — Unit 11a 5/7 — Linguarama

Decide on the budget — Pass Cambridge BEC 1 — Unit 11a 6/7 — Linguarama

Arrange a date — Pass Cambridge BEC 1 — Unit 11a 7/7 — Linguarama

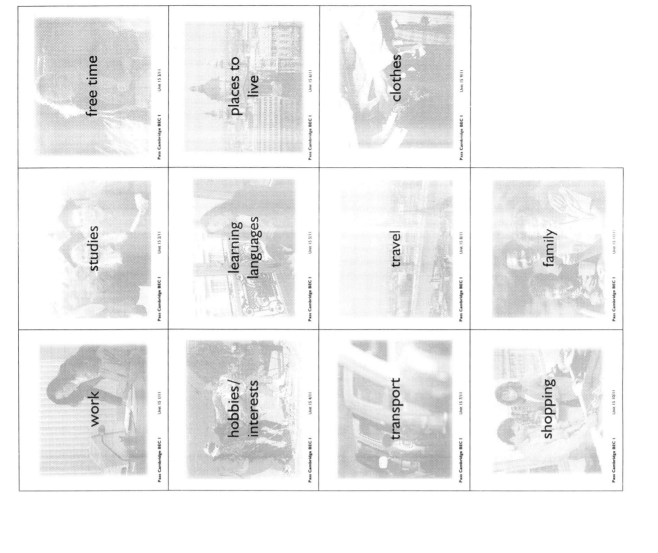

Topic cards

free time
Pass Cambridge BEC 1 — Unit 15 3/11

studies
Pass Cambridge BEC 1 — Unit 15 2/11

work
Pass Cambridge BEC 1 — Unit 15 1/11

places to live
Pass Cambridge BEC 1 — Unit 15 6/11

learning languages
Pass Cambridge BEC 1 — Unit 15 5/11

hobbies / interests
Pass Cambridge BEC 1 — Unit 15 4/11

clothes
Pass Cambridge BEC 1 — Unit 15 9/11

travel
Pass Cambridge BEC 1 — Unit 15 8/11

transport
Pass Cambridge BEC 1 — Unit 15 7/11

family
Pass Cambridge BEC 1 — Unit 15 11/11

shopping
Pass Cambridge BEC 1 — Unit 15 10/11

Game cards

Card 1
Your company is growing fast. You have orders for more goods than you can produce. Do you …
- decide to increase production? (Go to Card 3)
- deliver some orders late? (Go to Card 2)

Pass Cambridge BEC 1 — Unit 13b 1/13

Card 2
Some of your customers are unhappy about the delays. They have told you that if you do not deliver soon, they will cancel their orders.
(Go to Card 1)

Pass Cambridge BEC 1 — Unit 13b 2/13

Card 3
You have decided to increase production. Do you …
- increase capacity? (Go to Card 4)
- increase overtime? (Go to Card 5)

Pass Cambridge BEC 1 — Unit 13b 3/13

Card 4
You have decided to increase capacity. Do you …
- build a new factory? (Go to Card 6)
- expand the existing factory? (Go to Card 7)

Pass Cambridge BEC 1 — Unit 13b 4/13

Card 5
You increase overtime but still find it hard to meet demand. Workers start complaining and taking more days off sick. You start having quality control problems.
(Go to Card 3)

Pass Cambridge BEC 1 — Unit 13b 5/13

Card 6
The new factory is ready! It's very expensive, very modern and far more productive than the old factory. Do you use the new factory …
- for all production? (Go to Card 8)
- only for the extra orders? (Go to Card 9)

Pass Cambridge BEC 1 — Unit 13b 6/13

Card 7
Expanding the factory reduces capacity even more as building work regularly stops production and causes quality control problems.
(Go to Card 4)

Pass Cambridge BEC 1 — Unit 13b 7/13

Card 8
The new factory now meets demand but does not need as many workers. Do you …
- sell the old factory and cut jobs to save money and pay for the new factory? (Go to Card 10a)
- stop overtime, stop pay rises and save money in other ways? (Go to Card 11)

Pass Cambridge BEC 1 — Unit 13b 8/13

Card 9
The repayments on the new factory and the extra workers are eating all your finances and sharply reducing profits. You have to save money.
(Go to Card 8)

Pass Cambridge BEC 1 — Unit 13b 9/13

Card 10
Business is booming! Your order books are full again and demand is still increasing. Production at the new factory is running at its limit again.
(Go to Card 4)

Pass Cambridge BEC 1 — Unit 13b 10/13

Card 11
Business is booming! The new factory is running at full production and the old factory is now at 70% capacity. Sales predict even more orders. Do you …
- modernise the old factory now? (Go to Card 12)
- wait for sales to increase further before investing in modernisation? (Go to Card 13)

Pass Cambridge BEC 1 — Unit 13b 11/13

Card 12
Congratulations! Modernising when the old factory was only running at 70% capacity meant no reduction in production. Demand has increased and your company has successfully carried out a major expansion programme. Well done!

Pass Cambridge BEC 1 — Unit 13b 12/13

Card 13
Sales have improved even further and both factories are now running at full capacity. Sales have just got a big contract with an important new customer. You cannot meet the order. What do you do?
(Go to Card 4)

Pass Cambridge BEC 1 — Unit 13b 13/13

Card C

Raupack receives the goods, translates any important documents and forwards the shipment to the UK client. Raupack pays the German supplier and then sends the client an invoice.

Pass Cambridge BEC 1   Unit 16b 3/9

Card B

A UK client has bought packing machines from Raupack. It now needs some spare parts for the machine so it sends Raupack a fax asking about the price and availability of the parts.

Pass Cambridge BEC 1   Unit 16b 2/9

Card A

Raupack translates the quotation into English and faxes it to the UK client.

Pass Cambridge BEC 1   Unit 16b 1/9

Card F

The client agrees to the price and sends Raupack a fax confirming the order in writing.

Pass Cambridge BEC 1   Unit 16b 6/9

Card E

The client pays Raupack.

Pass Cambridge BEC 1   Unit 16b 5/9

Card D

The German supplier sends a fax giving the price and information about availability and delivery times.

Pass Cambridge BEC 1   Unit 16b 4/9

Card I

Raupack receives confirmation and asks the supplier to begin production of the parts.

Pass Cambridge BEC 1   Unit 16b 9/9

Card H

The German supplier receives confirmation of the order and begins production of the spare parts. When the order is ready, the company despatches the parts and bills Raupack.

Pass Cambridge BEC 1   Unit 16b 8/9

Card G

Raupack sends a fax to a German supplier, asking for a quotation for the spare parts required by the customer.

Pass Cambridge BEC 1   Unit 16b 7/9

---

a photocopier

Pass Cambridge BEC 1   Unit 16a 3/16

a book

Pass Cambridge BEC 1   Unit 16a 2/16

a letter

Pass Cambridge BEC 1   Unit 16a 1/16

600 copies of your company brochure

Pass Cambridge BEC 1   Unit 16a 6/16

a desk

Pass Cambridge BEC 1   Unit 16a 5/16

a car

Pass Cambridge BEC 1   Unit 16a 4/16

Paris by Friday

Pass Cambridge BEC 1   Unit 16 9/16

200 computers

Pass Cambridge BEC 1   Unit 16a 8/16

urgent documents

URGENT

Pass Cambridge BEC 1   Unit 16a 7/16

Munich within 2 weeks

Pass Cambridge BEC 1   Unit 16a 12/16

Prague by Tuesday

Pass Cambridge BEC 1   Unit 16a 11/16

London tomorrow

Pass Cambridge BEC 1   Unit 16a 10/16

Sydney in 5 days

Pass Cambridge BEC 1   Unit 16a 15/16

Washington in a week

Pass Cambridge BEC 1   Unit 16a 14/16

Rome by the end of the month

Pass Cambridge BEC 1   Unit 16a 13/16

Moscow within 48 hours

Pass Cambridge BEC 1   Unit 16a 16/16